STUDIES IN MAJOR LITERARY AUTHORS

Edited by
William E. Cain
Professor of English
Wellesley College

A ROUTLEDGE SERIES

Studies in Major Literary Authors

William E. Cain, *General Editor*

"SOMEWHAT ON THE COMMUNITY-SYSTEM"

Fourierism in the Works of Nathaniel Hawthorne

Andrew Loman

Routledge
New York & London

Published in 2005 by
Routledge
Taylor & Francis Group
270 Madison Avenue
New York, NY 10016

Published in Great Britain by
Routledge
Taylor & Francis Group
2 Park Square
Milton Park, Abingdon
Oxon OX14 4RN

© 2005 by Taylor & Francis Group, LLC
Routledge is an imprint of Taylor & Francis Group.

Printed in the United States of America on acid-free paper
10 9 8 7 6 5 4 3 2

International Standard Book Number-10: 0-415-97551-4 (Hardcover)
International Standard Book Number-13: 978-0-415-97551-3 (Hardcover)
Library of Congress Card Number: 2005017626

Library of Congress Cataloging-In-Publication Data

Loman, Andrew, 1968-
  Somewhat on the community-system : Fourierism in the works of Nathaniel Hawthorne / by Andrew Loman.
      p. cm. -- (Studies in major literary authors)
  Includes bibliographical references and index.
  ISBN 0-415-97551-4 (acid-free paper)
  1. Hawthorne, Nathaniel, 1804-1864--Political and social views. 2. Socialism and literature--United States--History--19th century. 3. Fourier, Charles, 1772-1837--Influence. 4. Communitarianism in literature. 5. Utopias in literature. I. Title. II. Studies in major literary authors (Unnumbered)

PS1892.S6L66 2005
813'.3--dc22   2005017626

Taylor & Francis Group
is the Academic Division of T&F Informa plc.

Visit the Taylor & Francis Web site at
http://www.taylorandfrancis.com

and the Routledge Web site at
http://www.routledge-ny.com

Contents

Notes on Abbreviations

I have used the Centenary Edition of the Works of Nathaniel Hawthorne throughout this book. I cite them in the book by volume:

CE 1   *The Scarlet Letter*
CE 2   *The House of the Seven Gables*
CE 3   *The Blithedale Romance and Fanshawe*
CE 8   *The American Notebooks*
CE 9   *Twice-Told Tales*
CE 10 *Mosses from an Old Manse*
CE 11 *The Snow Image and Uncollected Tales*
CE 16 *The Letters, 1843–1853*
CE 23 *Miscellaneous Prose and Verse*

I have used the following abbreviations for other texts often cited in the book:

ACU   *America's Communal Utopias.* Ed. Donald E. Pitzer.
CR   *Nathaniel Hawthorne: The Contemporary Reviews.* Ed. John L. Idol, Jr., and Buford Jones.
OSL   *The Office of the Scarlet Letter.* Sacvan Bercovitch.
RA   *The Rites of Assent: Transformations in the Symbolic Construction of America.* Sacvan Bercovitch.
TFM   *The Theory of the Four Movements.* Charles Fourier.
UA   *The Utopian Alternative: Fourierism in Nineteenth-Century America.* Carl Guarneri.
UU   *Théorie de unité universelle.* Charles Fourier.
UV   *The Utopian Vision of Charles Fourier.* Charles Fourier.

Acknowledgments

I owe a great deal to Mark Jones and Laura Murray, who supervised this project.

Mary Carpenter provided early and useful advice on English writers interested in Fourierism. Robert Martin was the first academic outside of Queen's to find this project exciting. Bryce Traister has offered his support both professional and personal since we met in Boston.

Russell Field was always ready to run to Robarts on my behalf, single-handedly compensating for the gaps in Queen's American collections; at a crucial moment he also edited the manuscript from start to finish. That's friendship.

Doug Babington, Les Casson, and Maureen Garvie generously let me use office space in the Writing Centre while I was working on final revisions.

My fellow graduate students Neta Gordon, Erin Lemon, Ella Ophir, Alice Petersen, Lori Pollock, Antje Rauwerda, Stephen Ross, and Aaron Santesso are my own utopian community of four-year-ites. My new-found cousin and fellow survivor Antje has been an especially dear friend. Drinking lattes won't be the same now that she's moved to Halifax.

David Diamond has been a cherished friend since I met him in Boston a pair of years ago. On a particularly bad day, he made a timely phone call and told a salvific joke. Craig and Joan Jones have also been marvelous friends: the many play-readings and dinners they've hosted have provided much-needed relief from writing.

SSHRC provided a year of much-needed funding for this project; OGS provided a further two years of funding. Somewhere within the bureaucracies represented by these capital letters are people who resolved that my project deserved support, and I thank them.

My in-laws Hanna and Laurence (Kris) Kristmanson have been unfailingly generous. For two summers in a row, they acted as surrogate parents to my son while I remained in Kingston to finish this dissertation; without them I'd still be working on it.

My parents Catrina and Gus Loman have provided emotional support, baby-sitting, and financial assistance at various stages of this process, and over the years have mastered the trick of seeming interested when I drone on about Hawthorne and the Fourierist challenge to capitalism. See how you do.

My wife Lynn Kristmanson has given me the invaluable gifts of her companionship, her intelligence, and her humor. She has also made considerable sacrifices to allow me to undertake and complete graduate study. Lynn, from my heart, thank you.

My son Nathaniel Jay bears the trace of his father's obsession in his name. The Boy's impending birth made a doctorate seem like a good idea; his love made its completion possible. Darling Nathaniel, I dedicate this to you and your momma.

Herstmonceux Castle

Preface

Since the original version of this study was completed in the fall of 2002, several book-length studies have been published that would have had a significant influence on my arguments. The first is Sterling Delano's *Brook Farm: The Dark Side of Utopia*, a history of the famous utopian community which became Hawthorne's model for Blithedale. The second is Brenda Wineapple's *Hawthorne: A Life*, a new biography that incorporates the most recent decade of Hawthorne criticism. The third study is the first volume of Patricia Dunlavy Valenti's *Sophia Peabody Hawthorne: A Life*. Valenti's is the first biography ever to focus on Hawthorne's wife Sophia and to make Hawthorne himself a supporting player, and, although its interpretations are certain to be challenged and refined, it gives welcome autonomy and depth to Sophia. All of these studies offer arguments and data that would have modified or enriched this study. In the first part of this preface, I will briefly suggest how each of these studies relates to my own analysis of Hawthorne's representations of Fourierism.

Delano's history has an obvious applicability to any historicist reading of *The Blithedale Romance*. *Brook Farm: The Dark Side of Utopia* is the first full-length account of the community in a century, offering a much-needed contemporary perspective. When I was writing my dissertation, I derived my sense of Brook Farm primarily from Carl Guarneri's references in *The Utopian Alternative*, from Lyndsay Swift's 1900 account of the community in *Brook Farm: Its Members, Scholars, and Visitors*, and from Marianne Dwight's letters. (Dwight lived at Brook Farm from 1844 to 1847, and her correspondence is the best first-hand account of the community after its conversion to Fourierism.) The absence of a contemporary account devoted to Brook Farm had repercussions on my study, as it has likewise had on other readings of *The Blithedale Romance* (in fact, on readings of all of Hawthorne's post-Brook Farm fiction). Delano's history is thus certain to figure in studies of Hawthorne that take his social contexts seriously.

Brook Farm offers anecdotes that critics of *The Blithedale Romance* will find productive, as a single example may suggest. In Hawthorne's novel, the only funeral ever held at Blithedale is Zenobia's, following her apparent suicide in the later chapters of the novel. Coverdale uses the occasion to show the fundamental conservatism of the Blithedale colonists (and to suggest that tradition is preferable to reform). "She [Zenobia] was buried very much as other people have been for hundreds of years gone by," Coverdale writes;

> In anticipation of a death, we Blithedale colonists had sometimes set our fancies at work to arrange a funereal ceremony, which should be the proper symbolic expression of our spiritual faith and eternal hopes; and this we meant to substitute for those customary rites which were moulded originally out of the Catholic gloom, and by long use, like an old velvet pall, have so much more than their first death-smell in them. But when the occasion came we found it the simplest and truest thing, after all, to content ourselves with the old fashion, taking away what we could, but interpolating no novelties, and particularly avoiding all frippery of flowers and cheerful emblems. (*CE* 3:240)

Zenobia's death foreshadows Blithedale's as well: the community soon "dies" itself, which Coverdale blames on its conversion to Fourierism. Delano's history reports that, as at Blithedale, so too at Brook Farm was there a single death and a single funeral, in December, 1844. Like Zenobia's, this funeral included "no pomp or rivalry of show, no gaudy deckings . . . but all was done decently, lovingly, peacefully, and well" (John T. Codman quoted in Delano 199). What makes this death interesting is that the woman who died, Marianne Williams, bore a far greater resemblance to Priscilla than to Zenobia. As Delano notes, Williams was a "seamstress and domestic servant whose admission to the community [. . .] was due to the persistence of Waldo and Lidian Emerson;" Williams was "already quite sickly when she arrived in West Roxbury" (198). And while the novel links Zenobia's death to that of reformist impulses, Brook Farmers saw Williams's death as vindication of their new moral world. According to Marianne Dwight, "Nowhere else could this poor woman, who has no near relatives and no property, have fared so well. Here is one of the pleasantest blessings of Association" (quoted in Delano 199). It is not likely that Hawthorne was personally acquainted with Williams—she arrived at Brook Farm in April, 1843, two years after Hawthorne's last visit to the community—and he may not even have known of her by report. However, it seems likely that Hawthorne did know of her: she travelled to Brook Farm in the first place thanks to the Emersons; the Brook Farmer who corresponded with the Emersons and ultimately arranged for Williams to join the community was Hawthorne's friend George Bradford; and in 1843 the Hawthornes were living in newly wedded felicity at the Emersons' Old Manse, playing host to both Bradford and Emerson on different occasions. In spite of Hawthorne's alienation from Brook Farm in 1844, he may well have been aware of her death: it seems probable that a death at the community would reach even the ears of someone estranged from it. Hawthorne may well have been thinking of Williams when planning to include a funeral at Blithedale, in other words. It is impossible to confirm or deny this, of course. Still, the parallels would make Priscilla's survival and Zenobia's death particularly interesting, the opposite of what those readers familiar with Brook Farm's history would expect. Such readers, recognizing the parallels between Priscilla and Williams, would expect the frail Priscilla—the novel's symbol of conservatism—to die, only to be confronted with the death of the robust Zenobia, the novel's symbol of reform. But even if one rejects this speculation, the case of Marianne Williams still shows how starkly Hawthorne's novel differs from the history of Brook Farm itself; the funerals of Zenobia and Marianne Williams are useful indices in this respect.

Delano's study will, in short, be useful as a treasury of anecdotes about Brook Farm that will relate productively to *The Blithedale Romance* (and, to a degree, *The House of the Seven Gables,* since Holgrave also spent time in a community of Fourierists); more broadly, it will be also be valuable for giving a nuanced portrait of Brook Farm's many trials. In Coverdale's narrative, Blithedale is a pastoral idyll until it converts to Fourierism, and then it dies. Delano's account of the ongoing financial crises at Brook Farm, by contrast, underlines how precarious the community's existence always was. These financial crises antedated Brook Farm's conversion to Fourierism (in fact precipitated that conversion). They intensified in the mid-1840s, but not because Brook Farm had entered its Fourierist phase. Delano argues that "[t]he two most immediate causes for Brook Farm's failure were the outbreak of smallpox in November 1845, followed just a few months later by the destruction of the phalanstery" (319). Both of these catastrophes, largely beyond the control of the Brook Farmers, caused irreparable financial harm to the community.

Delano's account of the class composition of Brook Farm is likewise relevant to *The Blithedale Romance.* Coverdale complains in the final chapters that Blithedale's conversion to Fourierism is a betrayal of its own higher spirit, but offers no explanation for why it is so: Fourierism, about which he has hitherto been ambivalent, suddenly becomes sufficient in itself to account for the demise of the community. Delano's analysis of the social transformations of Brook Farm attendant upon the conversion to Fourierism provides a different way of appraising Coverdale's character. Specifically, following the conversion to Fourierism the balance between middle- and working-class reformers shifted as the number of tradesmen and their families increased. As Delano notes,

> In the six months after the publication of its [Fourierist] constitution, eighty-seven applicants were admitted to the community. By July 31, fifty-eight of them had formally been elected members of the Association or were completing the two-month probationary period required by the constitution. Most of the thirty-two men who became associates were skilled or semiskilled workers. (157)

The temptation to read Coverdale's elegy for the higher spirit of Blithedale through the prism of these changes in Brook Farm's class composition is considerable.

But perhaps most importantly, Delano emphasizes how deeply engaged Brook Farm was in reform debates throughout its existence. Coverdale's description of Blithedale nowhere suggests that the experimenters were concerned with the world beyond their pastoral retreat. Blithedale's disengagement from the world was something at least one early reviewer found lacking in the novel. One of the English reviewers of *The Blithedale Romance* complained that by setting its socialists in a pastoral community removed from American cities the novel undermined the relevance of socialist arguments, all the while pretending not to offer an opinion on the merits of socialism. A reader unfamiliar with the history of Brook Farm might suppose that the English reviewer's complaint was not with Hawthorne but with Brook Farm itself, and perhaps more generally with American communitarianism; such a reader might suppose that Hawthorne's fictional treatment of Brook Farm reflected real political disengagement in the community. There was ample evidence to reject such a supposition even before Delano's study: the fact that Brook Farm published *The Harbinger* would in itself suggest a greater degree of political engagement than is evident in Coverdale's account of Blithedale. But Delano's study makes it absolutely clear that Brook Farm actively engaged with the wider currents of reform in spite of its agrarian setting. Either in the pages of *The Harbinger* or at the many conventions to which

Brook Farm despatched delegates and speakers, the Brook Farmers participated in most of the reform debates of the 1840s. One finishes Delano's
study persuaded that in this respect Hawthorne's portrait of the Blithedale
colonists calumniates the Brook Farmers.

Wineapple's new study of Hawthorne would not at first appear to have
much bearing on my project: she has little to say about Brook Farm and still
less about Fourierism. Her discussion of Hawthorne's sojourn at Brook Farm
is a brisk nine pages (pages that also include an extended sketch of Margaret
Fuller). She discusses Hawthorne's 1845 lawsuit against George Ripley and
Charles Dana in a single paragraph:

> Desperate for cash, Hawthorne sued George Ripley—do it "promptly
> and forcibly," he instructed Hillard—to recover the down payment he'd
> made on his Brook Farm house, a note for $530 plus interest.
> Hawthorne eventually won that suit, though not until the following
> year, and it's doubtful that he ever collected the money ($585.90)
> granted by the court. (190)

Several details are missing from this paragraph: most significantly she opts
not to mention that Hawthorne's suit was against Dana as well. And she
declines to mention their legal argument that the Brook Farm Phalanx—and
not Ripley and Dana—owed Hawthorne the money (they did not dispute
the existence of the debt). Nor, understandably enough, is she interested in
the circumstances obtaining at Brook Farm when Hawthorne sued them: her
aim is to show the Hawthornes' financial desperation in 1845, *tout court*.

But Wineapple concludes the discussion of Brook Farm with a valuable
single-sentence paragraph: she writes that Hawthorne "cursed the sense of
dependency—Brook Farmers called it cooperation—which the community
fostered no less than a Custom House sinecure" (154). One would not imagine
that a Custom House and Brook Farm would have many affinities, given their
considerable differences. Yet Hawthorne's treatment of them in *The Scarlet Letter* and *The Blithedale Romance* suggest that such affinities exist: placing "The
Custom House" alongside, for instance, Coverdale's valediction to the
Blithedale pigs would suggest that the government office and the alternative
community are more alike than either would be prepared to acknowledge.

As I note at greater length below, I registered this parallel while writing
my dissertation, along with further parallels between these sites and the asy-
lum, the prison, the almshouse, the boarding house, the hotel . . .—various,
seemingly disparate buildings whose unifying element is that they are all in
some sense communal, and all threaten the middle-class male. It is striking

how frequently in Hawthorne's writing such sites are condemned for their deleterious effects on his own masculinity or that of his characters. And it is also striking how pervasive they are; especially in *The Blithedale Romance* and *The House of the Seven Gables,* the only refuge from them is the middle-class home. That all these buildings have similar effects on the male subject has various implications, but chief among them is that Hawthorne did not object to Fourierism on moral or political grounds alone. In its emphasis on the communal, Fourierism included a character of antebellum culture that Hawthorne found both widespread and threatening. Wineapple's linkage of Custom-House sinecures and communitarian labour would have provided me with valuable corroboration.

Wineapple's biography also offers valuable details on the Hawthornes' relationships with other men and women, reflecting her participation in a critical project that gathered force through the 1990s. The tensions especially in Hawthorne's relationships with other men (and especially Melville) have become increasingly the focus of scholarly discussion since the rise of queer theory. For the most part Wineapple declines to join these discussions directly. She dismisses the debates on Melville's and Hawthorne's relationship almost as soon as she raises them, calling Edwin Havilland Miller's speculations "tired" (436n227). But in spite of Wineapple's evident boredom with queer readings of the Melville-Hawthorne relationship, the biography is nevertheless full of details about the Hawthornes' relationships with men and women that queer theorists will surely reference in future criticism. Sophia Hawthorne's friendship with Annie Fields is a case in point. It has not been accorded much attention in previous biographies; Wineapple's account is brief but emphasizes that friendship's intensity. Similarly, her account of the relationship between Hawthorne and Franklin Pierce emphasizes its tenderness: "Probably not even Pierce's wife," she affirms, "loved him as Hawthorne did" (354). I wish Wineapple had explicitly commented on the significance of these relationships: she adds a footnote to her discussion of Sophia and Annie Fields that directs her readers to debates on nineteenth-century same-sex relationships, but refrains from stating outright how, in her estimation, the "female sympathy" (354) Sophia derived from her friendship with Annie compared to the sympathy she derived from her marriage.

Wineapple's discussion of these relationships would have had a significant bearing on this study nonetheless. Early drafts of Chapter Four included a queer reading of *The Scarlet Letter* and *The Blithedale Romance* in light of Fourierist discourses on desire. Coverdale explicitly states that Blithedale "seem[s] to authorize an individual, of either sex, to fall in love with any other" (*CE* 3:72). As Robert Martin, Benjamin Scott Grossberg, and others have noted (most recently Robert S. Levine, in an article I discuss at greater length below), Coverdale implicitly includes same-sex relationships, implying that the utopianism of Blithedale is at least potentially queer. And even though *The Blithedale Romance* ends with a conservative retrenchment into heterosexual monogamy, it does not wholly retreat from its utopianism. Coverdale anticipates a time when Blithedale shall be resurrected and its reforms find more hospitable soil. (There are considerable problems with this utopianism, not the least of which is that it replicates Hawthorne's attitude towards slavery: we must wait, he argues with woeful pusillanimity, for an unspecified future where slavery will disappear on its own rather than fight for its dissolution in the present. But the crucial fact remains that the novel specifically includes homosexuality in its utopianism, a radical gesture that one should not discount.) In this respect, Hawthorne repeats Fourier's endorsement of same-sex desire. Wineapple's exploration of the relationships between the Hawthornes and various members of their circle offers new biographical contexts within which to understand the homoerotic currents of the novels.

Of these three studies, however, Patricia Valenti's biography of Sophia Hawthorne would have had the most significant influence on my dissertation, strictly because when I was writing it I had, in common with most Hawthorne scholars, at best a dim sense of Sophia's character. During my defense, one of my examiners asked if the dissertation altered our impression of Sophia; I had to admit that my understanding of Sophia derived from Hawthorne himself, and that Sophia was a phantom conjured up in his letters and his fictional portraits. To be sure, my impression was influenced by T. Walter Herbert's *Dearest Beloved,* a study of the Hawthornes that gave Sophia some psychic autonomy. But for the most part, Hawthorne himself constructed and controlled my understanding of his wife's character. The answer I gave to my interlocutor, then, was that the project might influence our understanding of Hawthorne's representations of Sophia, but it could do little to revise our understanding of the historical woman.

Valenti's biography restores to Sophia Hawthorne her depth and independence of character, and in doing so has transformed my understanding of the Hawthornes' marriage. In particular, I found her account of Sophia's enthusiasm for Transcendentalists like Alcott and Emerson productive. Valenti's account of Hawthorne's tenure at Brook Farm is still briefer than Wineapple's (and wrongly claims that Orestes Brownson was a member), and she does not speculate on what might have occasioned his participation, only noting that it was "uncharacteristic" (157). However, Sophia's interest in the Transcendentalists suggests that her fiancé's participation in the experiment—

a participation that has puzzled many—may well have been urged upon him by Sophia herself. In another vein, Valenti shows the stark differences between the Hawthornes when they were newly wedded and living in the Manse. Valenti traces the ways these differences expressed themselves in their responses to nature, to the birth of Una, and in many other instances. The second chapter of my study emphasizes how Nathaniel contrasted bourgeois marriage at the Manse with reformist communitarianism, praising the former and rejecting the latter. Valenti's study reveals the tensions informing the Hawthornes' marriage from its earliest days, explaining the anxieties that inform the many portraits of marriage in *Mosses from an Old Manse* and showing how fragile Nathaniel's own relationship was to the institution that he ultimately championed against its alternatives.

II.

One final recent study bears mentioning: in one of the essays in *The Cambridge Companion to Nathaniel Hawthorne* (2004), Robert S. Levine explores Hawthorne's meditation on the limits of sympathy in *The Blithedale Romance*. Aspects of this discussion parallel my discussion in Chapter Three of egotism and what Fourier called "Unityism" in *The Blithedale Romance*. I will therefore summarize Levine's argument here and relate it to my own analysis of *The Blithedale Romance*. I will focus on an instance, crucial for Levine's argument, when he chooses to read Coverdale's narrative naively. The virtue of his willed naivety in this instance is that it recuperates the novel from charges of unrelenting conservatism and cynicism. It is in this respect admirable, a show of the kind of solidarity and charity that a project like Blithedale would require if it hoped to be a success. But the text itself does not in fact justify this naivety: there are good reasons for reading Coverdale's every word sceptically. My argument in Chapter Three is that interpretive interventions of the kind that Levine makes reflect Coverdale's "reading" of the Blithedale communitarians and structure the critic's reading of Coverdale's narrative: sympathetic reading is one of the themes of the novel. Coverdale's general failure to read with "indefatigable human sympathy" (*CE* 3:163)—he is characteristically sceptical of the motives of his colleagues—is a sign of his conservatism, or, as I put it below, his is a reading practice that reflects the difficulties capitalist subjects have in theorizing altruism. Readers who replicate Coverdale's practices risk recapitulating his failure; as I read it, the book thematizes the extraordinary difficulty of escaping from such capitalist structures of thought.

Levine relates *The Blithedale Romance* to the cultural work of sympathy in antebellum reform culture. A "basic tenet of 1850s sentimental culture," Levine states, "celebrated the power of sympathy to link the self to unfortunate others" (208). Because the novel uses Coverdale as a first-person narrator, it raises a two-part question: "does sympathy help to connect the self to the other (and in this way contribute to social reform) or does sympathy create barriers between the self and other (and in this way thwart social reform)?" (208). In Levine's view, *The Blithedale Romance* answers in the affirmative to both questions: the wrong kind of sympathy creates barriers between the self and others, while the right kind of sympathy—"non-violative," "honest," and "potentially productive" (223)—will help to connect the self to others, and thereby conduce to reform. In thus acknowledging both the promise of the right kinds and the perils of the wrong kinds of sympathy, *The Blithedale Romance* "is participating in the sentimental project of the 1850s of imagining the other in terms of the self, while at the same time developing a critique of that project" (210). Levine wants to recuperate *The Blithedale Romance* from the many critics who see the novel as conservative: as he puts it, he wants to "re-radicalize *Blithedale*" (224). "In many respects," he affirms, "*Blithedale* is one of the boldest reform texts of the 1850s, powerfully exposing the hazards of trying to make the other into what Zenobia calls 'all self!'" (225).

That The Blithedale Romance critiques the sentimental project of the 1850s, I think, many readers will grant, and Levine's critique of writers like Harriet Beecher Stowe is forceful and persuasive; reservations about Levine's reading will likely arise over whether the novel can also be said to participate in the project it so effectively deconstructs. Levine finds a moment in the novel when Coverdale appears to have the "right" kind of sympathy: in the final chapter of the novel he meets Hollingsworth and Priscilla outside their domestic penitentiary; because Hollingsworth affirms that he has been trying to reform "a single murderer" (that is, himself) (CE 3:243), Coverdale bursts into tears and forgives him. For Levine, Coverdale's response is "moving and confused" (223), and emblematizes a preferable model of sympathy to the imperial kind that subordinates other to self. But conscripting this moment isn't straightforward, in part because Coverdale's forgiveness of Hollingsworth may not be honest. Coverdale's narrative has proven itself to be so unreliable that readers cannot be sure of his sincerity in this instance; readers may legitimately interpret his account of this seemingly spontaneous response to Hollingsworth as a cynical bid for his readers' sympathy rather than as a transparent description. And even if one grants that Coverdale's sympathy here is honest, it may still not be non-violative. After all, he only has the opportunity to feel it after seeking Hollingsworth in his retirement and, in defiance of Priscilla's unspoken plea that he leave certain questions unasked, violating the erstwhile reformer's privacy. And if his sympathy is neither honest nor non-violative, then it is hard to see how it could be productive. Coverdale's supposed discovery of "good" sympathy, in other words, arises from dubious actions and motives, and may itself be compromised insofar as Coverdale is too unsympathetic to his readers for them to ascribe generous motives to him. Such problems are not trivial: to an extraordinary degree, The Blithedale Romance demands that its readers attempt to see beyond the veils of Coverdale's narration, and to an extraordinary degree it prevents its readers from doing so. Levine's argument depends on finding an instance of sympathy in the novel that is positive. But the novel's powerful indictment of the wrong kinds of sympathy and its vexing narrative strategies together threaten to vitiate all instances of sympathy. It becomes an act of interpretive will to perceive any sympathy as productive. Such an intervention is an act of political faith, and needs to register that it is so.

My argument in Chapter Three has some bearing on Levine's in that it too responds to the problem of the self in the novel. Rather than discuss positive and negative models of sympathy, however, I approach *The Blithedale Romance* through the question of egotism and what Fourier called Unityism, egotism's inverse. In *The Theory of the Four Movements,* Fourier imagines that the gratification of one's idiosyncratic appetites in his communitarian utopia would conduce to social harmony. In his utopia, egotism would give way to Unityism, a passion for collective action. But he never defines what Unityism is—he cannot do so, he claims, because the capitalist self is too mired in egotism to imagine what Unityism might be—nor does he explain how indulging one's individual appetites in his utopia would nevertheless serve the interests of the community. The various relationships between individual appetite and collective good are the equivalent in his system of the invisible hand in Smith. But because he keeps the connections between individual appetite and social harmony obscure, Fourier offers a strong valorization of individual appetite but a weak demonstration of its socially salubrious effects. *The Blithedale Romance* explicitly notes this problem: Hollingsworth caustically remarks on Fourier's reliance on self-gratification as the mainspring of social regeneration, and claims to favour the eradication of the self instead. How to effect the leap from egotism to Unityism is arguably the central mystery of Fourierist theory. As I read *The Blithedale Romance,* it is deeply concerned with this mystery, and takes a deeply sceptical—not to say cynical—view of the chances of transforming egotism into Unityism. As distressed as the novel is with the status quo—as

I argue in the pages that follow, the novel's portrait of Boston evinces a real distress in the face of the cultural costs of capitalism—it is also doubtful of the ability of the capitalist subject to escape capitalist ideology. As Shaksan Bumas states in a recent article on Hawthorne and panopticism, the novel is about the pervasiveness of prisons. Among these prisons are structures of capitalist thought, in which altruism, especially, has no place.

The genius—or the deviltry—of *The Blithedale Romance* is that it implicates the reader in its critique of capitalist ideology, and does so through the device of its first-person narrator. The novel is rare among nineteenth-century novels both for the provisional character of its narrative and for its own insistence on that provisionality. The catalogue of events and relationships that remain a matter of speculation at the end of the book is long. We don't know the truth of Moodie's history: we neither know what the nature of his financial indiscretion was, nor even, since Coverdale admits to inventing much of Moodie's history, if there was any financial indiscretion at all. We don't know the nature of Zenobia's relationship with Westervelt. We don't know what transpired between Zenobia and Moodie. We don't know if Hollingsworth transferred his affections from Zenobia to Priscilla because of their changed fortunes. We don't know what happened at Eliot's Pulpit. We don't know if Zenobia really committed suicide. We don't know, finally, if Coverdale really was in love with Priscilla. In light of this catalogue (which is far from exhaustive), it becomes extremely difficult to evaluate the basic action of the novel, and evaluating the characters' conduct is still more fraught with problems. And in light of this catalogue, Coverdale's attribution of low motives to his fellow reformers is often staggeringly precipitate, not to mention singularly ungenerous. After praising Hollingsworth for his "more than brotherly care" during Coverdale's convalescence, for instance, Coverdale suggests that Hollingsworth nursed him only to gain a proselyte; after introducing Zenobia as the symbolic centre of Blithedale, Coverdale suggests that her heart was never with her fellow and sister communitarians. Even though Coverdale never conclusively demonstrates the legitimacy of his many suspicions, the reader is continually invited to subscribe to his characterizations of Zenobia, Hollingsworth, and Priscilla, not to mention Coverdale himself. It is extremely difficult for the reader to resist these continual attributions of low motives. Levine usefully suggests (213) that we take Coverdale seriously when he claims to "exaggerate [his] own defects" (*CE* 3:247) and we should likewise suspect that Coverdale exaggerates the defects of all the other characters at Blithedale. The reason to be scrupulously fair-minded as we read the novel is ultimately political: the moment we assent to Coverdale's characterizations of himself and others, we risk participating in an ideology that finds it convenient to asperse the motives of those purporting to be altruists. Coverdale's general inability to escape from this tendency is one crucial sign of his conservatism. The kind of "indefatigable human sympathy" that he champions but so rarely practices is a model for readers consciously to adopt.

III.

When I defended my dissertation in the fall of 2002, my external examiner asked me which aspects of the study had fallen by the wayside in the course of revision. I have already mentioned the disappearance of the queer reading of all three American romances: in my chapter on property and sexual exchange (Chapter Four), I had originally emphasized the queer dynamics of the relationships between both male and female characters; I truncated that discussion when my first readers found my specific interpretations unpersuasive. In what remains of these prefatory remarks, I will offer a brief survey of a second major discussion that, to my subsequent regret, I eliminated in the name of timely completion. The subject is the role of architecture in the latter two American romances, an inquiry I structured around the figure of the Fourierist phalanstery, the visionary building to which Coverdale refers in *The Blithedale Romance*.

My interest in the representations of Fourierism in Hawthorne's fiction derives in part from my reading of Michel Foucault's *Discipline and Punish*. Foucault represents the French Fourierists as forgotten heroes resisting the disciplinary turn, and himself as their descendant. His history of early opponents of the "monotonous discourse on crime, which sought both to isolate it as a monstrosity and to depict it as the work of the poorest class" (Foucault [1979] 228–229) gives pride of place to the Fourierists. There is "no doubt," Foucault writes, that the Fourierists "went further than any of the others" (Foucault [1979] 289) in contesting penal discipline. Not only did the Fourierists address the classism of discourses on crime, they also inaugurated the concept of criminality as a potential weapon against the existing social order. "*La Phalange* analyses penal affairs," Foucault writes,

> as a confrontation coded by 'civilization,' the great crimes not as monstrosities but as the fatal return and revolt of what is repressed, the minor illegalities not as the necessary margins of society, but as a rumbling from the midst of the battle-field. (Foucault [1979] 289–290)

Foucault in effect makes proto-Foucauldians of the Fourierists.

In both *The Blithedale Romance* and *The House of the Seven Gables,* Hawthorne sets Fourierism and "penal affairs" in opposition to one another. Hollingsworth, the designer of a model reformatory, vehemently declares his enmity to Fourier. And in the modern incarnation of the Pyncheon-Maule rivalry—between Judge Pyncheon and Holgrave—there is another expression of the same opposition: Pyncheon controls access to the prisons and Holgrave has spent time in a Fourierist community. The question with which I began my inquiry was whether Hawthorne anticipated Foucault's attitude towards discipline and punishment or if he used the same opposition to different ends.

Foucauldian readings of Hawthorne's fiction have characteristically insisted that he anticipates Foucault by resisting the disciplinary turn. To take two relatively recent examples, E. Shaskan Bumas has argued that *The Blithedale Romance* is, "like much of Hawthorne's fiction, about the omnipresence of prisons, real and imagined, their inevitability. But it is also about the possibility of escape" (Bumas 138). And Stephen Knadler has argued that *The House of the Seven Gables* recognizes that "amid a new configuration of power invested in systems of classification, political action has to begin with the self's social construction and work through the mind's release from the 'normal' rules of mental hygiene" (Knadler 282).

Although I won't develop my reading in detail here, my own view is that Hawthorne is not a proto-Foucauldian, and that his treatment of the Fourierists, whose provocations he repeatedly contains (at least for the present), marks his rejection of their anti-disciplinary arguments. Although the critique of the prison in *The House of the Seven Gables* is forceful, and although Clifford is the emblematic victim of prison discipline, still Hawthorne is not prepared to reject discipline altogether. Against readings that see a continuum between Hawthorne and Foucault, I suggest that Hawthorne wants not to escape the prison but to domesticate it. When Hollingsworth abandons public reform after Zenobia's suicide the novel strongly intimates that he is finally behaving appropriately; Coverdale can approve of him because he disciplines himself rather than imposes his discipline on others. *The Blithedale Romance* suggests both that reformers should first reform themselves and that the home and not the institution will best reform the criminal.

It remains interesting, however, that reformers on both sides of the disciplinary divide seek to embody their projects in architecture. Hollingsworth is again the best example of this tendency: throughout the novel he seeks funds to build a "grand edifice for the reformation of criminals" (*CE* 3:242).

The Blithedale communitarians also hope, in Coverdale's words, "to erect a Phalanstery [. . .] where the great and general family should have its abiding-place" (*CE* 3:128). Neither is built, but the shared aspiration is nonetheless significant. Among other things it suggests that a relationship exists between the visionary architecture of the reformers and the material architecture of Boston. In my reading of *The Blithedale Romance,* I suggested that buildings like the hotel where Coverdale stays when he returns to Boston, the nearby boarding-house where he espies Zenobia, Priscilla, and Westervelt, the tenement where Priscilla spends her childhood, and others, all share qualities of the visionary buildings of Hollingsworth and the Fourierists. The visionary buildings represent competing ideological positions; the material buildings are imperfect reifications of these positions, and suggest that the rivalries at Blithedale are distilled versions of broad tensions within antebellum culture.

Significantly, both the visionary edifices of Hollingsworth and the Blithedale colonists and also the urban architecture of Boston are communal. As I suggest in my discussion of Wineapple's biography, communal architecture both visionary and material is at odds with the middle-class home. When Hollingsworth and Priscilla retreat to a cottage at the end of the novel, they are spurning not only reformatories and phalansteries but also boarding-houses, tenements, and hotels. The middle-class home is not only a bulwark against reform, in other words; it is also a bulwark against the modern city.

The House of the Seven Gables is generally continuous with *The Blithedale Romance* in its architectural narrative, but it has one significant difference. Unlike *The Blithedale Romance,* where the surviving protagonists disperse and only Priscilla and Hollingsworth take refuge in the domestic home (leaving Coverdale woeful in isolation), *The House of the Seven Gables* allows all the protagonists to take refuge in the late Jaffrey Pyncheon's country home. What makes this ending especially interesting is that it includes Uncle Venner: although he is, after a fashion, adopted into the Pyncheon-Maule family, he is nevertheless not a blood relation. In a highly attenuated sense, then, the Pyncheon country home is itself a communal building, a kind of bourgeois phalanstery. The differences in tone between *The House of the Seven Gables* and *The Blithedale Romance* have many explanations, but one of them, I suspect, is that the earlier novel manages to achieve harmony between the domestic retreat and the communalism of the city. The later novel does not sustain this utopian synthesis. The difference between the utopian conclusion of *The House of the Seven Gables* and the bleak, exhausted conclusion of *The Blithedale Romance* is partly a matter of real estate.

Chapter One

Introduction

I.

Nathaniel Hawthorne read several of the works of the pre-Marxian socialist Marie François Charles Fourier (1772–1837), and was familiar or intimate with a number of the preëminent American Fourierists[1] of the 1840s. A founding participant in George Ripley's communitarian experiment at Brook Farm, he was aware of its later conversion to Fourierism; he may, in fact, have lost $500 because of this conversion, at a time when his personal finances were in crisis. Representations of Fourier are crucial to the logic of two of the American romances, *The House of the Seven Gables* (1851) and *The Blithedale Romance* (1852), and I will argue that Hawthorne implicitly challenges Fourierist theory in *The Scarlet Letter* (1850).

These facts notwithstanding, no critic has written a study that attends sufficiently to the function of Fourier in Hawthorne's work. Many have made note of Fourier's presence in *The Blithedale Romance,* and some have built powerful arguments about it which acknowledge and incorporate Hawthorne's representations of Fourier.[2] But Fourier's function in *The House of the Seven Gables* has been almost entirely ignored, even though he is as often invoked in that romance as in *The Blithedale Romance*.[3] Critics have treated *The Scarlet Letter*'s critique of reform only in general terms, for the novel makes no direct mention of Fourier. Nevertheless, Fourierist discourses influence *The Scarlet Letter* in its treatment of its major theme, adultery. A study is long overdue which makes Hawthorne's engagement with Fourierism its focus. Given the recent distinguished work attending to communitarianism[4] in general and to American Fourierism in particular, preëminent among which is Carl Guarneri's *The Utopian Alternative: Fourierism in Nineteenth-Century America,* such a study is also now possible.[5]

A Fourierist focus promises to enrich our understanding of the aesthetic complexities and historical situation of Hawthorne's fiction, and hence to clarify what Jane Tompkins calls their "cultural work." By this term, Tompkins refers to authors' "designs upon their audiences" and their efforts "to make people think and act in a particular way" (Tompkins xi); she argues that literary works participate actively in the *mêlée* of politics. The representations of Fourier in Hawthorne's romances are ineluctably political. When Hawthorne was writing his romances, the Fourierist experiments of the 1840s, and such distant communitarian cousins as the Alcotts' Fruitlands, were mostly over, typically having ended in bankruptcy. This might suggest that in *The Blithedale Romance* Hawthorne was writing a satiric elegy for an already discredited reform movement. Nevertheless, Fourierist phalanxes were not wholly a thing of the past in 1852. When the Oneida *Circular*, the journal of John Humphrey Noyes's Perfectionist community, reviewed *The Blithedale Romance*, it also ran an article on the Fourierist North American Phalanx, testimony to the persistence of Fourierism. And the existence of colonies such as Oneida and the free-love community Modern Times, which in different ways evinced Fourierist influence, suggests that Fourierism continued to exert an influence on American society well into the 1850s. To take one further example, Hawthorne's preoccupation with mesmerism in both *The House of the Seven Gables* and *The Blithedale Romance*, and his direct correlation of it with Fourierism, does not derive from his memories of Brook Farm. Rather, it responds to allegiances made between Fourierists and spiritualists in the late 1840s and early 1850s.[6] One can say, therefore, that Hawthorne's representation of Blithedale as safely interred in the past is not just an aesthetic representation of social reality, but also a political strategy, couched in the form of fiction, in an as-yet-unresolved contest.[7]

Understanding the cultural work of Hawthorne's fictions depends upon having a subtle sense of their historical situations. By historical situation I mean not only the context in which Hawthorne produced his work, but also the ways in which his work negotiated with other discourses to participate in that context. Historicist readings of literary texts are no longer new; literary criticism no longer needs to be told that one must "[a]lways historicize" (Jameson 9), or that without understanding the historical circumstances in which works are produced one cannot understand the works themselves. Still, much of this historicizing remains to be done. We have been able to perceive, for instance, that Hawthorne's works criticize Fourierism. But we have not understood well how they do so, or how even in the midst of their critique they covertly appropriate elements of Fourierist theory. The benefit of situating the works in their historical moment extends in two directions: we emerge with an enriched understanding not only of the texts, but also of the historical moment. Carl Guarneri's magisterial *The Utopian Alternative* has subtilized our understanding of American Fourierism.[8] But Guarneri approaches the issue as an historian, not as a literary scholar, and so his study's forays into literary analysis are limited. Studying the ways in which literature portrays Fourierism gives additional insight into the period. Hawthorne's works provide an appropriate starting point in such an enterprise because they are by far the best known works in English to engage with Fourierism.[9] Hawthorne is, however, only one of many authors representing Fourier.[10]

Hawthorne's representations of Fourier and Fourierism are not neutral signs indicating that he wrote at a time when there were such things as Fourierists. Hawthorne was conscious of the political effects of his works, and his representations of Fourier aim to persuade his reader of the merits of his own position—one largely hostile to Fourierism. This rhetorical enterprise is subtle, and so one must approach the texts with interpretive care as great as that of the most ardent formalist (as, indeed, all of the best politically oriented literary critics do). Such care not only discloses the nuances of Hawthorne's political enterprise, however. It has the additional virtue of subtilizing our understanding of the texts themselves: attending to the function of Fourier in Hawthorne's romances can disclose textual complexities heretofore unregistered.

The challenges such an enterprise faces, however, are various. One fundamental error would be to read the romances as Fourierist allegories. Such is the strategy of Gerard Nawrocki in a recent article on *The Blithedale Romance*. For Nawrocki, Fourierist theory makes the relations of the romance's characters intelligible: Fourier's complex equations for the ideal interaction of individuals within his social system inform the romance's deployment of its characters; Fourier's psychological theory explicates the romance's characters. As we shall see, Hawthorne's documented reading of Fourier's texts justifies Nawrocki's assumption that Hawthorne engaged with the intricacies of Fourierist theory. But Nawrocki's claims depend upon his own arbitrary schematizing of the romance. He writes, for instance, that "the group structure of *The Blithedale Romance* fits the basic group structure of Fourier's theory nearly perfectly" (Nawrocki 201); he can support this claim only by arranging the characters himself:

> there are seven characters with names: Zenobia, Hollingsworth, Priscilla, Coverdale, Mr. Moodie, Professor Westervelt, and Silas Foster. They are all united in the common interest of the Blithedale experiment or in affinity to Zenobia and her money. These seven characters form

> three sub-groups: the center which consists of Zenobia, Hollingsworth
> and Priscilla; the wing from Blithedale related to Zenobia's present is
> made up of Coverdale and Silas Foster; and the wing from urban society
> related to Zenobia's past is made up of Mr. Moodie and Professor West-
> ervelt. (Nawrocki 201)

But Westervelt and Moodie never meet in the action of the romance, except,
perhaps, at Zenobia's funeral, and thus their conscription in a sub-group is
not of their own volition, defying Fourierist group theory. And Coverdale
cannot so neatly be conscripted into the "wing from Blithedale" given his
ambivalence about communitarianism and his own provenance in the city.

Nawrocki not only makes too rigid an application of Fourierist theory to
the romance's design, but also attributes to Hawthorne an implausible familiarity with details of Fourier's career. He draws unwarranted parallels between
Blithedale and the only Fourierist community with which Fourier was personally involved, Condé-sur-Vesgre (near Paris), trying to read as significant certain perceived similarities between Hollingsworth and that community's
architect, Colomb Gengembre. It is remotely possible that Hawthorne read
Charles Pellarin's 1849 biography of Fourier which reprinted Fourier's private
letters complaining about Gengembre.[11] But differences between
Hollingsworth and Gengembre far outweigh similarities; ultimately, reading
Gengembre as a source for Hollingsworth is not particularly fruitful.
Nawrocki's best point is that group dynamics in *The Blithedale Romance* are
more destructive than Fourier imagined, and this might have led to more productive insights—that Hawthorne and Fourier have fundamentally opposed
conceptions of innate virtue or depravity, for instance. As we shall see, Fourier
followed Rousseau in supposing that society was corruptive. By contrast, for
Hawthorne, as one of the characters in "Earth's Holocaust" puts it, schemes for
reform will always collapse until reformers "hit upon some method of purifying that foul cavern" (*CE* 10:403), the "human heart." As Herman Melville
put it in his review of *Mosses from an Old Manse*, Hawthorne had a "great
power of blackness in him [which] derives its force from its appeals to that
Calvinistic sense of Innate Depravity and Original Sin" (*CR* 107).

Nawrocki's allegorization of *The Blithedale Romance* is inadequate, but it
is just as problematic, and just as easy, to make the opposite mistake: because
Fourier's system is so grand in scope, a study of its relation to Hawthorne's fiction can easily become too diffuse in focus. Carl Guarneri has shown that the
Fourierists represented their own cultural critique as totalizing, subsuming all
varieties of reforms within their own. F. O. Matthiessen suggested long ago
that a study "concentrat[ing] on how discerning an interpretation our great

authors gave of the economic and social forces of the time" might be called "*The Age of Fourier.*" Such a study

> could by license be extended to take up a wider subject than Utopian socialism; it could treat all the radical movements of the period; it would stress the fact that 1852 witnessed not only the appearance of *Pierre* but of *Uncle Tom's Cabin;* it would stress also what had been largely ignored until recently, the anticipation by Orestes Brownson of some of the Marxist analysis of the class controls of action. (Matthiessen viii–ix)

Crediting Fourier with "all the radical movements of the period" would accord with the Fourierists' own view of their role in mid-century reform.[12] But the Fourierists' claims on behalf of their theory and the realities of mid-century reform plainly differ: Brownson, for instance, has been called "Fourierism's fiercest opponent in America" (Hill 92). Nor should one assume, just because Hawthorne used Fourierism as a metonym for what he took to be immoral reform, that he considered it coextensive with all reform. To understand the function of Fourier in Hawthorne one must distinguish between his references to Fourierism and his references to various other programs of reform, rather than assent to the Fourierists' own claims to subsume all reform. One might justly read Zenobia's commitment (however ambivalent) to both communitarianism and feminism as reflective of the appeal that Fourier held for a number of antebellum American feminists (a variety of whom, most notably the Grimké sisters, lived for stretches of time in Fourierist communities), but one can assume neither that Fourierism and feminism were entirely comfortable partners nor that the ideals of Zenobia and those of the Fourierist Blithedale are coextensive. Similarly, although Fourierists and Hawthorne both use the rhetoric of slavery to describe the condition both of women and wage laborers, it would be misguided to assume that this implies a Fourierist influence on Hawthorne. The danger, in short, is to simplify the relation and to obscure the differences between the varieties of reform represented in Hawthorne's work.

A further difficulty arises in distinguishing between possible Fouriers. Fourierist discourse in the United States in the 1840s did not derive exclusively from Fourier. In 1840, when Albert Brisbane transported Fourierism across the Atlantic, Fourier himself had been dead for three years. Although Brisbane had studied theory with Fourier, French Fourierism had already changed considerably by 1840. At that time, the leader of the Fourierist movement in France, Victor Considérant, was committed to creating a mass movement, which necessarily implied jettisoning the philosophical, libidinal, and cosmogonical extravagances of Fourierist theory (this had been happening, in fact, from the moment that Fourier began to acquire adherents, but with Fourier's death the disciples had one significant impediment fewer to making Fourierism widely palatable).[13] It is a commonplace of pro-Fourierist propaganda of all stripes to disclaim affiliation with some element of Fourier's speculations. Brisbane's own version of Fourierism—which he published in 1840 as *The Social Destiny of Man* and in a weekly column in Horace Greeley's New York *Tribune*—reflects, sustains, and carries further the efforts of French Fourierists: relative to Fourier's own writing, *The Social Destiny of Man* is a pallid document advocating little more than communitarianism. And as Brisbane's Americanized Fourierism started to become a mass movement, there arose yet another version of Fourierism, that constructed in the conservative press. Thus Hawthorne, who read newspapers avidly and on two occasions read Fourier in the original, had a multiplicity of Fourierisms from which to assemble his own portrait.

II.

Hawthorne often bases his own representations of Fourierism on contemporary portraits hostile to Fourier. But he would have encountered at least four distinct strains of Fourierism. The first is Fourier's own. Second is the Fourierism that developed out of Brisbane's efforts at establishing a movement in America, which had close ties with Hugh Doherty's abortive efforts in England and with the Fourierism of Victor Considérant. Third is Fourierism as portrayed by its enemies, as in the representations of Fourierism by pamphleteer Donald M'Laren and slavery apologist George Fitzhugh. Fourth is the Fourierism that persisted in the 1850s after the collapse of most phalanxes; it became increasingly intertwined with discourses on free love, spiritualism, and anarchism.

Fourier's theorizing spanned the first four decades of the nineteenth century, but its basic outline was consistent from his earliest publication: political economists had failed to solve the problem of poverty, and philosophers had failed to solve the problem of happiness, and all of them were therefore fundamentally wrong. "[T]hroughout all the twenty-five centuries for which the moral and political sciences have existed," wrote Fourier,

> they have done nothing for the happiness of humanity. They have served only to increase human wickedness through progressive scientific schemes of reform, all of which have ended up perpetuating poverty and

betrayal, merely reproducing the same scourges in different forms. After so many fruitless attempts to ameliorate the social order, philosophers are left with nothing but confusion and despair. For them, the problem of public happiness is an insurmountable obstacle: for is not the mere sight of the poor who fill our cities proof enough that these cascades of philosophical enlightenment are really only torrents of darkness? (*TFM* 19)

Fourier's theory was founded on a theodicy featuring a purely beneficent but passive God: "the improvements the sciences have made in luxury," Fourier wrote,

> have operated to the profit of the dishonest, who are more likely to become rich in barbaric and civilised society than truthful men. This strange fact leads us to opt for one of two possible interpretations: either God or Civilisation is maleficent. Only the latter can be rationally entertained, as it is not possible to suppose God to be maleficent; although indeed he would be if he had condemned us to vegetate for ever in the disastrous state of Civilisation. (*TFM* 22)

The problem of evil thus derived from an imperfectly constituted society. Were one to found a society that corresponded with God's plan (whatever that might be), one would solve the "problem of public unhappiness." Determining the form of this ideal society required negative interpretation of the existing one: since Civilization (that is, nineteenth-century European society) was obviously corrupt at every point, the ideal society would be its inversion. Fourier's skills as a parodist are often cited and celebrated, but his system was more than parody. A hermeneutics of inversion was the path to God, and away from the "disastrous state of Civilisation."

Unexpurgated Fourierism has several axioms. To begin with, Fourier makes the condition of women the index of social progress: "As a general proposition," he writes in his first published work,

> [s]ocial progress and changes of historical period are brought about as a result of the progress of women towards liberty; and the decline of social orders is brought about as a result of the diminution of the liberty of women. [. . .] [T]he extension of the privileges of women is the basic principle of all social progress. (*TFM* 132)

Nineteenth-century feminists from Flora Tristan in France to Elizabeth Cady Stanton in America cited this proposition. Stanton quotes Fourier in an epigraph to her memoir *Eighty Years and More* (1898), as does Tristan in *L'Emancipation de la femme* (1844). Stanton's first public speech, delivered at the 1848 Seneca Falls Convention, discloses a clear debt to Fourier when she states that "[a]s the nations of the earth emerge from a state of barbarism, the sphere of woman gradually becomes wider, but not even under what is thought to be the full blaze of the sun of civilization, is it what God designed it to be" (Stanton 28): in relating the "sphere of woman" to a narrative of historical progress Stanton is unmistakably influenced by Fourier. The practical extent of Fourier's feminism (and, at one remove, the feminist commitment of his various followers) is an enduring subject of debate; nevertheless, his stated principles are unambiguously feminist.[14]

A second axiom of Fourierism is that history is progressive—as the quotation above reflects. Fourier adopts the common eighteenth-century model of historical ascendance and decline, but is as ever uncommon in his precision. He imagines an eighty-thousand-year cycle of history divided into thirty-two periods, of which humanity had as yet traversed only the first five, and those inconsistently.[15] The first five periods, the only ones relevant to Fourier's critique, he calls Edenism, Savagery, Patriarchate, Barbarism, and Civilization. Unsurprisingly, no society remained in Edenism, although, influenced by the accounts of Bougainville, Fourier describes Tahiti as nearly so (he characterizes it as hovering between Edenism and Savagery).[16] Anticipating Marx's views on the inevitability of proletarian revolution, Fourier claims that his social reforms would only accelerate the inauguration of the next inevitable period in historical development.

Fourier assumes that the ideal society to come would be agrarian and limited in size: he stipulates joint-stock (as opposed to communally owned) corporations of 1600 residents. In his earliest work, *La Théorie des quatre mouvements,* he calls these corporations "cantons," but subsequently he begins to call them "*phalanges,*" or phalanxes. The residents were to cohabit in a phalanstery, a single building which combined space for labor, recreation, eating, and sleeping. Fourier's stipulations for the structure of the phalanstery are at once grandiose in ambition and minute in their attention to detail (and would become one of the central problems in American attempts to realize Fourierism, since fidelity to this element of Fourier's plans undermined economy).

Fourier's call for collective living is motivated partly by economy, and partly by his psychological theory, which holds that one can only be fulfilled in a group. For Fourier, the multiplication of tasks in what he calls "incoherent" or "isolated" households, and, more broadly, in industry, is in itself an inducement to find a better social structure: "[i]n a civilized village," he writes,

> there may be a hundred women who waste a whole morning going to town to sell a jug of milk. Instead of these hundred women, a Phalanx will send a carriage bearing a barrel of milk and accompanied by just one man to take care of the horse and the carriage. We might add that to pick up and purchase the milk brought to the city by a hundred village women, civilization sends out three hundred servant-girls who work in three hundred incoherent kitchens. So it takes one hundred village women and three hundred servants to perform a task which can be done by one man and a horse. (*UV* 130)

But more importantly, Fourier imagines that living communally is the best way to accommodate the play of what he calls the twelve "radical passions" (*TFM* 84). Five of these twelve correspond to the five senses; four, social "appetites of the soul" (*TFM* 84), are "Honour," "Friendship," "Love," and "Family" (*TFM* 80). The final three are "distributive" or "mechanizing passions" (*UV* 218). These, the "Cabalist," "Butterfly," and "Composite" passions—for intrigue, for variety, and for "the simultaneous enjoyment of two pleasures" (*UV* 218)—are the most important of the radical passions, because their gratification will spontaneously form and dissolve the social groups of Fourierist society. The radical passions in turn are "subdivided into a host of subtle variations which exercise a greater or lesser influence over every individual" (*TFM* 86). These variations are potentially infinite, but Fourier imagines "eight hundred principal types" (*TFM* 86). To allow for the full play of the passions, Fourier's phalanx needs two of each type, one man and one woman. Thus, to function optimally, the phalanx needs sixteen hundred people.

These twelve radical passions, once gratified, would give rise to a thirteenth, which Fourier calls "Unityism" (*TFM* 81). This is "the inclination of the individual to harmonise his own happiness with that of everything around him and of the whole human race" (*TFM* 81). But, in a deferral of specificity which is characteristic of Fourier, this passion cannot be positively defined prior to the establishment of a successful phalanx. In the existing society, it only expresses itself negatively as its "counter-passion, or Egotism, which is so universally dominant that ideology [. . .] has made [it] the basis of all calculations" (*TFM* 82). In keeping with Fourier's theory of negative interpretation, Unityism can be defined as everything which Egotism was not.

Significantly, Fourier does not dispense with class hierarchies: because of the foundational importance he attributes to variety, he holds that disparity in social condition is intrinsically good, and that social conflict arises not from disparity *per se* but from material scarcity: eliminate hunger, and one will eliminate class conflict. Fourier supposes that with the economies of collective living, the problem of scarcity would be resolved (he projects, instead, that phalanxes would have to contend with surpluses). And as a further safeguard, he stipulates a "minimum income sufficient for present and future needs" (*UV* 275); Fourier was thus an early advocate of a minimum wage.

Surviving class disparities notwithstanding, every resident of the phalanx was to labor. In the face of a near consensus in the nineteenth century maintaining that labor is necessarily enervating,[17] Fourier holds that labor properly organized could be pleasurable, and that people would therefore undertake it voluntarily, indeed enthusiastically. To achieve this, and in keeping with his theory of passions, Fourier declares that work must be varied. No single occupation should be pursued for more than two hours:

> [b]y working in very short sessions of an hour and a half, two hours at
> most, every member of Harmony can perform seven or eight different
> kinds of attractive work in a single day. On the next day he can vary his
> activities by taking part in different groups. This method is dictated by
> the eleventh passion, the Butterfly, which impels men and women to flit
> from pleasure to pleasure, to avoid the excesses that ceaselessly plague
> the people of civilization who prolong a job for six hours, a festival six
> hours, a ball six hours (and that during the night) at the expense of their
> sleep and their health. (*UV* 275–276)

As Jonathan Beecher has noted, Fourier's call for variety in work almost certainly influenced the Marx and Engels of *The German Ideology*.[18]

Most importantly, Fourier believes that work should be undertaken collectively by individuals whose interest in the work leads them spontaneously to collaborate. The ideal group would consist of seven to nine workers with a shared interest. These would ally themselves with other groups with similar—but slightly different—tastes, so that between the groups there would be an invigorating rivalry. Three or four of such groups leagued together Fourier called a "passionate series."

Pleasure is the mainspring of Fourierism. According to Fourier, pleasure is divinely endorsed: there cannot be an evil impulse, although, constrained by a pernicious society, impulse can be perverted into a negative expression. Most frequently cited by contemporary criticism as an example of perverted desire in Fourier's *oeuvre* is the case of Madame Strogonoff. Fourier writes that Strogonoff

> became jealous of the beauty of one of her young slaves. She had the slave tortured; she herself pricked her with pins. What was the motive for her cruel behavior? Was it jealousy? No, it was lesbianism. Madame Strogonoff was an unconscious lesbian; she was actually inclined to love the beautiful slave whom she tortured. If someone had made Madame Strogonoff aware of her true feelings and reconciled her and her victim, they might have become passionate lovers. But remaining unaware of her lesbian impulse, the princess was overcome by a counterpassion, a subversive tendency. She persecuted the person who should have been the object of her pleasure. (*UV* 353)

The repression of desire signals the failure of "Civilization." By contrast, Fourier imagines a society where repression, including (although not limited to) sexual repression, is unnecessary. The implications of this ought to be clear enough: as the Fourierist Victor Hennequin puts it (not disapprovingly), "[t]he word that could once be read on a palace in Ferrara, *Orgia*, ought to be inscribed on the pediment of his Phalanstery" (quoted in Beecher 269). It should come as no surprise, then, that Fourier disapproves of monogamous marriage, which was in his view simply the erotic corollary of the isolated household.

The radicalism of his sexual theory begins to suggest what nineteenth-century interlocutors might have found outrageous or dangerous about Fourierism; Fourier's disciples tried, however imperfectly, to contain his visions of utopian eroticism. Indeed, the anecdote of Madame Strogonoff cited above is among the manuscripts repressed by French Fourierists and unpublished until 1967. On the other hand, Victor Hennequin's *Les amours au Phalanstère*, translated by Henry James, Sr., as *Love in the Phalanstery* and published in New York in 1849, set off a wave of rancorous debate among Fourierists about the relation of Fourier's erotic speculations and the American Fourierist movement.[19]

Fourier's sexual speculations, and the consternation and outrage they engendered, point to a recurring problem that his adherents faced. However brilliant Fourier's critique of capitalist culture, and however imaginative and often persuasive his alternatives, they would never be tolerable to the nineteenth-century mainstream to whom Fourierists needed to appeal. Nor was sexual libertinage the only problematic element of Fourier's writing. What I have left unmentioned in the foregoing summary of Fourierist theory is its bizarre cosmogony. Fourier's cosmogonical speculations were so extravagant that they inevitably became an embarrassment to his enthusiasts; when Fourier's propagandists did not suppress his cosmogony altogether, they typically repudiated it. Fourier held, for instance, that the earth was hermaphroditic, its Northern hemisphere trying to copulate with the Southern (in vain until the earth was cultivated as far north as the Arctic Circle);[20] he imagined that human beings would eventually grow what he called an "archibras," a tail with an eye and a hand;[21] he supposed that the oceans would desalinate by passing through a stage in which they would taste like lemonade (a curiosity that, as we shall see, Hawthorne noted).[22] These *bizarreries* belatedly would lead the Surrealists to claim Fourier as a kindred spirit and precursor, but this was not a congenial solution for his nineteenth-century enthusiasts. The Fourier problem—how to relate the eccentricities to the rest of the theory—persists in contemporary scholarship, and will no doubt remain the central difficulty in apprehending his work ("I would not care to argue," Jonathan Beecher writes in the introduction to his recent biography of Fourier, "that the man was entirely sane" (Beecher [1986] 12)).

Beginning with the first enthusiasts who attempted to propagate Fourier's theory and to turn Fourierist communitarianism from an eccentric body of theory into a mass movement, the traditional solution to the problem has been simply to expurgate whatever is impractical or potentially offensive. Thus Albert Brisbane's *Social Destiny of Man*, the 1840 translation of Fourier that in concert with Brisbane's articles for Horace Greeley's New York *Tribune* inaugurated the Fourierist movement in America, is relatively speaking a modest document critiquing existing social conditions, advocating communitarianism as a corrective, and retaining a commitment to the idea of attractive labor and architectural reform. Flights of fancy are conspicuous by their absence, as are Fourier's erotic speculations, although Brisbane does not elide those critiques of the isolated household which are staged in purely economic terms. Guarneri describes this as the Americanization of Fourier, but it might more generally be called its *embourgeoisement*, since French and English Fourierists performed similar excisions and revisions.

This laundered version of Fourierism was the main one circulated in America in the early 1840s. Along with Brisbane's selective translation, however, the French Fourierists' new editions of Fourier's original texts circulated in America; thus Sophia Hawthorne showed familiarity with Fourier in the original in 1845.[23] Anti-Fourierists focused on these editions, while noting the disparity with the disciples' translations. Thus Donald C. M'Laren, in a pamphlet entitled *Boa Constrictor, or Fourier Association Self-Exposed*, could write

What does association mean to substitute in the place of marriage as it now is? Marriage, as an institution, cannot subsist in the combined order. How can it be maintained, when there is to be the greatest intimacy and freedom of intercourse between the sexes, and that intercourse regulated, not by conscience, or moral duty, or reason, but by the passions alone. The artful and unprincipled promoters of this passional scheme, give their views with caution and reserve on this point, and will, no doubt, be unwilling that association should *at present* be established in harmony with their theory. Still, they divulge enough to convict them of base duplicity in their profession of adherence to the marriage institution of civilized society. (M'Laren 23, his emphasis)

Fourierism as constructed by its fiercest critics was a sordid affair, surreptitiously attempting to seduce "the sprightly, robust nurseling of civilization in this Western World" into the embrace of "a dissolute, silly, imported, pauper hag" (M'Laren 9).

In the most perfervid denunciations of Fourierism, it appears as a brothel or prison in which property rights have been completely dissolved. George Fitzhugh's writing is representative; in *Cannibals All! Or, Slaves Without Masters,* his 1854 justification for slavery, he surveyed the various critiques-from-within of Northern society. Representing Fourierism in the person of Horace Greeley, Fitzhugh wrote that Greeley "proposed at once to coop mankind up in Phalansteries, where, in a few generations, all the distinctions of separate property, and of separate wives and children, would be obliterated and lost" (Fitzhugh 139). This is not entirely accurate: it was central to the self-definition of Fourierists that their system maintained individual property rights: it was Pierre-Joseph Proudhon who, famously maintaining that property is theft, recommended the abolition of private property. Such distinctions between socialists may have been too fine for their critics, or those critics may have been willing to blur distinctions to suit their own rhetorical ends. It is also possible that Fourier's critics were right about the implications of Fourierism on property ownership, Fourier's defense of property notwithstanding. To both Fourier and his critics, in any case, his system represented the absolute negation of "civilized society." Fourier took this to be the virtue of his theory, but it scandalized his critics. And where Fourier imagined a paradise of the senses, they imagined a nightmarish landscape of sensual excess.

Conservative hostility stemmed, in part, from legitimate suspicions that Fourierism was too mechanistic in its social prescriptions. The schematism of Fourier's theory led to Ralph Waldo Emerson's famous declaration, in

"Fourierism and the Socialists," that Fourierism was the "sublime of mechanical philosophy" (Emerson 72), and that

> Fourier had skipped no fact but one, namely, Life. He treats man as a plastic thing, something that may be put up or down, ripened or retarded, moulded, polished, made into solid, or fluid, or gas, at the will of the leader, or, perhaps, as a vegetable, from which, though now a poor crab, a very good peach can by manure and exposure be in time produced, but skips the faculty of life, which spawns and scorns system and system-makers, which eludes all conditions, which makes or supplants a thousand phalanxes and New-Harmonies with each pulsation.
> (Emerson 74)

This was a commonplace in critiques of Fourierism. In Elizabeth Barrett Browning's *Aurora Leigh,* for instance, the Fourierist Romney Leigh describes the destruction of his phalanstery thus:

> My vain phalanstery dissolved itself;
> My men and women of disordered lives,
> I brought in orderly to dine and sleep,
> Broke up those waxen masks I made them wear,
> With fierce contortions of the natural face,–
> And cursed me for my tyrannous constraint
> In forcing crooked creatures to live straight [. . .].
> (Barrett Browning 8.888–894)

Hawthorne seems to have shared this response: when in *The Blithedale Romance,* Coverdale attacks Westervelt's lyceum presentation as "eloquent, ingenious, plausible, with a delusive show of spirituality, yet really imbued throughout with a cold and dead materialism" (*CE* 3:200), what follows is a vision distinctly influenced by Fourier. In *The House of the Seven Gables,* Holgrave characterizes Fourier as "the systematizing Frenchman" (*CE* 2:156). Elsewhere in the novel, another systematizing European presents his own mechanistic utopia in a box to the tune of a barrel-organ and accompanied by a monkey; this may represent an indirect attack on Fourierism as animated by a morbidly materialist philosophy.

Responses to Fourierism in the 1850s were not, however, universally negative. In certain circles in the late 1840s and early 1850s, the writings of Fourier remained influential, chiefly through the writings of free-love theorists such as Thomas Low Nichols, Mary Gove Nichols, and Marx Edgeworth

Lazarus. Following James's translation of Victor Hennequin's *Les amours au Phalanstère,* these writers began to publish attacks on monogamy in works such as *Woman in all Ages and Nations* (1849) and *Love vs. Marriage* (1852). Although, as Guarneri notes, few free-love writers seconded Lazarus's advocacy of communitarian contexts for the exploration of their theories, their vocabulary remained palpably inflected by Fourier's critique of the isolated household and the contemporary condition of women.[24]

There were also certain ties between Fourierists and spiritualists. Henry James, Sr.'s enthusiasm for both Fourier and Emmanuel Swedenborg led him to try harmonizing them. Arguably the chief document in the literature of spiritualized Fourierism (or Fourierized spiritualism) was Andrew Jackson Davis's *Principles of Nature* (1847), which turned in its concluding chapter to what Guarneri calls "an extensive vision of a Fourierism-tinged utopia" (*UA* 351). One might assert the relation between Davis's utopian vision and Fourierism more positively than Guarneri does here, for Davis makes specific reference to Fourier in this chapter, ranking him alongside Swedenborg and Jesus:

> Recurrence to the writings of Charles Fourier is necessary for the purpose of bringing his social system before the world, so that mankind may investigate it, and give a just verdict as to its truth, morality, and practicability. It is impossible to escape the conclusion that he revealed many truthful causes and principles of reform that must be in some degree practised before the kingdom of heaven can be established on earth. (Davis 777)

In its particulars, Davis's vision of the "kingdom of heaven" consistently owes a stronger debt to Fourierism than to any other contemporary theory.

III.

These, then, are the main varieties of Fourierism which circulated in Hawthorne's America. In what follows I speak more comprehensively of Hawthorne's direct engagement with Fourierist theory and practice, from his earliest acquaintance with Fourierism up to the late 1840s, when he began to write *The Scarlet Letter.* I make two challenges to current understandings of Hawthorne's attitude towards communitarianism in general and specifically to his apprehension of Fourier. First, I suggest that Hawthorne's departure from Brook Farm did not, as has been maintained, signal the end of his interest in participating in communitarian experiments. Hawthorne's surviving correspondence with David Mack, one of the founding members of the (non-Fourierist) Northampton Association, shows that Hawthorne did not rule out the possibility of communitarian life even after Brook Farm; indeed, he was contemplating a move with Sophia to the Northampton Association shortly before he arranged for their tenancy at the Emerson manse. Second, I question the date conventionally assigned for Hawthorne's first reading of Fourier's own writing, the spring of 1845. The editors of the *Centenary Edition* of Hawthorne's works arrive at that date on the basis of a letter sent from Sophia to her mother on April 6, 1845, and quoted by Julian Hawthorne in his exercise in filiopiety, *Hawthorne and His Wife*. But in his notebooks Hawthorne first refers to Fourier in the summer of 1844,[25] and short stories from as early as 1843 reflect an engagement with Fourierism. I incline to see the spring of 1845, then, as the last possible date at which Hawthorne could have read Fourier.

Hawthorne never again lived in a communitarian society following his departure from Brook Farm in October of 1841. This fact has generally been taken to imply his renunciation of communitarianism as a social theory, but such an inference is unwarranted. Hawthorne's departure from Brook Farm derived in part from his rejection of George Ripley's ambition to "insure a more natural union between intellectual and manual labor than now exists" (quoted in *UA* 47), and in part from his pessimism about Brook Farm's prospects. But he seems principally to have left because he found himself incapable of writing there. The first and last reasons are related. D. H. Lawrence is only paraphrasing Hawthorne himself when he states in *Studies in Classic American Literature* that "You *can't* idealize hard work" (Lawrence 112, his emphasis); in a letter to Sophia composed at Brook Farm, Hawthorne complains that "labor is the curse of the world, and nobody can meddle with it, without becoming proportionably brutified." In "providing food for cows and horses" Hawthorne found that he was not "free to think and feel" (*CE* 15:557–558). Hawthorne, in effect, rejected the possibility of uniting manual labor with intellection. But in the early 1840s, this appears to be the sum of his critique of socialism.

A letter Hawthorne wrote to David Mack on May 25, 1842, demonstrates that he did not reject the communitarian principle along with Brook Farm: to the contrary, "I have," he states, "much faith in the general good tendency of institutions on this principle" (*CE* 15:624). The object of writing the letter was to excuse himself from joining the Northampton Association of Education and Industry:

> I am troubled with many doubts (after my experience of last year) whether I, as an individual, am a proper subject for these beneficial

influences. In an economical point of view, undoubtedly, I would not do so well anywhere else; but I feel that this ought not to be the primary consideration. A more important question is, how my intellectual and moral condition, and my ability to be useful, would be affected by merging myself in a community. I confess to you, my dear Sir, it is my present belief that I can best attain the higher ends of life, by retaining the ordinary relation to society. (*CE* 15:624)

The letter shows Hawthorne's disenchantment with Brook Farm did not lead to a disenchantment with all communitarian practice.

I insist upon the relevance of this letter to Mack because I see Hawthorne's choice of the Old Manse over the Northampton Association reflected in his fiction. I develop this in greater detail in the second chapter, and here only insist that the Old Manse ought to be read (borrowing Michel Foucault's term) as a heterotopia representing "the ordinary relation to society."[26] That is to say, Hawthorne's recurrent references to the Old Manse in *The American Notebooks* as an Eden, and to him and Sophia as a new Adam and Eve, should be related to the communitarian moment just as Walden has been. Richard Francis has characterized Walden as Thoreau's utopian community of one,[27] and the Old Manse ought similarly to be considered the Hawthornes' utopian community of two (or, after the birth of Una, of three). But this utopia, rather than being a challenge to contemporary society, as were the alternative societies proliferating in the 1840s, was rather its apotheosis: Hawthorne idealized it, and the marriage relation around which it was organized, in opposition to communitarian Edens.

It is probable that Hawthorne was first acquainted with Fourier at least in name during the months he spent at Brook Farm, and even possible that he read *Social Destiny of Man,* since Ripley among others had become familiar with Fourier by way of Brisbane before inaugurating Brook Farm. During their three years at the Old Manse, however, both of the Hawthornes read Fourier in the original: the first direct reference to Fourier in Hawthorne's work appears in an entry in *The American Notebooks* for July 27, 1844, in which he describes Sleepy Hollow, near Concord. The source for the tradition that Hawthorne first read Fourier in 1845 is the letter that Sophia Hawthorne wrote to her mother in May of that year. Writing in response to her mother's tentatively advanced opinion that Fourier had "lost all true ideas relative to women" and was "undermining the very foundations of the social order" (Peabody in Julian Hawthorne 1:266–267), Sophia replied that she had read Fourier herself, and that though [the fourth volume of Fourier's works] was so abominable, immoral, irreligious, and void of all delicate sentiment, yet George Bradford says it is not so bad as some other volumes. Fourier wrote just after the Revolution;[28] and this may account somewhat for the monstrous system he proposes, because then the people worshipped a naked woman as the Goddess of Reason. But I think that the terrific delirium that prevailed then with regard to all virtue and decency can alone account for the entrance of such ideas into Fourier's mind. It is very plain, from all I read (a small part), that he had entirely lost his moral sense. To make as much money and luxury and enjoyment out of man's lowest passions as possible,—this is the aim and end of his system! To restrain, to deny, is not suggested, except, alas! that too great indulgence would lessen the riches, luxury, and enjoyment.

This is the highest motive presented for not being inordinately profligate. My husband read the whole volume, and was thoroughly disgusted. (Sophia Hawthorne in Julian Hawthorne 1:268–269)

As Robert Martin notes in his reading of this letter,[29] its hostility is directed at Fourierism's sexual economy. It is possible that Sophia is overstating her outrage for rhetorical effect: her mother's concern that Fourier was undermining the foundations of the social order may have veiled concern for the Hawthornes themselves. By 1845, Brook Farm had converted to Fourierism, and Elizabeth Peabody may have been seeking reassurance that her daughter and son-in-law were not like-minded, his communitarian past notwithstanding; as T. Walter Herbert has shown, Sophia was not at other moments above twitting her mother for her sexual conservatism, and this may have been a corollary moment of reassurance.[30] It is also possible that Hawthorne's reaction was more nuanced than Sophia's letter suggests, and that "disgust" was not his only reaction. All in all, however, there is no reason not to assume that the letter gives us a generally accurate reading of the Hawthornes' response to Fourier.

What the letter definitely does not give is a specific date for their reading of Fourier's fourth volume, *Théorie de l'unité universelle*. Sophia's letter only provides the latest possible date: she specifies neither when she nor Hawthorne read Fourier, and it is certainly credible to suppose that Hawthorne was directly familiar with Fourier when he wrote his passage in Sleepy Hollow, or even earlier. *Theorie de l'unité universelle* was originally published in 1822, and was republished by the French Fourierists between 1841 and 1843. The Hawthornes, then, might well have read Fourier several years earlier than

1845. Hawthorne's reference in *The American Notebooks* to "the very model of a community, which Fourierites and others are stumbling in pursuit of" (*CE* 8:249) suggests that he was familiar with Fourier already in 1844.

The mid-1840s are unquestionably, however, a period when Hawthorne was souring on communitarianism, as his deteriorating relations with Brook Farm suggest. On or around February 21, 1846, he wrote a letter[31] in which he states that "Brook Farm, I suspect, is soon to see worse times than it ever has yet—at least, so men of business appear to think. Let it sink, say I;—it has long since ceased to have any sympathy from me, though individually I wish well to all concerned" (*CE* 16:144). A measure of this lack of sympathy is a court case he initiated in September 1845. While he was a resident at Brook Farm, he had not only paid $1000 for shares for himself and Sophia, but had loaned the community a further $500. In 1845, facing eviction from the Manse and in desperate financial circumstances, Hawthorne finally decided to sue Brook Farm—that is to say, George Ripley and Charles Anderson Dana—to recover the money. He included, improbably, a calculation for his 1841 summer of labor, so that in sum he was seeking compensation of more than $800. Ripley and Dana did not dispute the existence of a debt; their defense was to rest on the claim that since its conversion to Fourierism, the Brook Farm Phalanx as a whole and not they as individuals owed Hawthorne the money. The case began on March 7, 1846, after the Hawthornes had left the Old Manse for Salem, but before he was awarded the position at the Salem Custom-House.

The timing of the court case was particularly unfortunate for the community. Four days before the case began, on March 3, the phalanstery burned to the ground when one of its chimneys caught fire. Brook Farm had gone into debt financing the phalanstery; when it burned down it was neither finished nor insured against fire.[32] Although Brook Farmer Marianne Dwight Orvis wrote at the time that the fire was a welcome purgation and, she hoped, represented a new beginning,[33] the community only survived one year more. In August 1847 it would sell its assets to the town of Roxbury, which converted the community's farmhouse into an almshouse.[34]

IV.

In the same year that Hawthorne sued the Brook Farm Fourierists, his own work was appropriated as Fourierist propaganda. As Guarneri has shown, American Fourierists were at pains to show how Fourier's Eurocentric critique applied in a country where the inequities of Europe were, at least in the view of some, not as acute (*UA* 107). In an August 1846 edition of *The Harbinger,*

John Sullivan Dwight conscripted Hawthorne's "The Prophetic Pictures" (1837) to press the Fourierist point that the inequities of Europe were latent in the American social structure, and would in time become manifest. In "The Prophetic Pictures," Walter and Elinor, a young couple on the eve of marriage, commission a painter to capture their likeness. The two paintings he produces seem to prefigure a tragic end to their marriage: the painter imagines that Walter is insane and will ultimately turn violently on Elinor; he includes a subtle prophecy of this in the images he produces. At the story's end, the painter appears to be vindicated, for the assault only fails to take place owing to the intervention of the painter himself. Dwight uses the story as an analogy: just as the painter saw behind the façades of Walter and Elinor to their authentic and essential character, so too did Fourier see the essential character of American capitalism; as it developed it would vindicate Fourier's critique, just as the painter's portraits of Walter and Elinor "[a]t first [. . .] displeased them" (Dwight in *UA* 107) but were later proven accurate.

If Hawthorne was aware of this appropriation of "The Prophetic Pictures," which is probable, it must have been galling in light of the law suit. No evidence survives to prove that Hawthorne knew of Dwight's conscription of his story. Nevertheless, the two were acquainted—Hawthorne names him in the preface to *The Blithedale Romance* (*CE* 3:3)—and it is probable that Hawthorne, always alert to reviews of his fiction, was familiar with the article in *The Harbinger,* inasmuch as it referred to his own work. He would thus be presented with the spectacle of his own fiction being conscripted in support of a movement with which, as he said, he no longer sympathized.

More troubling still, Dwight misreads the story, ignoring or failing to register its critique of the painter. Hawthorne suggests that the painter is mad with excessive speculation. "It is not good," Hawthorne writes,

> for man to cherish a solitary ambition. Unless there be those around him, by whose example he may regulate himself, his thoughts, desires, and hopes will become extravagant, and he the semblance, perhaps the reality, of a madman. Reading other bosoms, with an acuteness almost preternatural, the painter failed to see the disorder of his own. (*CE* 9:180)

Hawthorne tenders the possibility that the artist has in fact manufactured the assault in accordance with his own interpretation of the husband's pathology: his paintings suggest to the pliable Walter and Elinor how Walter's madness will express itself. In a particularly telling sentence, Hawthorne writes that "[s]o much of [the painter] himself—of his imagination and all other powers—had been lavished on the study of Walter and Elinor, that he almost regarded them as creations of his own" (*CE* 9:179). This lavishing—literally, flooding—of self on other complicates the painter's "preternatural" insight.[35] The equation Dwight draws between Fourier and the painter is an unwitting critique of Fourier himself, inasmuch as it suggests that Fourier's critique only reifies his own madness.

More importantly still, Dwight ignores the story's subversion of the painter's insight. If the painter misreads Walter's madness, but because of his rhetorical power is able to persuade Walter and Elinor of his perspicuity, then the story fails to serve Dwight's political purposes. Rather, it subverts them, because the analogy would suggest that Fourier's critique of capitalism is a similar misreading, and similarly threatens to mislead those who accept it. Dwight's conscription of "The Prophetic Pictures" is only useful as propaganda as long as the story's ironies are ignored or elided.

In light of this appropriation it is no coincidence, I think, that in *The House of the Seven Gables* Hawthorne once again represents an artist whose work is purported to disclose hidden character. Dwight's misreading of "The Prophetic Pictures" may well have confirmed Hawthorne's decision to identify Holgrave with both art and Fourierism, finding in daguerreotypy a medium still more mimetic than painting: "[t]here is a wonderful insight in heaven's broad and simple sunshine," Holgrave tells Phoebe; "[w]hile we give it credit only for depicting the merest surface, it actually brings out the secret character with a truth that no painter would ever venture upon, even could he detect it" (*CE* 2:91). But Holgrave's insightful art does not make him a committed Fourierist: instead, he abandons reform and embraces Phoebe's conservatism. I read this as Hawthorne's recuperation of his own art: granted Hawthorne's familiarity with Dwight's article, *The House of the Seven Gables* becomes a thrice-told tale, reclaiming "The Prophetic Pictures" from the appropriations of *The Harbinger.*

Such a recuperation would seem more urgent given events intervening between 1846 and Hawthorne's composition of the American romances beginning in 1849. In 1848 Europe was convulsed with liberal revolutions, and in articles in *The Harbinger,* American Fourierist leaders not only declared their allegiance with the French revolutionaries, but even (wrongly) declared that the French Fourierists led by Victor Considérant were influential among them.[36] In light of the Fourierists' readiness to appropriate Hawthorne's work, Hawthorne was in a politically ambiguous position: conservative reviewers of *The Scarlet Letter* would accuse him of being a fellow-traveler of the Fourierists.[37] Beginning in *The House of the Seven Gables,* Hawthorne made his disagreement with Fourierism clear.[38]

Hawthorne cannot have failed to see the Fourierists in America as colleagues of the Republicans in France. Larry Reynolds's study of the influence of the 1848 revolutions upon *The Scarlet Letter* amply demonstrates Hawthorne's lack of sympathy; both *The House of the Seven Gables* (*CE* 2:156) and *The Blithedale Romance* (*CE* 3:53) call attention to Fourier's nationality, emphasizing the relationship between American Fourierists and the European left. *The Blithedale Romance* goes so far as to suggest that Fourierism is peculiarly French: Coverdale remarks that "in consideration of the promised delights of his system—so very proper, as they certainly are, to be appreciated by Fourier's countrymen—I cannot but wonder that universal France did not adopt his theory, at a moment's warning" (*CE* 3:54). In the American romances, Fourierism figures emphatically as a foreign presence in the United States. If the American romances are hostile responses to Europe's 1848, American Fourierism bears the brunt of the attacks.

Hawthorne's hostility to Fourierism by the 1850s is strongly suggested by a series of passages in the *American Notebooks* that culminate in an attack on the Shaker community at Hancock, Massachusetts. On July 31, 1851, Hawthorne borrowed three volumes of Fourier's works from Caroline Tappan as part of his preparatory research for *The Blithedale Romance,* and he spent the next week reading them. His notebook entries record little by way of response to this reading. He notes on August 7, 1851, that "Fourier states, that, in the progress of the world, the ocean is to lose its saltness, and acquire the taste of a peculiarly flavored lemonde—limonade a cedré [*sic*]" (*CE* 8:310) (a comment that Coverdale repeats, more or less, when he explains Fourierism to Hollingsworth in *The Blithedale Romance* (*CE* 3:53)). On the same day he records that he discussed Fourierism "and kindred subjects" with a neighbor, Mr. Waldo (*CE* 8:461). These mild comments do not in themselves suggest how Hawthorne was responding to his reading of Fourier. The next day, however, Hawthorne traveled to the Hancock Shakers in the company of his son Julian, Herman Melville, and the Duyckincks. Hawthorne's description of the community is a rare instance in which his *Notebooks* are frankly and unambiguously critical. The passage is worth quoting at length, for after his descriptions of life at Brook Farm, it is the most comprehensive and unmediated response to communitarianism in his writing:

> After a smoke under the trees, and talk about literature and other things, we set forth again, and resolved to go and visit the Shaker establishment at Hancock, which was but two or three miles off. I don't know what Julian expected to see—some strange quadruped or other, I suppose—at any rate, the term "Shakers" was evidently a subject of great puzzlement with him; and probably he was a little disappointed when I pointed out an old man in a gown and a gray, broad-brimmed hat, as a Shaker. This old man

was one of the fathers and rulers of the village; and under his guidance, we visited the principal dwelling-house in the village. It was a large brick edifice, with admirably convenient arrangements, and floors and walls of polished wood, and plaster as smooth as marble, and everything so neat that it was a pain and constraint to look at it; especially as it did not imply any real delicacy or moral purity in the occupants of the house. There were spit-boxes (bearing no appearance of ever being used, it is true) at equal distances up and down the long and broad entries. The sleeping apartments of the two sexes had an entry between them, on one side of which hung the hats of the men, on the other the bonnets of the women. In each chamber were two particularly narrow beds, hardly wide enough for one sleeper, but in each of which, the old elder told us, two people slept. There were no bathing or washing conveniences in the chambers; but in the entry there was a sink and wash-bowl, where all their attempts at purification were to be performed. The fact shows that all their miserable pretence of cleanliness and neatness is the thinnest superficiality; and that the Shakers are and must needs be a filthy set. And then their utter and systematic lack of privacy; their close junction of man with man, and supervision of one man over another—it is hateful and disgusting to think of; and the sooner the sect is extinct the better—a consummation which, I am happy to hear, is thought to be not a great many years distant. (*CE* 8:464–465)

Hawthorne adds, momentarily, that the Shakers "are certainly the most singular and bedeviled set of people that ever existed in a civilized land; and one of these days, when their sect and system shall have passed away, a History of the Shakers will be a very curious book" (*CE* 8:466). The sooner the "filthy," "hateful and disgusting" Shakers can be contained in a "very curious" history, the better.

On the few other occasions that Hawthorne refers to the Shakers, he is not nearly so critical. Twenty years earlier he had visited a Shaker community in Canterbury, New Hampshire; in a subsequent letter to his sister he characterized the Shaker ceremonies as "ridiculous" but spoke more positively of their living conditions (*CE* 8:563n4.13). Hawthorne's two pieces of short fiction involving the Shakers—"The Canterbury Pilgrims" and "The Shaker Bridal"—are both critical, characterizing their communities as a flight from life and Shaker celibacy as *contra naturam*, but again, there is nothing in them to suggest the coming acerbity.

T. Walter Herbert has suggested that Hawthorne's animus in the Hancock passage derives in part from "the presence of Melville, with whom he shared a male friendship offering satisfactions that were anathematized in the emerging organization of male sexualities" (Herbert 262), and this suggestion has a certain cogency. Melville's presence might well have compounded Hawthorne's anxiety. But the propinquity of this attack on the Shakers to his reading of Fourier suggests an additional explanation. The sexual politics of Fourierist theory were horrifying to conservatives, and charges of sexual excess were often directed at Fourierist communities: as Guarneri writes, Brook Farm took special pains to guard against charges of sexual incontinence.[39] In light of such charges, what is important in the Hancock incident is that Hawthorne perceives sexual excess in a communitarian context specifically: the problem for Hawthorne is not that individuals are pretending to be "clean" when in fact their relations are "disgusting," but that an entire community is maintaining the "pretense." Why Hawthorne would have had this reaction in 1851 and not in 1831 is only partly explained, it seems to me, by the presence of Melville. Hawthorne's reading in Fourier during the week immediately prior to his visit may also have influenced his response: the Shaker community was a near analogue to a Fourierist community. Hawthorne's emphasis on the disjunction between Shaker "pretense" and Shaker "reality" may reflect his attitude toward the disjunction between the Americanized Fourierism of Brisbane and others and its reality as expressed in Fourier's own works; Hawthorne's critique of the Shakers recalls an 1844 critique of Fourierists as practicing "base duplicity in their profession of adherence to the marriage institution of civilized society" (M'Laren 23). It is significant, in any case, that what Hawthorne expresses here as a wished-for "consummation," the extinction of a community, becomes in *The Blithedale Romance* a fact. As I have already suggested, we need to consider Blithedale's extinction—which Coverdale specifically describes as resulting from its conversion to Fourierism (*CE* 3:246)—as a tactic in a political contest.

V.

Although, as I shall argue, Fourierism is an absent presence in certain Hawthorne stories of the 1840s and in *The Scarlet Letter,* it comes into plain sight, as it were, in *The House of the Seven Gables* and *The Blithedale Romance.* In *The House of the Seven Gables,* Holgrave has

> the strangest companions imaginable;—men with long beards, and
> dressed in linen blouses, and other such new-fangled and ill-fitting gar-
> ments;—reformers, temperance-lecturers, and all manner of cross-looking
> philanthropists;—community-men and come-outers [. . .] who

acknowledged no law and ate no solid food, but lived on the scent of
other people's cookery, and turned up their noses at the fare. (*CE* 2:84)

And Hepzibah has read a newspaper report "accusing [Holgrave] of making a
speech, full of wild and disorganizing matter, at a meeting of his banditti-like
associates" (*CE* 2:84). Holgrave has "spent some months in a community of
Fourierists" (*CE* 2:176); in conversation he refers both to Fourier and Fourierism, telling Phoebe that he and she will "be fellow-laborers" in the Pyncheon garden "somewhat on the community-system" (*CE* 2:93), and that
Venner's anti-property reveries derive from "the principles of Fourier," the
"systematizing Frenchman" (*CE* 2:156).

In *The Blithedale Romance,* Fourierism is referred to often. Coverdale
falls ill upon arriving at Blithedale, and while convalescing reads

> interminably in Mr. Emerson's Essays, the Dial, Carlyle's works, George
> Sand's romances, (lent me by Zenobia,) and other books which one or
> another of the brethren or sisterhood had brought with them. [. . .]
> Fourier's works, also, in a series of horribly tedious volumes, attracted a
> good deal of my attention, from the analogy which I could not help but
> recognize between his system and our own. (*CE* 3:53)

From this catalogue of social theorists and artists, Coverdale singles out
Fourier for special comment. In conversation with Hollingsworth, Coverdale
"proceed[s] to explain [. . .] several points of Fourier's system [. . .] and
ask[s] Hollingsworth's opinion as to the expediency of introducing these
beautiful peculiarities into our own practice" (*CE* 3:53). Hollingsworth's
response is vituperative: Fourier

> has committed the Unpardonable Sin! For what more monstrous iniquity
> could the Devil himself contrive, than to choose the selfish principle—the
> principle of all human wrong, the very blackness of man's heart, the por-
> tion of ourselves which we shudder at, and which it is the whole aim of
> spiritual discipline to eradicate—to choose it as the master-workman of
> his system? [. . .] [H]is consummated Paradise [. . .] would be worthy of
> the agency which he counts upon for establishing it. [. . .] [L]et [Fourier]
> make a Paradise, if he can, of Gehenna, where, as I conscientiously
> believe, he is floundering at this moment! (*CE* 3:54).

In spite of this repudiation, and in spite of Coverdale's claim that "there [is]
far less resemblance [. . .] than the world [chooses] to imagine" (*CE* 3:53)

between Blithedale's system and Fourierism, the community still borrows vocabulary from Fourierism. Its "permanent plans" seem to consist exclusively of "erect[ing] a Phalanstery (as I think we called it, after Fourier)" (*CE* 3:128). When Coverdale first emerges from his convalescence

> into the genial sunshine, [he] half fancie[s] that the labors of the brotherhood had already realized some of Fourier's predictions. [. . .] In [his] new enthusiasm, man look[s] strong and stately!—and woman, oh, how beautiful!—and the earth, a green garden, blossoming with many-colored delights! (*CE* 3:61–62)

Coverdale's ironic tone is subversive, here—clearly, it implies, "the labors of the brotherhood" have not "realized [. . .] Fourier's predictions." Still, Fourierism seems to be latent in Blithedale's theory: at the end of his narrative, Coverdale affirms that, like Brook Farm, Blithedale "laps[ed] into Fourierism" before "dying, as it well deserved, for this infidelity to its own higher spirit" (*CE* 3:246).

There is thus ample reference to Fourier in the later American romances. Significantly, however, in neither *The House of the Seven Gables* nor *The Blithedale Romance* is it simple to find anyone genuinely committed to Fourierism. Holgrave discloses that he was formerly resident in "a community of Fourierists" (*CE* 2:176), but the narrator almost immediately cants away from attributing to Holgrave a commitment to Fourierist doctrine: however much he may have "put [. . .] off one exterior, and snatch[ed] up another, to be soon shifted for a third—he had never violated the innermost man, but had carried his conscience along with him" (*CE* 2:177): Fourierism has been one of a number of surfaces that can be assumed or discarded without altering the "essential" Holgrave. This pattern of simultaneous identification and distancing is consistent across both romances. Holgrave may perceive Fourierism at the root of Venner's rejection of individual property in favour of a collective "farm" (*CE* 2:155), but Venner's speculations are not formalized, lacking "systematizing" Fourierist "distinctness" (*CE* 2:156). And when Holgrave proposes to Phoebe that they work together in the Pyncheon garden, he immediately limits his analogy with Fourierist collaboration: their shared enterprise will be only "somewhat on the community-system" (*CE* 2:93).

In *The Blithedale Romance,* none of the central characters are Fourierists, even though Fourier is frequently invoked, nor is Blithedale, apparently, a phalanx, at least to begin with. Hollingsworth is the most openly hostile to Fourier, but Coverdale, although he invokes the "beautiful peculiarities" of

Fourier's system, nevertheless dismisses Fourier's works as "horribly tedious" (*CE* 3:53). Zenobia, who appears to be the genius of Blithedale in spite of her abandonment of its precincts in the latter half of the romance, never expresses any familiarity or affinity with Fourier (she does not lend the convalescent Coverdale any of Fourier's work, for instance; she lends him her copies of George Sand's fiction).[40] Even Blithedale itself, although its residents begin planning a phalanstery far earlier in its history than occurred at Brook Farm, is only analogous to a Fourierist community: "the two theories differed, as widely as the zenith from the nadir, in their main principles" (*CE* 3:53), Coverdale reassures his readers. Thus, although Fourier is by far the most frequently invoked of anyone other than the principal characters in either romance, he floats more or less free from any individual or practice actually represented in the texts. Each romance is already profoundly preoccupied with ghosts, but one can still say of both that a specter is haunting them—the specter of Fourierism.

This spectralization of Fourier serves a similar rhetorical function in each romance: Fourierism becomes the sign of that component of reform which must be rejected. In the case of *The House of the Seven Gables*, the distance between the principal characters and the spectral Fourier allows Hawthorne to imbue his protagonists with Fourier's aura of social critique while still drawing them back into the liberal democratic mainstream. Holgrave can make his conservative turn because only his outermost self has been committed to the "moonshine" of reform (*CE* 2:214). Venner's critique of individual property, ostensibly derived from Fourier, is so inchoate that he can assert it and yet not appear revolutionary, still serving as the romance's exemplar of evolutionary change.

The worst qualities of characters in *The Blithedale Romance* tend to be associated with Fourierism. Coverdale's sybaritism (a quality he shares with Clifford Pyncheon) is especially palpable when he waxes eloquent about the "beautiful peculiarities" (*CE* 3:53) and the "promised delights" (*CE* 3:54) of Fourierism. And when Zenobia accuses Hollingsworth of being a "cold, heartless, self-beginning and self-ending piece of mechanism," "nothing but self, self, self!" (*CE* 3:218), she echoes Hollingsworth's earlier excoriation of Fourier for choosing "the selfish principle [. . .] as the master-workman of his system" (*CE* 3:53). Buried in Blithedale pasture, Zenobia is closely associated with Fourierism, in spite of her wavering commitment to Blithedale. Zenobia seems to threaten sexual license. Because of her past "entanglement" with Westervelt (whatever it may be), Coverdale suspects her of contemplating adultery or polyandry with Hollingsworth (*CE* 3:127): conservative critics of Fourierism feared that it would produce just such a multiplication of partners. Zenobia's trajectory through *The Blithedale Romance* echoes that of Blithedale. Coverdale's first representations of Zenobia imbue her with almost excessive vitality, epitomized in the fresh hot-house flower she wears in her hair. Coverdale's narrative subjects her to an aestheticizing petrification: first, she replaces the real flower with one "exquisitely imitated in jeweller's work" (*CE* 3:164); following her suicide she herself becomes "the marble image of a death-agony" (*CE* 3:235). But even as she declines into materiality, Coverdale imagines her as a ghost haunting Hollingsworth, exacting penitential meditation from him and thereby containing him in Priscilla's domestic sphere. Similarly, Blithedale takes a Fourierist turn which culminates in its "dying, as it well deserved, for this infidelity to its own higher spirit" (*CE* 3:246). And yet Coverdale, too, is haunted by the memory of Blithedale.

Characters in *The House of the Seven Gables*, then, are recuperable within the dominant ideology to the extent that they are dissociable from Fourierism, while in *The Blithedale Romance* Coverdale justifies isolating or expelling characters by intimating that they too closely resemble Fourierism. Not, clearly, Fourierism as nineteenth-century Fourierists understood and practiced it, nor as Fourier himself would articulate it: the Fourierism that the romances repudiate is aligned with the conservative, dysphemistic construction of it. To equate Fourierism with materialism, for instance, overemphasizes that Fourier saw society as being susceptible to scientific analysis while it understates its spiritualism—for, as recent critics of Fourier have argued, Fourierist theory began "as an attempt to discover a successor, not to capitalism, but to the Christian Church" (Jones in *TFM* xxvi). Fourierist literature—the *Harbinger* is the obvious example—consistently affirms the Fourierists' Christianity; Marianne Dwight Orvis speaks in her letters from Brook Farm of their attempt to establish a Fourierist church.[41] Calling Fourierism "the sublime of mechanical philosophy," as Emerson does in "Fourierism and the Socialists," is therefore an aspersion that the Fourierists themselves would and did resist.

Although in both *The House of the Seven Gables* and *The Blithedale Romance* Fourierism is ostensibly expelled from the social body, it is nevertheless not the case that Fourierism is wholly denounced. In its conservative conclusion, *The House of the Seven Gables* absorbs various elements of Fourierist doctrine that it fails to identify as such. And precisely because it declines to identify the provenance of its utopian gestures, the romance can propound them without the aspersions that the invocation of Fourier's name would beget. Our intimations of the social arrangements at the Pyncheon estate derive from the social arrangements in the garden of the Pyncheon house, ones which Holgrave himself characterizes as "somewhat on the community-system" (*CE* 2:93). Phoebe's ability to give domestic "labor [. . .] the easy and flexible charm of play" (*CE* 2:82) borrows the Fourierist ideal of attractive industry in order to give a utopian flavor to the domestic labor of the "true woman." The romance's attempt simultaneously to preserve class difference and to resolve class conflict, dramatized in the readiness of Uncle Venner and Clifford Pyncheon to reside within "five minutes' saunter" (*CE* 2:317) of each other, reflects Fourier's social ideal. Finally, the rejection of the city in favor of a small but socially varied community is the logic behind the Fourierist phalanx (it is not coincidental that *The Blithedale Romance* begins where *The House of the Seven Gables* ends, with the departure from the city for a utopian community). The tacit appropriation of elements of Fourierism in *The House of the Seven Gables* reflects an attitude at odds with the disavowal of Fourier himself.

Likewise, *The Blithedale Romance* finds much in Fourierism to admire. Coverdale's belated regret and nostalgia converge with his testament to the "beautiful peculiarities" of Fourierism and his early enthusiasm for a world where Fourier's predictions seem to be realized. These suggest a positive attitude towards Fourierism that Hollingsworth's invective cannot wholly exorcise. In this regard, Coverdale's claim that Blithedale "seem[s] to authorize any individual, of either sex, to fall in love with any other, regardless of what would elsewhere be judged suitable and prudent" (*CE* 3:72) is emblematic. In this, Blithedale is alien to the values of "America." The "genuine American," according to Zenobia, "never dreams of stepping across the inappreciable air-line which separates one class from another" (*CE* 3:170). But the novel never retreats from installing this vision of love as a utopian ideal. In his belated expressions of nostalgia and regret, Coverdale may be merely disingenuous. But the key note of *The Blithedale Romance* is ambivalence: sardonic about the possibility of realizing Blithedale's utopian vision the novel nevertheless recognizes its attractions.

Their different treatment of Fourierism, then, also accounts for the difference in tone between *The House of the Seven Gables* and *The Blithedale Romance*. In the former, Fourierist utopianism can like Holgrave be conscripted into the social body and domesticated: with respect to Fourierism the text's cultural work is essentially assimilative, reminiscent of Sacvan Bercovitch's characterization of Emersonian liberalism as "a wholesale appropriation of utopia, all the hopes of reform and revolution nourished on both sides of the Atlantic by the turmoil of modernization, for the American way" (*RA* 335). Because it can succeed in this, *The House of the Seven Gables* is in essence a comic novel, and can conclude with a utopian flight to a kind of suburban New Jerusalem. In *The Blithedale Romance,* by contrast, Fourierism like Zenobia is expelled from the social body. But those who remain behind, like Hollingsworth and Coverdale, are never at ease with these expulsions: both men linger obsessively over their losses. Bercovitch has argued that in *The Scarlet Letter,* Hawthorne offers gradualism as a balm for contemporary injustice: in the face of gender inequity, Hester can rest easy in the "firm belief" in a better future (*CE* 1:263). In *The Blithedale Romance,* by contrast, Hawthorne argues that progress is a chimera, one whose promises inadequately compensate for present-day misery.[42]

VI.

This project is divided into four chapters. Chapter Two reads Hawthorne's writings from the 1830s and 1840s to examine his earliest representations both of communitarianism in general and of Fourierism in particular. The first part of this chapter reads three stories from the 1830s—"The Canterbury Pilgrims" (1833), "The May-Pole of Merry Mount" (1836), and "The Shaker Bridal" (1838). The Shaker stories interest me especially in light of Hawthorne's August 1851 response to the Shaker community at Hancock. These early stories represent the Shakers as unnaturally repressive of the libido; they are analogous, in this regard, to Hawthorne's Puritans. No study of Fourierism in *The Blithedale Romance* can ignore "The May-Pole of Merry Mount," for the critique of Blithedale repeats the critique of Merry Mount. "The May-Pole of Merry Mount" suggests that already in the 1830s Hawthorne had developed techniques to contain groups at odds with the dominant culture.

The latter part of Chapter Two focuses on the 1840s, when Fourierism was at its height as a national movement. I focus on the preface to *Mosses from an Old Manse*—"The Old Manse" (1846)—and "Egotism; or, the Bosom-Serpent" (1843) to argue that Hawthorne tacitly appropriates both the Fourierist critique of capitalist culture and the utopianism of the Fourierist alternative: these are tactics that Hawthorne will again resort to, *mutatis mutandis,* in *The House of the Seven Gables.* What Hawthorne produces as a result is a conservative utopianism organized around the domestic sphere: that is, Hawthorne buttresses separate-spheres ideology as an ideal by selectively borrowing from Fourierism.

Chapters Three and Four examine the American romances. Chapter Three further explores the relationship of Fourierism to the mainstream through a reading of egotism and Fourierist "Unityism" in *The House of the Seven Gables* and *The Blithedale Romance.* Fourier defined "Unityism" as the opposite of capitalist egotism, but at the same time he enthusiastically endorsed the gratification of individual appetite. Fourier's theory therefore shares certain qualities with that of radical individualists like Emerson and Max Stirner. This suggests in turn that capitalism and Fourierism are uncannily similar. The representations of the capitalist Jaffrey Pyncheon and the working-class Matthew Maule as kindred figures of dangerous virility derive from this similarity. Likewise, the similarity explains Hollingsworth's indictment of Fourier for his commitment to the "selfish principle" (*CE* 3:53) in a quasi-Fourierist community aimed at overcoming "selfish competition" (*CE* 3:19).

Chapter Four examines the relationship of sexuality and property, seeing them as deeply interconnected. Beginning with George Fitzhugh's claim that the Fourierists sought to dissolve "all the distinctions of separate property, and of separate wives and children" (Fitzhugh 139), I read the American romances as dramas in which such distinctions are under threat of dissolution. The romances all contend with the specter or the reality of multiple sexual partners, beginning with Hester Prynne's two partners and ending with the supposed entanglement of Zenobia with Westervelt; the romances are never more anxious than when paternity or title are in doubt. Fourierism, I argue, represents the extreme form of the threat to individual title and monogamy, but Fourierism is also a convenient scapegoat for mainstream society, the legitimacy of which can never be guaranteed.

Chapter Two

Dreamers' Utopias: Communitarianism and Fourierism in Hawthorne's Works Prior to the American Romances

The World was all before them, where to choose
Thir place of rest, and Providence thir guide:
They hand in hand with wandring steps and slow,
Through *Eden* took thir solitarie way. (*Paradise Lost* XII: 646–649)

The lovers drank at the Shaker spring, and then, with chastened hopes, but more confiding affections, went on to mingle in an untried life. ("The Canterbury Pilgrims" *CE* 11:131)

They went heavenward, supporting each other along the difficult path which it was their lot to tread, and never wasted one regretful thought on the vanities of Merry Mount. ("The May-Pole of Merry Mount" *CE* 9:67)

In fine, we gathered up our household goods, drank a farewell cup of tea in our pleasant little breakfast-room [. . .] and passed forth between the tall stone gate-posts, as uncertain as the wandering Arabs where our tent might next be pitched. ("The Old Manse" *CE* 10:33)

I. SHORT FICTION OF THE 1830S

Long before fictionalizing Brook Farm in *The Blithedale Romance*, Hawthorne visited separatist communities and used communitarianism as a theme for his fiction. His preoccupation with such communities is one of his most enduring. Already in his earliest fiction he used "utopian" communities as the setting for "phantasmagorical antics."

When he began representing Fourierism in the 1840s and 1850s, then, Hawthorne already had a history of appropriating communitarianism for his fictional purposes. He was inclined to make certain assumptions about the nature of Fourierism, for instance, on the basis of his earlier experience with the United Society of Believers in Christ's Second Appearing, known better as the Shakers. The later preoccupation with Fourierism, must be understood in light of the representations of other communitarian societies in his earlier fiction. The later fiction subjects Fourierist experiments to critiques reminiscent of those the early tales apply to the earlier communitarian societies. His earlier engagements with "utopian" communities suggest that Fourierism appeared to him in part as a symptom of historical forces which already preoccupied him.

The three stories from the 1830s that use a "utopian" community as the principal setting dramatize conflicts that Hawthorne would revisit when he came to write the American romances. "The Canterbury Pilgrims" (1833), "The May-Pole of Merry Mount" (1836), and "The Shaker Bridal" (1838) are set in communities that are, or try to be, outside of history. Edens after the Fall, they are necessarily delusive and corrupt their members in differing ways. Remaining within the community, as the protagonists of "The Shaker Bridal" do, is psychically devastating, and possibly fatal; following Milton's Adam and Eve and leaving "Eden," as the couples do in the other stories, exposes them to the mutability of postlapsarian life, but also promises a measure of fulfillment beyond the grasp of those whom they leave behind. In "The Shaker Bridal" and "The Canterbury Pilgrims," both of which depict Shaker communities, what corrupts—or threatens to corrupt—is the Shaker code of celibacy, which Hawthorne believes to be too strict. Conversely, in "The May-Pole of Merry Mount," the hedonism of the Merry Mount colonists threatens to corrupt the Lord and Lady of the May, Edith and Edgar. Though "The May-Pole of Merry Mount" describes a hedonistic utopia, discipline remains an issue: the postlapsarian world which Edith and Edgar enter is in the power of the Puritans, disciplinary utopians *par excellence.* The Shaker stories would suggest that such discipline is as pernicious as is the Merry Mounters' licentiousness. Hawthorne proposes the marriage of Edith and Edgar as a middle path. Nevertheless, if monogamy synthesizes hedonism and discipline, containing sexuality but still allowing it expression, the synthesis favors the disciplinary pole of the dyad.

"The May-Pole of Merry Mount" also complicates this binary opposition by staging the contest of utopias as a foundational conflict in New England history: because the Puritans rather than the Merry Mount colonists prevail, subsequent models of self-management will tilt towards the disciplinary. Read in light of Michel Foucault's account of the disciplinary turn, "The May-Pole of Merry Mount" appears as a genealogical myth, nationalizing and naturalizing disciplinarity by representing a foundational contest in which discipline prevails against its obverse.

In short, Hawthorne uses separatist communities in his early fiction to develop and critique extreme models of the management of the body, and posits monogamy as a more effectively managerial alternative to them. The meanings Hawthorne imposes upon these communities do not necessarily have much bearing on their actual social practices. Michael Colacurcio's claims for Hawthorne as a moral historian notwithstanding, it is clear enough that Hawthorne's constructions of the Puritans, however consistent with other nineteenth-century representations of them, were not especially accurate portraits of seventeenth-century New England culture. Neither does Hawthorne's negative representation of the Shakers in his fiction accurately represent Shaker communities. His two stories of the 1830s do not appear to reflect even his own initial response to these communities. In 1831, Hawthorne wrote a letter to his sister Louisa, in which he wrote:

> I walked to the Shaker village yesterday, and was shown over the establishment, and dined there with a squire and a doctor, also of the world's people. [. . .] Our dining-room was well furnished, the dinner excellent, and the table attended by a middle-aged Shaker lady, good looking and cheerful. [. . .] This establishment is immensely rich. Their land extends two or three miles along the road, and there are streets of great houses painted yellow and tipt with red. [. . .] On the whole, they lead a good and comfortable life, and, if it were not for their ridiculous ceremonies, a man could not do a wiser thing than to join them. Those whom I conversed with were intelligent, and appeared happy. I spoke to them about becoming a member of their society, but have come to no decision on that point. (quoted in Waggoner 40)

It has been generally assumed that Hawthorne's claim to have spoken to the Shakers about joining them is a joke for Louisa. Still, Hawthorne is far from the unequivocal condemnation that he later expressed, and one might plausibly see in his admiration of the Shakers' communitarian lifestyle—"ridiculous ceremonies" excepted—the sentiment that would move him to join Brook Farm a decade later.

His representation of Shakers in fiction is much more critical. In "The Canterbury Pilgrims" (1833) and "The Shaker Bridal" (1838), the Shaker settlements are equated with a living death, and the characters who join them are in effect committing suicide. The Shaker settlement is outside of history: the pilgrims approaching Canterbury see a couple dressed in "a strange old fashioned garb" (*CE* 11:120). The man seems "to have inherited his great-grand-sire's square skirted coat, and a waistcoat that extended its immense flaps to his knees" (*CE* 11:121); the woman's "close, long waisted gown [. . .] might have been worn by some rustic beauty who had faded half a century before" (*CE* 11:121). This extrahistorical space has utopian resonance. The couple leaving the Shaker settlement resemble Milton's Adam and Eve leaving Paradise: "[t]he lovers drank at the Shaker spring, and then, with chastened hopes, but more confiding affections, went on to mingle in an untried life" (*CE* 11:131). But given the postlapsarian realm of human action, this Eden is necessarily false. Those wanting to join the Shakers, Hawthorne writes, seek "a home where all former ties of nature or society [shall] be sundered, and all old distinctions levelled, and a cold and passionless security be substituted for human hope and fear, as in that other refuge of the world's weary outcasts, the grave" (*CE* 11:131). The only critic to have attended to these stories at length, Hyatt Waggoner long ago likened the portrait of the Canterbury Shaker community to a "Protestant monastery" (Waggoner 41). But Hawthorne's reference to the grave suggests that the Shakers are less monastic than spectral.

Still, the comparison to monks remains apt: in both stories, the insufficiency of Shaker life is especially apparent in the fate of marriage, understood as not just legal or spiritual but sexual union. The Shakers practiced celibacy as a form of religious devotion: as Lawrence Foster explains, "[o]nly by giving up all 'carnal' propensities—including sexual intercourse and close family attachments—and devoting oneself wholly to the worship of God within a supportive communal setting could salvation ultimately be achieved" (Foster 20). In his fiction, Hawthorne critiques the Shakers less for their "ridiculous ceremonies" than for their celibacy: in his view the Shakers themselves cannot bear it. Josiah and Miriam, the young protagonists of "The Canterbury Pilgrims," surreptitiously leave the Shaker community at Canterbury rather than renounce their "'carnal' propensities." In "The Shaker Bridal," when Adam Colburn and Martha Pierson—two former lovers—venture to solemnize in a mock-wedding ceremony their position as spiritual leaders of the Goshen Shaker community, Martha collapses "like a corpse in its burial clothes." "[A]fter many trials firmly borne," Hawthorne writes, "her heart could endure the weight of its desolate agony no longer" (*CE* 9:425). Shaker celibacy demands too great a physical repression.

Hawthorne suggests that such repression cannot conquer but only displace the libido. In "The Shaker Bridal," Ephraim, who officiates at the bridal of Adam and Martha, "had been a most dissolute libertine, but was converted by Mother Ann herself, and had partaken of the wild fanaticism of the early Shakers" (*CE* 9:424). Hawthorne suggests that Ephraim has translated sexual energy into religious enthusiasm, and supplements this etiology with a rumor that Ephraim's conversion stems from torture: "Tradition whispered, at the firesides of the village, that Mother Ann had been compelled to sear his heart of flesh with a red-hot iron, before it could be purified from earthly passions" (*CE* 9:424). In this subtle sentence, Hawthorne not only intimates that the Shakers' "earthly passions" have taken on a sadomasochistic form, but that the fireside narrations (presumably complete with their own pokers) themselves function as sexual displacement, a kind of filiopietistic erotica. In "The Shaker Bridal," celibacy does not suppress libidinal impulses but transmutes them into violent fantasy.

The Shakers, however, are not the sole objects of Hawthorne's critique. Both stories represent characters turning to the Shakers for economic reasons. If in Hawthorne's view the Shakers are deluded in their choice of refuge, their need for refuge is real. Such a need is the principal reason for the success of Shaker communitarianism: "converts of this sect," Hawthorne writes, "are oftener driven [to the Shakers] by worldly misfortune, than drawn thither by fanaticism" (*CE* 9:422). Certainly, two of the Canterbury pilgrims are objects of satire: a poet and a merchant who have experienced disasters in their literary and economic speculations retreat to the Shakers animated principally by outraged dignity. The poet ostentatiously composes a valediction to his art which he promptly arranges for publication; the merchant begins to calculate the value of the Shakers' property with an eye to "doubl[ing] their capital in four or five years" (*CE* 11:127). The disappointments of neither are sufficient, Hawthorne suggests, to warrant their removal to the Shakers, nor is their withdrawal from society complete. Other pilgrims are sketched with greater sympathy, but still as motivated by material needs: a farmer, his wife, and their two surviving children have resolved to join the Shakers because of economic hardship. "I have labored hard for years," the farmer states, "and my means have been growing narrower, and my living poorer, and my heart colder and heavier, all the time; till at last I could bear it no longer" (*CE* 11:128). In "The Shaker Bridal," Adam Colburn joins the Shakers for like reasons.[1] He and Martha defer marriage until their circumstances have improved; eventually, "that calm despair, which occurs only in a strong and somewhat stubborn character, and yields to no second spring of hope, settle[s] down on [Adam's] spirit" (*CE* 9:422). Adam imposes his despair upon Martha and so shares responsibility for her collapse, but Hawthorne does not belittle the circumstances which led him to join the Shakers (even as Hawthorne deliberately overstates the Shakers' immunity from economic cycles).

Crucially, neither the farmer and his wife in "The Canterbury Pilgrims" nor Adam Colburn and Martha Pierson in "The Shaker Bridal" are wholly justified in abandoning the private realm of marriage to escape market vagaries. In both cases, their flight to the Shakers is premature. In spite of their complaints that economic hardship has permanently compromised their marriage, the married couple in "The Canterbury Pilgrims" could have remedied their own affairs: "one word fitly spoken," Hawthorne writes,

> or perhaps one peculiar look, had they had mutual confidence enough to reciprocate it, might have renewed all their old feelings, and sent them back, resolved to sustain each other amid the struggles of the world. But the crisis past, and never came again. (*CE* 11:130)

Similarly, Hawthorne states unambiguously that Adam and Martha might have successfully married even without absolute economic security. The fault lies with Adam, whose "calm and cautious character" makes him "loath to relinquish the advantages which a single man possesses for raising himself in the world" (*CE* 9:421). It is not the economic market itself which is to blame, but the characters who flee it in hopes of finding a life without vicissitudes.

Given the choice between the Shaker community and the society which circumscribes it, Hawthorne opts for the latter, which permits what he takes to be a more natural relationship between the sexes. In spite of being subject to the vagaries of economic cycles, in spite, too, of the persistence of "old [social] distinctions" (*CE* 11:131) among "the world's people" (*CE* 11:121), Josiah and Miriam are more likely to find a chastened happiness in their self-imposed exile from the Shakers than are Adam Colburn and Martha Pierson, who remain among them. The Shakers' asceticism overweighs in Hawthorne's consideration their supposed freedom from the market.

The Shaker stories thus depict a communitarianism that arises in response to the economic crises among the "world's people." Shaker settlement and "mainstream" America relate to each other dialectically. Each in its own way, however, debilitates its members. To the extent that Blithedale too responds to a society it characterizes as "false and cruel" (*CE* 3:19) in its principles, it resembles these Shaker communities. Unlike them, however, it is predicated not on repression but license: it damages, Hawthorne suggests, by permitting too much.

Historians of American communal societies have traditionally distinguished between pietistic and secular communities.[2] Another distinction has been drawn between exemplary communities such as the Fourierists,' which sought to inspire general structural changes in society, and quietist ones like the Shakers, uninterested in broad social change. Hawthorne's representation of the Shakers and his later portrait of Blithedale suggest a different opposition between discipline and hedonism, or repression and expression. The Shakers are at the former pole, Blithedale towards the latter.

This polarization plays throughout Hawthorne's fiction, but its *locus classicus* is "The May-Pole of Merry Mount," which allegorizes the quarrel between Thomas Morton and the Pilgrims as "[j]ollity and gloom [. . .] contending for an empire" (*CE* 9:54). This is a foundational moment, Hawthorne gives us to understand, in New England's history. The seventeenth-century contest between Puritan and Cavalier is the origin of contemporary American subjectivity: "[t]he future complexion of New England," he writes,

> was involved in this important quarrel. Should the grisly [Puritan] saints establish their jurisdiction over the gay [Cavalier] sinners, then would their spirits darken all the clime, and make it a land of clouded visages, of hard toil, of sermon and psalm, forever. But should the banner-staff of Merry Mount be fortunate, sunshine would break upon the hills, and flowers would beautify the forest, and late posterity do homage to the May-Pole! (*CE* 9:62)

The puritanism that, as Colacurcio puts it in *The Province of Piety,* "overcomes the only credible challenge to a local hegemony aspiring to become totalized" (Colacurcio 252) sets New England on the path to its nineteenth-century form. Blithedale, which has a May Day ceremony almost identical to the one in "The May-Pole of Merry Mount," belatedly recapitulates this contest: as Colacurcio says, the trouble with Blithedale is that it "has forgotten its history" (Colacurcio 33).

This begs the question of what New England's history actually is, of course. Even by the standards of the documents available to him—Thomas Morton's *New English Canaan* and Nathaniel Morton's *New Englands Memorial*[3]—Hawthorne's version of what happened at Merry Mount is not historically accurate. In keeping with their provenance on opposite sides of the conflict, these histories offer contrary accounts. But Hawthorne's story draws on them selectively, to say the least. Rather than navigate between the two Mortons, Hawthorne allegorizes the conflict, and, like the Puritans themselves, exaggerates the carnivalesque elements of Merry Mount. This allegorization elides the complexities of the ideological contest waged between Puritans and Cavaliers, but also eliminates the political issues. The story omits any reference, for instance, to Thomas Morton's readiness to sell weapons to nearby Native tribes, or his alleged leveling of social classes at Mount Wollaston. Much of the historical matter resists simplification; Hawthorne's response is to eliminate elements that complicate the binary opposition.[4]

Hawthorne's allegorization of the Puritan-Cavalier contest privileges Puritanism. Edith, the Lady of the May, suggests that Merry Mount is a kind of hallucination (thereby anticipating Coverdale in his characterization of Blithedale as illusory (*CE* 3:21)). "I struggle as with a dream," she says, "and fancy that these shapes of our jovial friends are visionary, and their mirth unreal, and that we are no true Lord and Lady of the May" (*CE* 9:58). By definition carnival comes to an end (just as prelapsarianism ends in the Fall). But the Merry Mount carnival is not an authorized release from discipline that ends with a peaceful restoration of authority. It is rather a denial of reality, a May-Day "at sunset on midsummer eve" (*CE* 9:55). As such, the story gives Puritanism the greater claim to understand things as they "really" are.

Hawthorne's moral allegory depends upon the elision of the history of Merry Mount. Hawthorne's narrator refers to the "true history" of Merry Mount (*CE* 9:60) even as he distorts it for the sake of emphasizing the carnivalesque: Merry Mount's leaders, the narrator states,

> were men who had sported so long with life, that when Thought and Wisdom came, even these unwelcome guests were led astray, by the crowd of vanities which they should have put to flight. Erring Thought and perverted Wisdom were made to put on masques, and play the fool. The men of whom we speak, after losing the heart's fresh gaiety, imagined a wild philosophy of pleasure, and came hither to act out their latest daydream. They gathered followers from all that giddy tribe, whose whole life is like the festal days of soberer men. In their train were minstrels, not unknown in London streets; wandering players, whose theatres had been the halls of noblemen; mummers, rope-dancers, and mountebanks, who would long be missed at wakes, church-ales, and fairs; in a word, mirthmakers of every sort, such as abounded in that age, but now began to be discountenanced by the rapid growth of Puritanism. (*CE* 9:59)

Nowhere in this representation of Merry Mount's history is there anything which approaches the Mortons' accounts, except, perhaps, for Nathaniel Morton's characterization of Thomas Morton as a Lord of Misrule. Nathaniel Morton's charge is not that Thomas Morton gathered at Mount Wollaston some proto-Bohemian throng, but rather that he "receive[d] [servants] as [his] partners and consociates" (Nathaniel Morton 69) and made life anxious for other colonists by, among other things, selling weapons to the Indians. "[L]et this pestilent fellow [Thomas] Morton," Nathaniel Morton writes, "bear a great part of the blame and guilt of [Indian warfare] to future Generations" (71). Hawthorne elides those elements which have led others to see in the Merry Mount episode a moment in the development of American democracy.[5] In making the rebellious servants a giddy tribe of artists who "counterfeit [. . .] Indian hunter[s]" (*CE* 9:56) but do not sell them weapons, Hawthorne's narrator aestheticizes the community: if Nathaniel Morton's history of Merry Mount points, anxiously, to the spectre of seventeenth-century class and racial warfare, the narrator of Hawthorne's version presents nothing that physically threatens.

If Hawthorne cannot be said to be writing "true" history, then what is he doing? If we understand how the concerns of Hawthorne's present influence "The May-Pole of Merry Mount," we may see the story as having a genealogical function. Hawthorne's references to "[t]he future complexion of New England" (*CE* 9:62) and Endicott as the "severest Puritan of all who laid the rock-foundation of New England" (*CE* 9:66) make it clear that he is creating a genealogy for the conditions of his present. As a belatedly formulated myth of origins "The May-Pole of Merry Mount" not only transposes into the past the contemporary contests of nineteenth-century America, but fixes the fight, as it were, in this "historical" past.

The Puritan-Cavalier conflict is in essence one between discipline and unruly desire. Nancy Armstrong explicates such dyads in *Desire and Domestic Fiction,* her Foucauldian history of the domestic novel. She reads the novel as developing alongside the proliferation of disciplinary technologies in the eighteenth and nineteenth centuries, arguing that the rise of self-disciplining heroines such as Jane Eyre and the containment of non-bourgeois social and sexual practices reflect and participate in the consolidation of middle-class culture, and that oppositional political practices become pathologized as alternative sexual practices: "It may be with some regret," Armstrong writes,

> that we feel the passion depart as the first generation of lovers dies out
> of *Wuthering Heights* or when a much subdued Rochester reappears in

> *Jane Eyre* without his hand, eye, and lunatic wife, but there is no ques-
> tion that these figures of desire have become obsolete. (203)

Armstrong's application of Foucault's disciplinary thesis to the history of the
English novel is clearly germane to "The May-Pole of Merry Mount."
Hawthorne's Puritans exaggerate the disciplinary turn of the eighteenth and
nineteenth centuries; the Merry Mount colonists exaggerate fringe groups as
figures of excessive sexuality.

Just as Hawthorne finds fault both with the Shakers' separatism and
with the economic crises that lead subjects to resort to it, he submits to critique both Puritan discipline and the "systematic gaiety" of the Merry
Mount colonists. The Puritans deal out their punishments with such
enthusiasm that they begin to look not like principled moralists, but like a
sadistic inversion of the Merry Mount revellers. After the fall of the May
Pole, Endicott has his own version of postlapsarian nostalgia and wishes for
its restoration, since "it would have served rarely for a whipping-post!" (*CE*
9:64). The festive Merry Mount community, meanwhile, is either deluded
or repressing disbelief: "the youngest deemed themselves happy," the narrator affirms;

> [the] elder spirits, if they knew that mirth was but the counterfeit of happi-
> ness, yet followed the false shadow wilfully, because at least her garments
> glittered brightest. Sworn triflers of a lifetime, they would not venture
> among the sober truths of life, not even to be truly blest. (*CE* 9:59–60)

Both poles are not equally the objects of critique, however. The Puritans may
be sadistic, but Endicott nevertheless carries Edith and Edgar out of a false
Eden into the realities of this world. The Puritans may be hypocrites in their
condemnation of hedonism, but their Calvinism has a better grasp of the
way things are: their Puritanic gloom reflects and emerges out of "the moral
gloom of the world," which, like Endicott at Merry Mount, "overpowers all
systematic gaiety" (*CE* 9:66).[6] If by definition the carnival must end with
Lent, with the return of its protagonists to a conservative social order, then
Endicott's condemnation of Merry Mount imposes from without what is
already structurally intrinsic to carnival itself. Moreover, however much
Hawthorne asperses Endicott, attributing his disciplinary enthusiasm to sexual sadism rather than piety—or suggesting, perhaps, that Calvinist piety is
predicated on sadism[7]—Endicott's action is anticipated and so affirmed by
nature. When Edith and Edgar feel a presentiment of doubt about the
ephemerality of Merry Mount,

Just then, as if a spell had loosened them, down came a little shower of withering rose leaves from the May-Pole. Alas, for the young lovers! No sooner had their hearts glowed with real passion, than they were sensible of something vague and unsubstantial in their former pleasures, and felt a dreary presentiment of inevitable change. (*CE* 9:58)

The story culminates, of course, in the absorption of Edith and Edgar into the Puritan "Israel" (*CE* 9:66). "Real passion" disenchants the "wild philosophy of pleasure"; Puritan discipline, Hawthorne supposes, is a social mode that better accommodates postlapsarian nature, and on this ground he rationalizes patriarchal monogamy.

Edith and Edgar negotiate the poles of Hawthorne's carefully constructed binary as the exemplars of a disciplinarity that avoids the implicit sadism of Puritanism's public version. Edith and Edgar go "heavenward, supporting each other along the difficult path which it [is] their lot to tread, and never [waste] one regretful thought on the vanities of Merry Mount" (*CE* 9:67). Like the emergent bourgeois subjects in Nancy Armstrong's account of the history of the novel, they do so within the private domain of their marriage: Endicott may officially incorporate them into the Pilgrim community, but Hawthorne suggests that they remain largely independent of it. Their marriage functions both to dispel the hedonistic ephemerality of Merry Mount— or to restrict it to the bedroom—and to preempt Endicott's excessive public penality. Domesticity displaces both licentious May-Pole and sadistic whipping post as a third term. Critics have often faulted the portraits of Edith and Edgar for their banality, and as characters, it is true, they are neither especially differentiated nor memorable. Their importance lies in their ideological function as embodiments of domesticity. In the seventeenth-century setting of the story, they are anachronistic, since they are familiar nineteenth-century types. It is as though Hawthorne includes in Edith and Edgar a projection of the relationships that Endicott's destruction of Merry Mount will generate, the flowers that will grow in the long shadow cast by the New England Way. Endicott is to Edith and Edgar as the women who hurl animadversions at Hester Prynne are to their nineteenth-century descendants:

Morally, as well as materially, there was a coarser fibre in those wives and maidens of old English birth and breeding, than in their fair descendants, separated from them by a series of six or seven generations; for, throughout that chain of ancestry, every successive mother has transmitted to her child a fainter bloom, a more delicate and briefer beauty, and a slighter physical frame, if not a character of less force and solidity, than her own. (*CE* 1:50)

Edith and Edgar are domesticated Endicotts; Endicott is an atavistic Edgar.

Reading "The May-Pole of Merry Mount" alongside the Shaker stories is useful because it forestalls the inclination to read it purely as historical fiction. However vivid Hawthorne's portrait of colonial history, and however extensive his reading in New England histories, his portraits of the Puritans are not different in kind from his portrait of the Shakers. In part, this may be Hawthorne's point: the anachronistic clothes of Josiah and Miriam suggest the deep similarity between Shaker and Puritan public discipline, both obsolete in the context of nineteenth-century domesticity.

The more general point to insist upon is that Hawthorne uses communitarianism in his fiction of the 1830s to represent social structures against which he can posit an ideal in conventional marriage. Marriage responds both to experimental modes of social management and to economic crisis. "The May-Pole of Merry Mount" demonstrates the former point in its dialectical representation of discipline and hedonism, between which marriage negotiates. The Shaker stories dramatize the latter point: Hawthorne does not belittle the Shakers for seeking a refuge from economic contractions; instead, he suggests that the communitarian solution is mistaken. The appropriate response, as Josiah and Miriam's example demonstrates, is not to seek a public sphere immune to market cycles, but to distinguish between public sphere and private sphere, and find refuge from the former's volatility in the stability of the latter.[8]

The representations of communitarianism in Hawthorne's writings of the 1840s and 1850s differ from those of the 1830s in emphasis, but they are not radically dissimilar. In *The House of the Seven Gables* and *The Blithedale Romance*, marriage at least superficially remains the appropriate solution to market fluctuations: Holgrave abandons communitarian reform when he marries Phoebe; and the rural cottage to which Hollingsworth and Priscilla retreat replaces Blithedale's phalanstery. Communitarianism remains, that is, an inadequate alternative. But Hawthorne's portrait of marriage as balm and source of stability is subtler in the romances, particularly *The Blithedale Romance*. This development is owing not only to Hawthorne's personal experience of marriage to Sophia, but to a decade in which Fourierists and others articulated a sustained critique of marriage.

II. THE AMERICAN NOTEBOOKS, JOURNAL OF AN AFRICAN CRUISER

In the 1840s Hawthorne did not set any fictions in communitarian contexts, but his interest in the subject did not disappear. Given his explanation to David Mack on the eve of moving to Concord and the Manse with Sophia that "I can best attain the higher ends of my life by retaining the ordinary relation to society" (*CE* 15:624), he viewed the Manse specifically as an alternative to communitarian experiments, and his representations of it should be read as responses to such experiments. But if the Manse represents "the ordinary relation to society," Hawthorne's representations of it are nevertheless utopian. The Manse is a synecdoche of an idealized society, representing "institutions" such as marriage that in Hawthorne's view have "grown out of the heart of mankind" (*CE* 10:26). It is, in other words, at once a "rebuke [to] the speculative extravagances of the day" (*CE* 10:25) and also a utopian community of two.

The earliest specific example of Hawthorne's imaginative appropriation of Fourierism is in an extended and carefully composed passage in *The American Notebooks* from July 1844—a passage Hawthorne would later mine both for "The Old Manse" and for his edition of Horatio Bridge's *Journal of an African Cruiser.* Like the communitarian fictions of the 1830s, the passage associates communitarianism with a utopian scene that must be abandoned. Hawthorne sets himself the task of recording "such noticeable points as the eyes fall upon around [him]" while sitting down "in Sleepy Hollow, a shallow space scooped out among the woods" near Concord (*CE* 8:245). Towards the end of this *jeu d'esprit,* he notices

> a whole colony of little ant-hills, a real village of them; they are small,
> round hillocks, formed of minute particles of gravel, with an entrance in
> the centre; and through some of them blades of grass or small shrubs have
> sprouted up, producing an effect not unlike that of trees overshadowing a
> homestead. Here is a type of domestic industry ? perhaps, too, something
> of municipal institutions—perhaps, likewise (who knows?) the very
> model of a community, which Fourierites and others are stumbling in
> pursuit of. Possibly, the student of such philosophies should go to the ant,
> and find that nature has given him his lesson there. (*CE* 8:249)

Instants after having recorded this, he notices "clouds, voluminous and heavy, [. . .] scattered about the sky, like the shattered ruins of a dreamer's Utopia" (*CE* 8:250), and (presumably fearing rain) concludes the exercise.

The passage thus follows a general trajectory from enchantment to disenchantment. And just as Hawthorne first characterizes the hollow as the "lap of bounteous Nature" (*CE* 8:245) but eventually associates it with a "shattered [. . .] Utopia," so too does he begin by trying to record "noticeable points" (*CE* 8:245) and ends by lamenting the insufficiency of language: he states in conclusion that the "distinct and expressed thought" of his "record of observation" is a "shallow and scanty [. . .] stream [. . .] compared with the broad tide of dim emotions, ideas, associations, which were flowing through the haunted regions of imagination, intellect, and sentiment" while he was writing (*CE* 8:250). "Utopia" and "the haunted regions of imagination, intellect, and sentiment" are allied in the Sleepy Hollow exercise, ideals of which Fourierism and text are "stumbling" pursuers and "shallow" transcriptions.

Hawthorne uses two catalogues to adumbrate the disenchantment with which the exercise concludes. The first of these is drawn from nature: the sounds of three animals increasingly disturb Hawthorne's "tranquility" (*CE* 8:248). He first hears a bird whose "long, melancholy note [. . .] [complains] of some wrong or sorrow, that worm, or her own kind, or the immitigable doom of human affairs has inflicted upon her," and then hears a squirrel with a "sharp, shrill chirrup" (*CE* 8:248). Finally, "terrible to the ear, [t]here is the minute but intense hum of a musquito," an insect which Hawthorne crushes: its "grim and grisly corpse" is "the ugliest object in nature" (*CE* 8:248). Hawthorne follows this sequence of progressively disruptive animal sounds with the noises of human labor. Echoing his catalogue of animal sounds, Hawthorne alludes in sequence to four different sounds of culture penetrating Sleepy Hollow: the "striking of the village-clock;" mowers "whetting their scythes;" "the tinkling of a cow-bell;" and finally, "the whistle of a locomotive" (*CE* 8:248). With increasing effort, Hawthorne reconciles the first three with his Edenic landscape. The clock, although it "tells of human labor," represents "the sacredness of the Sabbath;" the sounds of the mowers' labor "increase the quiet of one who lies at his ease;" and the cow-bell, "a noise peevishly dissonant, were it close at hand," is "even musical" from a distance (*CE* 8:248). The noise of the locomotive, however, cannot be "mollif[ied] into harmony," since it bespeaks "busy men, citizens, from the hot street [. . .] and the noisy world" (*CE* 8:248–9). The noise of the mosquito and the noise of the locomotive are similar, but while Hawthorne can crush the mosquito, he must attempt to mollify the locomotive's noise. But crucially, this attempt fails: he is obliged to wait until the noise dissipates.

Hawthorne discovers the ant-colony—and alludes to Fourierism—when a "slumbrous peace" has been restored after the locomotive's whistle. In invoking Fourierism at this moment Hawthorne comments ironically upon human attempts to pastoralize labor. The Fourierists sought mechanisms to make work attractive. The locomotive's intrusive whistle represents what Hawthorne takes to be the impossibility of doing so: human labor is an intrusion into the utopian space of Sleepy Hollow, and by implication it is irreconcilable with it; the idyll depends upon labor being elided. Hawthorne thus recapitulates his complaint to Sophia at the end of his tenure at Brook Farm (in 1841) that "labor is the curse of this world" (*CE* 15:558). In the anthill labor is pastoral—but the laborers are ants. The immediate transition from intrusive human labor to the "domestic industry" of the ants suggests that only animals can experience labor as anything but a "curse." Inevitably, then, the Fourierists are "stumbling" (*CE* 8:249).

James Mellow argues that Hawthorne's reference to Fourier in this passage is a "mild criticism" (Mellow 249). Hawthorne's real response was far harsher, Mellow states, citing Sophia Hawthorne's letter to her mother. But Hawthorne's point in the Sleepy Hollow exercise is not that Fourierists are vicious, but that their ideals are impossible to realize. The Fourierists function as an analogy to Hawthorne himself, or at least to his narrator, who also stumbles, in his case in pursuit of an ideal transcription of Nature and Imagination: "When we see how little we can express," Hawthorne writes, "it is a wonder that any man ever takes up a pen a second time" (*CE* 8:250). Hawthorne's criticism may be mild precisely because he enlists Fourierist reform as an analogue to the aspirations of the artist.

This analogy is obviously relevant to understanding the artist-reformers in the latter two American romances, Holgrave and Coverdale, who each struggle to define the relationship between reform and art. (One of the unanswerable questions raised by *The House of the Seven Gables* is whether Holgrave abandons daguerreotypy—and fiction—when he abandons reform; Coverdale's struggle to find a way to represent reform is one of the recurrent problematics of *The Blithedale Romance*.) The analogy also represents a departure from the Shaker stories and, to a lesser extent, from "The May-Pole of Merry Mount." Although a disappointed poet is among the pilgrims to the Shaker community at Canterbury, that story does not suggest a parallel between the poet's artistic aspirations and those of the Shaker community. In "The May-Pole of Merry Mount," the relationship of art to utopian community is more complex. But the Merry Mount colonists are a "giddy tribe" (*CE* 9:59) of artists, which distinguishes them from Hawthorne in the Sleepy Hollow passage: Hawthorne is not frivolous, like them, but he is nevertheless unable to remain in the utopian scene.

Hawthorne's criticism of Fourierism is still more mild in the version of this passage he published in Horatio Bridge's *Journal of an African Cruiser*. Bridge, who had sponsored the 1837 publication of *Twice-Told Tales*, served in the early 1840s on an American sloop, the *Saratoga*, which policed the illegal transatlantic traffic in slaves. Before Bridge left on the expedition, he and Hawthorne agreed to publish excerpts from Bridge's maritime journal in the *Democratic Review,* with Hawthorne acting as editor; then, changing their plans, they opted to publish it as a book. In the preface to *Mosses from an Old Manse,* Hawthorne claims that editing Bridge's work was "an easy task" (*CE* 10:34); this is not to say, however, that he was a passive editor. His letters to Bridge give tutelage in the art of writing, and probably indicate the nature of his own editorial interventions: "Allow your fancy," he writes,

> pretty free license, and omit no heightening touches because they did not chance to happen before your eyes. If they did not happen, they at least ought—which is all that concerns you. This is the secret of all entertaining travellers. (*CE* 23:626)

As the editors of the *Centenary Edition* show, Hawthorne's local changes to the Bridge manuscript can be substantial: in one passage, his emendations double the length, adding literary allusions and polishing the style.[9] In at least one instance Hawthorne added material from his own notebooks to the *Journal of an African Cruiser:* a version of the Sleepy Hollow episode's comparison of ants to Fourierists appears late in the book, still to the detriment of the Fourierists, but now describing not the ants of Massachusetts but those of Liberia:

> At the present day, when the community-principle is attracting so much attention, it would seem to be seriously worth while for the Fourierites to observe both the social economy and the modes of architecture of these African ants. Providence may, if it see fit, make the instincts of the lower orders of creation a medium of divine revelations to the human race: and, at all events, the aforesaid Fourierites might stumble upon hints in an ant-hill, for the convenient arrangement of those edifices, which, if I mistake not, they have christened Phalanxteries [*sic*].[10] ("Bridge" 159)

The description of the ants is peripheral to the main concerns of the *Journal,* a digression whose principal function is to provide comic relief. But its satire would hardly seem savage to anyone unfamiliar with Hawthorne's later representations of Fourier. And to most readers the passage's author was an anonymous "Officer of the U. S. Navy" (Bridge's name having been suppressed, and Hawthorne's editorship alone acknowledged). Charles Anderson Dana, ever attentive to representations of Fourierism, protests only at the characterization of Associationists as "Fourierites." "'Fourier*ist,*'" he writes, "is sufficiently disagreeable [. . .] but [. . .] 'Fourier*ite*' excites in us a kind of intellectual nausea" (Dana's emphasis, *Harbinger* 1:58). His review concludes approvingly by citing a passage in the *Journal* "full of good sense" (*Harbinger*

1:58), and inviting the anonymous author to write again. The communitarian movement would vigorously object to Hawthorne's satire in *The Blithedale Romance,* but the Fourierist response to the *Journal* was to enlist its presumed author as an ideological ally.

However mild its satire, the *Journal's* allusion to Fourierism is a caution against inflated expectations. As a kind of socialist colonialism, Fourierism resembled in certain respects the American Colonization Society's "repatriation" of emancipated slaves to Liberia; this resemblance probably informed Hawthorne's decision to incorporate his allusion to "Fourierites." The *Journal* explicitly represents itself as an authoritative and impartial report on Liberia's prospects of success: as the preface puts it,

> If, in any portion of the book, the author may hope to engage the attention of the public, it will probably be in those pages which treat of Liberia. The value of his evidence, as to the condition and prospects of that colony, must depend, not upon any singular acuteness of observation or depth of reflection, but upon his freedom from partizan bias, and his consequent ability to perceive a certain degree of truth, and inclination to express it frankly. A northern man, but not unacquainted with the slave institutions of our own and other countries—neither an Abolitionist nor a Colonizationist—without prejudice, as to prepossession—he felt himself thus far qualified to examine the great enterprise which he beheld in progress. ("Bridge" v–vi)

The allusion to Fourierism occurs moments before the *Journal* begins its principal commentary on the prospects of Liberia. The American Colonization Society, it argues, ought not to exaggerate the virtues of the Liberian colonies, because colonists drawn there by overheated ACS rhetoric "will find it very far from a paradise" ("Bridge" 163). Periodically the *Journal* uses racist stereotypes of indolence to characterize the emancipated slaves who have colonized Liberia. They have, it states in one instance, "high notions of freedom and exemption from labor (ideas which with many are synonymous)" ("Bridge" 34), and thus arrive ill suited to the difficulties of "planting" a colony. According to the *Journal,* for Liberia to prosper the colonists "must cultivate their minds, be willing to exert themselves, and not look for a too easy or too rapid rise of fortune" ("Bridge" 163): they must, in short, adopt a Franklinian work ethic.

Cautions against expectations of the easy and rapid success of reformist colonies would resonate with a readership becoming familiar by 1845 with the collapse of Fourierist communities. At first, Brisbane and other Fourierist propagandists had adopted the perfervid and immediatist rhetoric of Fourier's writings, which stated that a single phalanx would effect a transformation from "Civilization" to "Harmony." On the one hand, promises of a society quickly perfected through attractive industry contributed to American Fourierism's initial success at attracting recruits; on the other hand, these promises caused problems once the phalanxes were operating because participants expected the Fourierist miracles to begin instantly.

By invoking a reform movement whose utopian rhetoric was not confirmed by its results, the *Journal* prepares the ground for its own, more qualified utopianism. Although those first arriving in Liberia will find it "far from paradise," it stands to be a "black man's paradise" insofar as it restores to the formerly American African male "his long-lost birthright of equality" ("Bridge" 164): "The white man, who visits Liberia," the *Journal* states, "be he of what rank he may, and however imbued with the prejudices of hue, associates with the colonists on terms of equality" ("Bridge" 163–164). The utopian promise of Liberia is not that it will free its colonists from labor, nor that it will eliminate racial prejudice, and it does not imply social transformation akin to Fourierist explorations of the "community-principle" ("Bridge" 159). As the *Journal* conceives it, Liberia's "great enterprise" is restorative, not progressive. This is the kind of conservative utopianism that Hawthorne also propounds in "The Old Manse."

III. "THE OLD MANSE"

Hawthorne interpolated text from the Sleepy Hollow passage not only into the *Journal of an African Cruiser,* but also into "The Old Manse" (1846), the description of his tenure at Concord which prefaces *Mosses from an Old Manse.* Near the preface's conclusion Hawthorne defends himself against the imputation of being an "egotist" on the grounds that "[s]o far as I am a man of really individual attributes, I veil my face" (*CE* 10:33). He buttresses this claim by stating that writing is an insufficient medium for accurate representation, and here interpolates and modifies his climactic lament from the Sleepy Hollow passage. The Sleepy Hollow passage concludes with the following complaint:

> And now how narrow, scanty, and meagre, is this record of observation, compared with the immensity that was to be observed, within the bounds which I prescribed to myself. How shallow and scanty a stream of thought, too,—of distinct and expressed thought—compared with the broad tide of dim emotions, ideas, associations, which were flowing

through the haunted regions of imagination, intellect, and sentiment, sometimes excited by what was around me, sometimes with no perceptible connection with them. (*CE* 8:250)

The modified passage in "The Old Manse" reads:

How narrow—how shallow and scanty too—is the stream of thought that has been flowing from my pen, compared with the broad tide of dim emotions, ideas, and associations, which swell around me from that portion of my existence! How little have I told!—and, of that little, how almost nothing is even tinctured with any quality that makes it exclusively my own! (*CE* 10:32)

When Hawthorne was writing the Sleepy Hollow passage, he related the writer's awkward attempts to represent nature to the Fourierists' awkward attempts to contrive an ideal social economy. In "The Old Manse" he elides the Fourierists entirely and relates the failure of language to the end of his tenure in the Manse. And just as the Sleepy Hollow passage concludes with Hawthorne's recognition that "it is time to move" (*CE* 8:250), "The Old Manse" concludes with Hawthorne's departure from the Manse: "we gathered up our household goods, drank a farewell cup of tea [. . .] and passed forth between the tall stone gate-posts, as uncertain as the wandering Arabs where our tent might next be pitched" (*CE* 10:33). Like the Canterbury Shaker community and the Merry Mount colony, the Manse is an Eden from which this latest version of Adam and Eve must depart.

But the utopianism of the Manse is categorically different from that of Merry Mount or the Shaker colonies. Where these are in one way or another at odds with "American" identity, the Manse is deeply intertwined with American history. "The Old Manse" situates itself in American literary, political, and religious history by invoking the previous inhabitants of the Manse and the historical events—especially those associated with the Revolution— that occurred in its vicinity. "The Old Manse" describes the battle at Lexington Bridge in Concord, emphasizing the propinquity of the Manse to the inaugural battle of the Revolution: "there needed," Hawthorne writes, "but a gentle wind to sweep the battle-smoke around this quiet house" (*CE* 10:6). Similarly, Hawthorne calls attention to the Puritan ministers who previously lived in the Manse, thus situating it within the history of New England as a Puritan colony (even while insisting upon a categorical difference between the previous occupants and himself). Hawthorne freights the Manse with both the political and the religious history of New England.

The Manse is not, then, a reformatory which seeks to contest the values of society; it is rather a synecdoche for an idealized America. Certainly, Hawthorne evokes the social critiques originating with Fourierists and others. After describing a fishing trip on the Assabeth with William Ellery Channing, Hawthorne refers to "custom and conventionalism" and the "fettering influences of man on man" (*CE* 10:25) from which their flight has liberated them. But the "custom and conventionalism" of the Manse is not pernicious. To the contrary, the Manse is "a stately edifice" representing "the institutions that [have] grown out of the heart of mankind" (*CE* 10:26); it is an organicist utopia that deserves supernatural protection: "it had grown sacred," Hawthorne writes, "in connection with the artificial life against which we inveighed" (*CE* 10:25). The Manse is a utopia, but it is not an oppositional one.

Although "The Old Manse" refers to Brook Farm, which by 1846 was in its Fourierist phase, nowhere does it mention Fourierists specifically. But reading the Sleepy Hollow passage alongside "The Old Manse" suggests that Fourierism is an absent presence in the latter. The text's reference to the summer islands is instructive in this regard. Describing the Manse's orchard and the idea it confers of an "infinite generosity and exhaustless bounty, on the part of our Mother Nature," Hawthorne compares it positively to the "summer islands, where the bread-fruit, the cocoa, the palm, and the orange, grow spontaneously" (*CE* 10:13). This allusion, which almost certainly derives from his reading in Melville's *Typee* (which he reviewed in late March of 1846), may also be a displacement of Fourierist theory. Hawthorne probably was not directly familiar with Fourier's representation of Tahiti as the society which most nearly approximated the conditions of Eden, and which was a foretaste of the pleasures of Harmony. Hawthorne may well have read, however, Charles Dana's long polemical review of *Typee* in *The Harbinger* for April 4, 1846.[11] Dana resorts to conventional apostrophes to an Eden hitherto exempt from Western corruption in order to repeat Fourier's description of Polynesia as a forerunner of a Fourierist paradise:

> Such are these gems of the ocean, in which Nature, prodigal and unhindered, has hinted the extent of her possibilities, and by a kind of material diffraction has prophecied her own future perfections;—perfections which she shall possess in infinite and universal variety when, through the combined industry and wealth and power of a United Race, she shall have become but the image and expression of the Kingdom of God abiding in the souls and societies of Man! (*Harbinger* 2:263)

Typee affords Dana the opportunity to speculate on the conditions requisite for social harmony, and he located these conditions in the natural abundance of the Marquesan Islands, whose fecundity left none wanting. Quoting Melville's descriptions of the harmonious and healthy Typee (but declining to mention the intimations of cannibalism that haunt Melville's narrator), Dana attributes their well-being to the "*abundance* [that exists] *for every person*" (*Harbinger* 2:265, Dana's emphasis), and proceeds to argue for the institution of "associated, coöperative labor" (*Harbinger* 2:266). According to Dana, only Fourierist theory with its federated labor and its guarantee of social minimums can bring plentitude to "civilized communities." Such abundance, Dana argues,

> is not possible in the midst of social and political institutions which are mostly forms of organized selfishness, where every thing is subjected to greedy, fraudulent and uncertain commerce, and where Slavery in some one of its disgusting and inhuman forms is a necessary and constant fact. (*Harbinger* 2:266)

If Hawthorne was familiar with this passage, then his reference to the summer islands does more than reflect his reading of Melville. It also appropriates for the Manse the tropical plentitude the Fourierists saw as a precondition for Harmony, making the Manse an American utopia.

The Fourierists were quick to appropriate the utopianism of accounts of the South Pacific.[12] In "The Old Manse," Hawthorne draws on these same accounts to describe the utopianism of the Manse. One need not assume that "The Old Manse" refers directly to Fourier in order for it to be coherent. But together with the deprecatory reference to Brook Farm that immediately follows this passage (*CE* 10:13), Hawthorne's allusion to the summer islands implicitly rebuts Fourierism's claims on behalf of cooperative labor. Not the communal and radical Brook Farm but the isolated and conservative Manse is the source of utopian abundance in Massachusetts.

Reading "The Old Manse" as influenced by Fourierist discourse allows one to situate it in a wider continuum of antebellum social debate, as espousing a moderate path between various "speculative extravagances." If the Fourierists function invisibly in "The Old Manse," the antipode to their communitarianism does not. Hawthorne's representations of Emerson and the enthusiasts who follow him burlesque the liberal individualism of "Self-Reliance." Emerson, a "great original Thinker," attracts "[y]oung visionaries" and "[g]ray-headed theorists" who try either to "seek the clue that would lead them out of their self-involved bewilderment" or "to invite this free spirit into their own thraldom" (*CE* 10:30). Anticipating Hollingsworth in his recapitulation of the Puritan exemplary city on a hill, Emerson is a "beacon burning on a hill-top," but one who attracts "bats and owls, and the whole host of night-birds, which [flap] their dusky wings against the gazer's eyes, and sometimes [are] mistaken for fowls of angelic feather" (*CE* 10:31). Hawthorne's portrayal of "hobgoblins of flesh and blood attracted" to Concord by Emerson's "wonderful magnetism" (*CE* 10:30) recalls Emerson's own claim in "Self-Reliance" that a "mind of uncommon activity and power [. . .] imposes its classification on other men, and lo! a new system" (Emerson 521): Emersonian self-reliance gains currency, Hawthorne suggests, precisely through such an imposition.

Hawthorne disavows the "false originality" and "triteness of novelty" (*CE* 10:32) that derives from Emersonian individualism, claiming that "being happy, I [. . .] admired Emerson as a poet of deep beauty and austere tenderness, but sought nothing from him as a philosopher" (*CE* 10:31). Hawthorne also has to contain the irruption of individualism into his work: he almost immediately curtails his sketch of the Manse. He needs to conclude "The Old Manse," he says, lest his readers "vilify the poor author as an egotist" (*CE* 10:32). Hawthorne is articulating a recognition that he develops more fully in *The Blithedale Romance:* a first-person narrative rests upon an individualist poetics. He denies egotism in "The Old Manse" through the duplex claim that he remains invisible to the reader and has "appealed to no sentiment or sensibilities, save such as are diffused among us all" (*CE* 10:32–33). Just as the Manse is a synecdoche for "the institutions that had grown out of the heart of mankind" (*CE* 10:26), Hawthorne's I-narrator is a synecdoche organically connected to his readers.

Hawthorne situates the Manse, then, on a conservative foundation that equally resists the blandishments of communitarianism and individualism. The ideal society is that of the middle path. While "The Old Manse" never directly refers to Sophia—either out of patriarchal oversight or patriarchal calculation—it is nevertheless clear that what organizes the conservative utopia—its heart—is marriage, from which Hawthorne derives the happiness that makes Emerson's individualism superfluous. As in the Shaker stories and "The May-Pole of Merry Mount," marriage mediates the extremes. But in "The Old Manse" it mediates between Emersonian atomism and Fourierist collectivity.

The critique of Emerson is more direct than that of the generalized "speculative extravagances of the day" (*CE* 10:25) that presumably include Fourierism. One reason for this is that, just as marriage in "The May-Pole of

Merry Mount" cleaves more closely to disciplinarity, marriage in "The Old Manse" cleaves towards individualism: compared with Fourierism, with its radical prescriptions for social change, Emersonian individualism is a conservative force. If it is an engine of appropriation, as Sacvan Bercovitch has argued,[13] it stages its appropriations from within the existing social structure. Emerson declined to join Brook Farm. But another reason for mystifying the Fourierist presence in "The Old Manse" is that Hawthorne can thereby borrow the Fourierist critique of individualism even as he offers a different corrective—marriage rather than socialist communities. Thus, for instance, "Egotism; or, the Bosom-Serpent," composed in 1843 near the apex of Fourierism's American career, makes use in its title of a term—"egotism"—from the Fourierist lexicon.

IV. "EGOTISM; OR, THE BOSOM-SERPENT"

Although "Egotism; or, the Bosom-Serpent" is often assumed to comment on the exaggerated individualism of Emerson or Jones Very, no one has considered how it relates to the socialism that prompted Emerson's formulation of salubrious individualism to begin with.[14] Although Hawthorne probably had not read Fourier by 1843, his comment that "the snake in [Roderick's] bosom seem[s] the symbol of a monstrous egotism, to which everything [is] referred" (*CE* 10:274) is comparable to Fourier's characterization of egotism as an "odious [. . .] mania for subordinating everything to our own individual convenience" (*TFM* 82). Hawthorne does not, however, offer Fourier's communitarian corrective to individualist excess. Rather, as in "The Old Manse" he promotes the virtues of the private sphere organized around a marriage: only in marriage, he suggests, can one "forget [one]self in the idea of another" (*CE* 10:283) and retain moral health. Once again, Hawthorne appropriates the Fourierist lexicon and critique of modernity, but in place of the solutions of communitarianism proposes conventional marriage as solace.

Egotism is not merely a moral condition in the story: Roderick Elliston's pathology is tied to the market. This association is suggested in an apparently incidental description of the Elliston property. The Ellistons are a family in decline, living in a "spacious and once magnificent family-residence" (*CE* 10:280). "[E]arly in the past century," Hawthorne states, "land being of small comparative value, the garden and other grounds had formed quite an extensive domain." But subsequently "a portion of the ancestral heritage had been alienated" (*CE* 10:280). Such alienation of property, or the threat thereof, occurs throughout Hawthorne's portraits of New England families. It is virtually certain that families of any longevity in Hawthorne's *oeuvre* will be economically embattled in their contemporary incarnation. Alienation of hereditary property—or the threat that someone will invade it and displace the family—is a central concern in "Peter Goldthwaite's Treasure" and *The House of the Seven Gables,* and appears in *The Blithedale Romance* and even, arguably, in "The Old Manse" (where, however, the Hawthornes themselves are interlopers).[15] The dilapidated or alienated ancestral house emblematizes the displacement of an older social order by a new one.

Like the Pyncheons of *The House of the Seven Gables* and Peter Goldthwaite in "Peter Goldthwaite's Treasure," the "distinguished gentleman, Roderick Elliston, Esq." (*CE* 10:272) is troubled by the encroaching forces of modernity. He is an aristocrat learning to be a bourgeois. He is not, his doctors conclude, insane: "[h]is eccentricities were doubtless great," they state, "but the world was not, without surer ground, entitled to treat him as a madman" (*CE* 10:280). But faced with the disorienting obsolescence of a society ordered around the family estate and the rise to preëminence of another society ordered around the city, Roderick descends into something that closely resembles madness: the market revolution of the nineteenth century threatens to dehumanize those caught unprotected in its economic and cultural transformations.

Roderick's affliction manifests itself most clearly in his ambivalent relation to the new society. He cannot decide whether to obtrude upon others or withdraw from them. After he separates from Rosina, he begins to distance himself from his "associates" (*CE* 10:270) until he "estrange[s] himself from all companionship" (*CE* 10:271). But presently, he "solicit[s] and force[s] himself upon the notice of acquaintances and strangers" (*CE* 10:273): he turns from familiar social networks to anonymous ones. But soliciting the attention of strangers proves also to be an inconstant impulse: depending upon his mood, he either removes himself from "the ordinary experience of mankind" or, "yearning for fellowship," aims "to establish a species of brotherhood between himself and the world" (*CE* 10:274). Roderick seems incapable of achieving a salubrious balance between individual and community; the "species of brotherhood" that he aspires towards is a distortion of those communitarian designs animating contemporary socialism.

Roderick is like the I-narrator of Hawthorne's "The Procession of Life" (1843), who also seeks to discover "a true classification of society" (*CE* 10:208). Roderick does this by "making his own actual serpent—if a serpent there actually was in his bosom—the type of each man's fatal error" (*CE* 10:277). Whether or not his characterization of "each man's fatal error" reflects genuine insight or is merely Roderick's speculation, the conceit of parasitic serpents derives from his own ostensible bosom-serpent, and to this extent, he undertakes what Hawthorne describes as an "exercise of ventriloquism" (*CE* 10:277): he projects his own classifying system on others. Terry Eagleton has related modern philosophy's preoccupation with the relationship of subject and object to the "economic and political practice" of the bourgeoisie, and argues that a philosophical imperialism "follows logically" therefrom: it is no surprise, he writes, "[t]hat the individual subject should come to occupy centre stage, reinterpreting the world with reference to itself" (Eagleton 70). This is an apt description of Roderick, who wants to be autonomous and at the same time remake the world in his image. Hawthorne seems to assert that the condition of the public man is to obtrude upon his fellow citizens and colonize them with his own pathology: Roderick looks for "his own disease in every breast" (*CE* 10:274).

Roderick shares his propensity to interpret others with reference to himself with other characters in the story. At the beginning of Roderick's decline, "more than one elderly gentleman, the victim of good cheer and slothful habits, magisterially pronounce[s] the secret of the whole matter to be Dyspepsia!" (*CE* 10:271). The man who first diagnoses the presence of "a SNAKE in [Roderick's] stomach" is himself one of "the noted quacks that [infest] the city" (*CE* 10:272); he is himself, that is, a manner of parasite in the body politic.[16] Roderick's appearance reminds the sculptor George Herkimer of "a species of marble out of which he [Herkimer] had once wrought a head of Envy, with her snaky locks" (*CE* 10:269); at the end of the story, Herkimer diagnoses Roderick's malady as "[a] tremendous Egotism, manifesting itself [. . .] in the form of jealousy" (*CE* 10:283), in effect imposing his own interpretation in his judicial summation of the "moral of the story" (*CE* 10:283).[17] The way that Roderick's egotism manifests itself is by no means unique to him; it is, instead, the common condition of the modern subject in the marketplace.

Hawthorne's corrective to the pathological self-involvement of Roderick Elliston is not communitarian. Against the dehumanizing market, Hawthorne posits marriage as restorative. Anticipating Phoebe Pyncheon, Rosina is an "ideal of gentle womanhood" (*CE* 10:270); she offers Roderick her "unselfish love" (*CE* 10:283) undergirded by her Christian faith (*CE* 10:281). Hawthorne thereby tenders a profoundly conservative solution to problems noted in radical critiques of the *status quo*. With the resuscitation of Roderick's marriage to Rosina, Hawthorne supplants the communal "Unityism"—the Fourierist converse to egotism—with marital "Unityism."

The similarity between the Fourierist alternative to the market and that of Hawthorne is suggested by the space in which Rosina and Roderick finally reconcile. It is an urban garden, a "shadowy enclosure" in the rear of Roderick's "spacious and once magnificent family-residence" where "a student, or a dreamer, or a man of stricken heart, might lie all day upon the grass, amid the solitude of murmuring boughs, and forget that a city had grown up around him" (*CE* 10:280–281). The Elliston garden is a hybrid space, circumscribed by a city and yet capable of eliding it, at once transcending history and situated squarely in the present, and emblematized by its fountain, "born at every moment, yet of an age coeval with the rocks" (*CE* 10:281). In *The House of the Seven Gables,* such a garden is the scene of Holgrave and Phoebe's labor, which they agree to undertake "somewhat on the community-system" (*CE* 2:93). The garden in "Egotism; or, the Bosom-Serpent" is similar; both clearly are types of recuperated Edens. As a *rus in urbe,* however, the garden also recalls the Fourierist attempt to reconcile city and nature in what Guarneri characterizes as "the phalanx's orderly blending of urban and rural forms" (*UA* 399): as Engels states in *Anti-Dühring* (1878), Fourier demanded "the abolition of the antithesis between town and country" (Engels 719).[18] In "Egotism; or, the Bosom-Serpent," the regenerative garden is analogous to those demanded by Fourierist theorists. Here, however, it is allied not with communitarianism but with monogamy: marriage is a sufficient balm, the story implies, for the depredations of the market.

It is not accurate to say that Hawthorne discovers the social function of marriage in the wake of his engagement with Fourierism. It is fair, however, to argue that Fourierism spurred him to extol the virtues of marriage as a superior corrective to capitalist atomism, and that in Hawthorne's view it was preferable to Fourierism precisely because of its conservatism. Thus in the fiction which Hawthorne composed during or after the Fourierism's major phase, marriage must be seen as negotiating between extremes. To put it another way, "Egotism; or, the Bosom-Serpent" is not only an attack on Emersonian individualism; it is also a containment of Fourierist communitarianism.

"Egotism; or, the Bosom-Serpent" thus anticipates *The House of the Seven Gables* in proposing a utopian marriage as the solution to the excesses of capitalism. But because it offers no fundamental revision of the premises of market society, it is in effect a mystification of societal problems that persist. That is, the egotism that the story purports to dispel is in fact only mystified by recourse to marriage; Rosina's love must indeed be unselfish, because in accordance with the patriarchal codes of antebellum America, she will be legally subordinate to her husband. The ending of the story, when George Herkimer imagines that he sees the serpent escape from Elliston's mouth, may contain a latent irony. "If report be trustworthy," the narrator states, "the sculptor beheld a waving motion through the grass, and heard a tinkling sound, as if something had plunged into the fountain" (*CE* 10:283).

The fountain, "born at every moment, yet of an age coeval with the rocks, and far surpassing the venerable antiquity of a forest" (*CE* 10:281), is like the serpents who reportedly persist through the Elliston line: "My sable friend, Scipio, has a story," Roderick states,

> of a serpent that had lurked in this fountain—pure and innocent as it looks—ever since it was known to the first settlers. This insinuating personage once crept into the vitals of my great-grandfather, and dwelt there many years, tormenting the old gentleman beyond mortal endurance. But, to tell you the truth, I have no faith in this idea of the snake's being an heirloom. He is my own snake, and no man's else. (*CE* 10:282)

Escaping from Roderick, the serpent returns to the fountain. But the fountain is in the midst of this renovated, domestic Eden. However concealed, in other words, egotism persists within the middle-class home.

Although both "The Old Manse" and "Egotism; or, the Bosom-Serpent" portray a utopian domesticity that posits itself as compensation for the marketplace, marriage is not always a panacea in *Mosses from an Old Manse*. The marriages that Hawthorne portrays therein are more commonly post-utopian than utopian, not only in the sense that they follow Hawthorne's account of his departure from the Manse, but also in the sense that they are typically unhappy. Hawthorne composed his most chilling portraits of marital discord while living in the Manse in what has been mythologized as perfect marital felicity. This points to tensions in the Hawthornes' marriage that Hawthorne imperfectly sublimated, and that return in his fiction.[19] One might add that the Manse did not provide respite from market forces, the "free gifts of Providence" in its garden notwithstanding: the Hawthornes left the Manse in dire economic straits, with a new-born son, Julian, to feed and the surveyorship at the Salem Custom-House not yet secured.[20]

But marriage in *Mosses from an Old Manse* has a significance greater than the details of Hawthorne's biography alone can explain. At the symbolic "heart" of society (*CE* 10:26), idealized marriages symbolize Hawthorne's ideal society; the corrupted marriages which proliferate in *Mosses from an Old Manse* correspondingly symbolize society's corruption.[21] Unsurprisingly, corrupted marriages predominate: for all that Hawthorne fetishizes the Manse as a utopian synecdoche for the perfect society, his more common premise is that society, after the Fall, remains corrupt. In "Earth's Holocaust," reformers burn symbols of crime and corruption in a massive fire on "one of the broadest prairies of the West" (*CE* 10:381); with "a portentous grin," however, a "dark-visaged stranger" predicts that the reform will not last long because of inexpungeable flaws in "the human heart": "And," he says,

> unless they hit upon some method of purifying that foul cavern, forth from it will re-issue all the shapes of wrong and misery—the same old shapes, or worse ones—which they have taken such a vast deal of trouble to consume to ashes. [. . .] Oh, take my word for it, it will be the old world yet! (*CE* 10:403)

Hawthorne's portraits of marriage oscillate, then, between the utopianism of "The Old Manse" and the kind of anti-utopianism expressed in "Earth's Holocaust." Especially in the American romances, these marriages will be threatened by market egotism and Fourierism alike. Understanding the logic of this paired threat is the concern of the next two chapters.

Chapter Three

The Unpardonable Sin: Egotism as Ideology in *The House of the Seven Gables* and *The Blithedale Romance*

I.

Discussing egotism in Fyodor Dostoevsky's short fiction of the 1840s, Joseph Frank writes that its "revaluation [. . .] was very much in the fore-ground of Russian awareness in 1847: the combined influence of Fourier and Max Stirner had been working to transform this idea from the nega-tive to the positive" (Frank 233). Associating Fourier and Stirner as Frank does here is at first glance startling: Stirner's *The Ego and its Own* was a radical defense of the individual and a critique of socialism. But Fourier in his earliest work denounces egotism as an "odious characteristic," the demonic parody in "Civilization" of the salubrious passion of "Unityism" (*TFM* 82). Stirner seems more comparable with figures like Emerson who were appropriating and revaluating terms like "individualism" from socialists.

Nevertheless, Frank's association of Fourier with the defence of egotism finds a kind of corroboration in *The Blithedale Romance*. When Coverdale suggests introducing Fourierist "peculiarities" into Blithedale's communitar-ian practice, Hollingsworth explodes: "Let me hear no more of it!" He exclaims:

> I never will forgive this fellow! He has committed the Unpardonable
> Sin; for what more monstrous iniquity could the Devil himself contrive
> than to choose the selfish principle—the principle of all human wrong,
> the very blackness of man's heart, the portion of ourselves which we

shudder at, and which it is the whole aim of spiritual discipline to erad-
icate—to choose it as the master-workman of his system? To seize upon
and foster whatever vile, petty, sordid, filthy, bestial, and abominable
corruptions have cankered into our nature, to be the efficient instru-
ments of his infernal regeneration! And his consummated Paradise, as
he pictures it, would be worthy of the agency which he counts upon for
establishing it. The nauseous villain! (*CE* 3:53–54)

Hollingsworth's invective is freighted with irony; Zenobia will later
denounce Hollingsworth for his own egotism. Nevertheless, it suggests that
at least some of Fourierism's American critics considered it to be predicated
on "the selfish principle."

In fact this representation of Fourierism is well founded. Although in
his writings Fourier repudiates egotism as a perversion of Unityism, he envisions a social structure that can fully gratify individual appetite. Indeed, grat-
ifying one's inclinations is the foundation of Fourierist theory. Although,
Fourier writes, "[o]ur desires are so boundless in relation to the limited
means we have of satisfying them that God seems to have acted rather
thoughtlessly when he gave us passions so eager for pleasure" (*TFM* 74) and
although "moralists" (*TFM* 74) argue that these passions must consequently
be repressed, "there is nothing vicious in your passions" (*TFM* 72). Because
these passions derive from a beneficent God, Fourier argues, they cannot be
vicious: to the contrary, a social structure that depends upon their repression
must itself be vicious. In Fourier's renovated society, he writes in *The Theory
of the Four Movements,* it will be "necessary to protect everything we call vice,
such as greed and sexual intrigue" (*TFM* 72). These "vices," Fourier main-
tains, proceed from healthy sources; they only take a vicious form because
the repressions demanded by "Civilization" distort them.

What reconciles the apparent contradiction in Fourierist theory
between the indulgence of individual appetite and social cohesion is Fourier's
assumption that the "trunk" of the "tree of passion" is "Unityism" (*TFM* 78).
Unityism, one infers, is an appetite for collective action, but Fourier defines
it only negatively: "This Prospectus," he writes in *The Theory of the Four
Movements,*

> does not offer a definition of Unityism, or the root-stock of the pas-
> sions, but as it is entirely undeveloped in Civilisation all that is neces-
> sary is to direct our attention to the counter-passion, or Egotism, which
> is so universally dominant that ideology [. . .] has made egotism or the
> *self* the basis of all its calculations. Studies of Civilised Man have as a

rule observed nothing but the subversive passions, which have a scale comparable to that of Harmony.

Our scholars are unaware of Unityism and boundless philanthropy. All they have been able to make out instead is that passion's subversive play or counter-development, the mania for subordinating everything to our own individual convenience. (*TFM* 82, his emphasis)

Only establish "Harmony," Fourier supposes, and egotism will transform into its salubrious and natural opposite, whereupon the indulgence of individual appetite will tend inevitably towards social harmony.

The failure to define unityism except negatively means, however, that the relationship between self-gratification and social harmony remains abstract in Fourier's theory. The difference between corruptive egotism and the constructive gratification of appetite, Fourier affirms, cannot be articulated because Unityism is unavailable to students of "Civilised Man." Along with a critique of repression, what remains is a powerful advocacy of appetite and a weak demonstration of its socially constructive effects. That Kropotkin saw Fourier as one of the intellectual progenitors of anarchism suggests that the Fourierist validation of individual appetite competed with his communitarianism for influence.[1] Frank's claim that Fourier and Stirner played comparable roles in changing the connotations of egotism is therefore plausible. Likewise Hollingsworth's critique of Fourierism: only ignore the claim that the subject will transform in Harmony from egotist to "Unityist," and it is easy to reduce Fourier's validation of impulse to "greed and sexual intrigue." And this in turn would seem to invalidate Fourier's critique of repression: if greed and sexual intrigue do not demonstrably conduce to social harmony, then their repression is a social good. Thus critics attacked Fourierism as mere sybaritism. In *The Theory of the Four Movements*, Fourier writes that "the diamond and the pig are hieroglyphs of the thirteenth passion [Unityism], which the inhabitants of Civilisation have no experience or understanding of" (*TFM* 284–285). The pig as a symbol of Unityism! By contrast, Coverdale characterizes the Blithedale pigs as "stifled and almost buried alive, in their own corporeal substance" (*CE* 3:144) in what seems to be a tacit satire on Fourier's symbolism.

As Jonathan Beecher has noted,[2] Fourier's claim that a relationship exists between self-gratification and the public weal repeats the arguments of the classical political economists, evoking Bernard Mandeville's validation of "Private Vices" and especially Adam Smith's defense of self-interest in *Wealth of Nations*. Repudiating the "regulation of commerce" (Smith i.475), Smith asserts that he has "never known much good done by those who affected to trade for the public good. It is an affectation, indeed, not very common among merchants, and very few words need be employed in dissuading them from it" (Smith i.478). A merchant who follows his own interest, who "neither intends to promote the public interest, nor knows how much he is promoting it," is often "led by an invisible hand to promote an end which was no part of his intention" (Smith i.477). "By pursuing his own interest," Smith states, "he frequently promotes that of the society more effectually than when he really intends to promote it" (i.477–478). Fourier shares with Smith and Mandeville the assumption that the gratification of private interest will redound to public benefit. The similarity reflects a more general propinquity between Fourierist and capitalist theory, despite Fourier's professed hostility to the latter (he attacked *laissez-faire*, for instance, as a sophism that meant "*let the merchants do whatever they like*" (*TFM* 239, his emphasis)). In light of this and other similarities, Carl Guarneri has argued that Fourierism failed in part because it differentiated itself insufficiently from the *status quo* to become a genuinely oppositional movement.[3]

That said, it bears repeating that Fourier differs from figures like Smith and Mandeville in his hostility to contemporary society. Both Smith and Mandeville are in effect apologists for the *status quo*. Mandeville, for instance, argues that

> *T'Enjoy the World's Conveniencies,*
> *Be fam'd in War, yet live in Ease,*
> *Without great Vices, is a vain*
> *EUTOPIA seated in the Brain.*
> *Fraud, Luxury and Pride must live,*
> *While we the benefits receive.*
> —(Mandeville 411–416, his emphasis)

If Mandeville anticipates Fourier in arguing that "man" is "a compound of various passions; that all of them, as they are provoked and come uppermost, govern him by turns, whether he will or no" (Mandeville 36), he would reject Fourier's social remedies as "vain" utopianism; like Hawthorne in *The Scarlet Letter*, he preaches patience rather than reform in the face of suffering.

Nevertheless, in both of the American romances which directly address Fourierism, Hawthorne draws parallels between Fourierists and capitalists. Holgrave, the former Fourierist, must demonstrate respect for the individuality of Phoebe, or he will be morally of a piece with Judge Pyncheon, ready to sacrifice Clifford for the sake of his own emolument: in repudiating Fourierism,

Hawthorne suggests, Holgrave abandons a "licentious system" equivalent to capitalism. On the other hand, the collapse of Blithedale owing (Coverdale alleges) to its conversion to Fourierism parallels the trajectory of Hollingsworth towards egotism and the trajectory of Zenobia from her advocacy of women's rights to her apparent betrayal of her political and biological sister Priscilla. Thus the supposed reformers act like or collude with Westervelt, who voices utopian slogans on stages in village halls, but purely for his own advantage. Reform enterprises that aspire to collective action disintegrate because of the ego's return.

II. *THE HOUSE OF THE SEVEN GABLES*

In the representative figure of Judge Pyncheon, *The House of the Seven Gables* confronts an immoral marketplace; the novel's central concern is with finding a moral alternative to the market system in which the material benefits of capitalism are retained. In this it is similar to Fourierism. But, as will be more clearly the case in *The Blithedale Romance, The House of the Seven Gables* suggests that Fourierism provides the wrong alternative: although with considerably more subtlety, *The House of the Seven Gables* anticipates Hollingsworth's attack on Fourierism for being predicated on egotism like the market system it strives to supplant. *The House of the Seven Gables* proposes bourgeois domesticity as a social ideal instead, its protagonists fleeing from Salem to an estate where Phoebe, the "little figure of the cheeriest household life" (*CE* 2:140), presides. Like the Manse, the Pyncheon estate is essentially a conservative space: it is an institution that has "grown out of the heart of mankind" (*CE* 10:26). But "conservative" in this novel means not only anti-Fourierist, it also means anti-capitalist.

The many limitations of Hawthorne's own utopia—its failure to guarantee the legitimacy of property; its insufficient disentanglement from the capitalist processes that produce its comforts; its reliance upon and pastoralization of women's work—have been the principal subject of literary criticism on the novel. Read as an attempt to envision a solution to the inequities of capitalism, *The House of the Seven Gables* seems to most contemporary readers, including me, patently inadequate. Hawthorne's critique of political economists remains illuminating, however. In *The Theory of Moral Sentiments,* Adam Smith disparages Mandeville's political economy as a "licentious system" (Smith 632). Hawthorne makes a similar judgment both of capitalism and of Fourierism; in *The House of the Seven Gables* both Fourierist and capitalist are characterized in terms of an exaggerated masculinity that is clearly a figure for unruly appetite. The challenge of the novel is to direct such appetites, be they sexual or material, into temperate courses, to envision enjoying wealth while at the same time living virtuously. In organizing his conclusion around the domestic angel Phoebe, Hawthorne propounds a chaste alternative to the "licentious systems" of capitalism and Fourierism alike.

Sexuality unquestionably carries economic resonances in *The House of the Seven Gables*. The most avaricious characters in the novel are also sexually dangerous: destructive erotic energy characterizes both the Colonel and Judge Pyncheon and, in Holgrave's historical fiction, Matthew Maule. According to the narrator, "the Puritan [. . .] had worn out three wives, and, merely by the remorseless weight and hardness of his character in the conjugal relation, had sent them, one after another, broken hearted, to their graves" (*CE* 2:123). When Jaffrey Pyncheon attempts to kiss Phoebe, she recoils, because "[t]he man, the sex, somehow or other, was entirely too prominent in the Judge's demonstrations of that sort" (*CE* 2:118). Alice Pyncheon admires the "remarkable comeliness, strength, and energy" of Matthew Maule; his artisan's clothing includes "a long pocket for his rule, the end of which protruded" (*CE* 2:201), a phallic symbol that foreshadows his mesmeric enslavement of Alice. The narrative associates these symbols of excessive masculinity with the organ grinder's monkey, whose "thick tail curl[s] out into preposterous prolixity from beneath his tartans" (*CE* 2:163–164), and specifically imbues the monkey with economic meaning: "take this monkey just as he was," the narrator states, "and you could desire no better image of the Mammon of copper-coin, symbolizing the grossest form of the love of money" (*CE* 2:164). The too prominent masculinity of the characters, then, involves not only sexual appetite but also "the love of money."

The monkey appears in one of the crucial episodes of the novel; taken as a whole, this episode demonstrates the novel's preoccupation with uncontained desire as a socially corruptive force. Spectating on the action in the streets below his window, Clifford's eye is drawn to an Italian street musician. The Italian's mahogany case discloses a "company of little figures, [. . .] whose principle of life was the music, which the Italian made it his business to grind out" (*CE* 2:162–163). This company, engaged in a "variety of occupation[s]," constitutes a "fortunate little society [which] might truly be said to enjoy a harmonious existence, and to make life literally a dance" (*CE* 2:163). Having appeared to celebrate this mechanical utopia, however, the narrator proposes that "some cynic, at once merry and bitter, had desired to signify, in this pantomimic scene, that we mortals, whatever our business or amusement—however serious, however trifling—all dance to one identical tune, and, in spite of our ridiculous activity, bring nothing finally to pass" (*CE* 2:163). Clifford watches with momentary delight, but presently begins to cry.

The ugliness of the scene so upsetting to Clifford derives from the reduction of all values to that of money. As Hawthorne criticism has understood,[4] the Sisyphean labor of the community in the organ case is necessitated by the monkey's hunger for money, which there is no "possibility of satisfying" (*CE* 2:164). In this light, what the narrator omits in his initial catalogue of the case's occupants is significant: the narrator describes the inhabitants twice, but on the first representation, alludes only to "the cobbler, the blacksmith, the soldier, the lady with her fan, the toper with his bottle, [and] the milk-maid sitting by her cow" (*CE* 2:163). Only at the culmination of the second iteration does the narrator add a "miser [who] count[s] gold into his strong-box" and "a lover [who] salute[s] his mistress on her lips!" (*CE* 2:163). The miser's absence from the first list allows the reader briefly to imagine an idyllic community unsullied by money; when the miser makes his appearance in the second catalogue, the commerce that the monkey entails irrupts, and the description of the inhabitants consequently becomes an anti-idyll. The lovers' appearance alongside the miser links sexuality to money. The narrator imagines a cynic contriving the scene to "signify [. . .] that we mortals [. . .] all dance to one identical tune" (*CE* 2:163), then rejects "the whole moral" because it implies that romance is an economic exchange bereft of love. This anticipates the romance's own conclusion, which likewise tries to forestall cynicism by carving out a place for (monogamous, heterosexual) love unsullied by the unrestrained appetite of the market. Stripped of love, sexual exchanges are mechanistic and bestial, no different from economic exchange.

Given the recurring allusions to Fourierism elsewhere in the text, the narrator's description of the "fortunate little society" and its "harmonious existence" in the mahogany case (*CE* 2:163) bears an indirect relation to Fourierism: the "company of little figures" constitutes a kind of utopian community, although clearly not a Fourierist one. As T. Walter Herbert rightly notes, the community nostalgically evokes "typical characters of village life" and "traditional patterns of social life" (Herbert 95). But the connection is clearer once we appreciate the Italian musician as a parodic representation of Fourier himself, whose visions of a harmonious society always depended on procuring a patron willing to spend extravagant sums of money. Certainly, the presence of the Italian, "rather a modern feature of our streets" (*CE* 2:162), points to the social changes of nineteenth-century New England;[5] Robert Martin has suggested that the organ grinder racializes the

intruding economic forces of modernity.⁶ But he is also a caricature of the
European social scientist, peddling sham utopias out of a box. Utopia, the
scene (like the novel as a whole) suggests, is no more than a commodity
which relies on the very processes it seeks to mystify.

The narrative of *The House of the Seven Gables* confirms the moral
made symbolically in the organ-grinder passage: the material and sexual self-
gratification of the Pyncheons and the Maules is never sublimated as a social
good. Hawthorne rejects the argument common to Fourier and to Smith
and Mandeville that private self-gratification might benefit the public. This
rejection is confirmed in the romance's various representations of spectral
and invisible hands. According to what the narrator characterizes as an
implausible popular "fable," when the Lieutenant Governor enters Pyncheon's
study and discovers the Colonel's body, he sees a "skeleton hand [. . .] at the
Colonel's throat, [. . .] which vanishe[s] away, as he advance[s] farther into
the room" (*CE* 2:16). The spectral hand reappears later in the romance, in
the narrator's account of Hepzibah's hesitations on the threshold of the market. Of Hepzibah's disinclination to be seen by the patrons of her cent-shop,
the narrator says that it "might have been fancied, indeed, that she expected
to minister to the wants of the community, unseen, like a disembodied
divinity, or enchantress, holding forth her bargains to the reverential and
awe-stricken purchaser, in an invisible hand" (*CE* 2:40). As in the instance of
the Lieutenant Governor's vision, the narrative retracts its supposition immediately and states that Hepzibah entertains no such fantasies of disembodi-
ment. But here, more clearly than in the first instance, the invisible hand
relates to the market, Hepzibah's vain attempt to preserve aristocratic privilege in the face of financial exigency. The reference to the invisible hand can
hardly be innocent. The narrative's two invocations of a ghostly hand are an
implicit critique of Smith, suggesting that the leap of faith connecting individual self-indulgence to collective benefit is at worst self-serving, at best
delusive.

That Hepzibah wants to become the philanthropic spirit of capitalism
in order to escape the sullying realities of the market suggests that
Hawthorne understands Smith's conceit in *The Wealth of Nations* as similarly
evasive. Smith's defense of self-interest, Hawthorne seems to imply, is as
delusive as is Hepzibah's attempt to avoid her patrons' eyes. In Hepzibah's
case, however, her pressing need to provide for Clifford demands that she
relinquish her fantasy before she can even enjoy it. Only the successful capitalist and the flush aristocrat can entertain such flights of fancy: only they are
sufficiently buoyed by economic success to ignore the processes upon which
that success is founded.

In the other passage, the Lieutenant Governor's hallucination inverts Smith's beneficent hand of capitalism: it entails a Gothic return of the repressed, where what has been repressed is the economic crime upon which the Pyncheon estate is founded. Whether or not we take the hand literally to belong to Maule, it also represents an abstract moral accountability: where the invisible hand leads the capitalist to act in the public interest in spite of himself, the skeletal hand attacks him. Where the invisible hand mystifies the potential brutality of capitalism, the skeletal hand is a nightmarish vision of retribution for economic crime. And, since the invisible hand is Smith's attempt to establish an organic relationship between private enrichment and public benefit, it is appropriate that the skeletal hand becomes visible when Pyncheon attempts to make manifest the benefit that the community has derived from his property theft: the day of his death is also the day on which he opens his house to the community at a "ceremony of consecration, festive, as well as religious" (*CE* 2:11). Such a housewarming party might be one way of making visible the otherwise unseen hand of *laissez-faire*. But Pyncheon's death, seemingly enacting Maule's curse, turns the spectacle of collective benefit into a spectacle of collective complicity.

Just as Colonel Pyncheon and his latter-day incarnation Jaffrey are sexual predators, so too is Matthew Maule as Holgrave represents him in his fiction, "Alice Pyncheon," and this, perhaps counter-intuitively, points to Hawthorne's critique of Fourier. As I elaborate at greater length in the next chapter, I read Holgrave's representation of his ancestor not solely as an historical portrait but also as a demonic self-portrait, Matthew Maule being the figure whom Holgrave must avoid becoming. In effect, this is to ascribe to Holgrave's agency the parallel that the novel establishes between them in any case: Phoebe's susceptibility to Holgrave's mesmeric powers clearly recapitulates Alice Pyncheon's susceptibility to those of Matthew Maule; the novel clearly implies that Holgrave does succeed in avoiding the unhappy fate of Maule. That Holgrave must learn to practice self-denial out of "reverence" for "another's individuality"—that he does not assault Phoebe's "free and virgin spirit" (*CE* 2:212)—earns the narrator's praise and points to the happy conclusion of the novel. And, in light of hostile accounts of sexual incontinence at Fourierist phalanxes, it is significant that this moral retreat from the mesmeric domination of Phoebe marks the beginning of the end of Holgrave's radicalism. "To a disposition like Holgrave's," the narrator states, "at once speculative and active, there is no temptation so great as the opportunity of acquiring empire over the human spirit" (*CE* 2:212). But were Holgrave, like Maule, to accede to this temptation and gratify his appetite for such empire, the result would be "as dangerous, and perhaps as disastrous" as it is in "Alice Pyncheon" (*CE* 2:212). Such self-discipline, however, runs contrary to the Fourierist theory ostensibly animating Holgrave's radicalism.

In contrast to the various characters, all male, guilty of or tempted to crime, Hepzibah and Phoebe ultimately are the novel's embodiments of unimpeachable virtue. Although both Hepzibah and Jaffrey Pyncheon are associated with the novel's critique of Adam Smith, for instance, a vast difference exists between the Lieutenant Governor's gothic vision of a spectral hand at Jaffrey Pyncheon's throat and Hepzibah's comically evasive delusion of being an invisible hand. Her fantasies about ministering invisibly to the patrons of her cent-shop are pathetic rather than malicious, the remnants of aristocratic pretension and not a sophistry to justify the indulgence of appetite. The difference between Colonel Pyncheon and Hepzibah lies both in their relative power and in their ethical probity: certain of his poor character, for instance, Hepzibah is immune to Jaffrey's various blandishments. And such virtue is figured once again in sexual terms: the Colonel's hypermasculinity not only leads him to steal Maule's property but also leads to the death of three wives; Hepzibah is an "old maid" (*CE* 2:30) who "never knew, by her own experience, what love technically means" (*CE* 2:32). Her ignorance of the technical side of love also implies, for Hawthorne, moral purity, an equation which holds true for the virginal Phoebe as well.[7]

The challenge of *The House of the Seven Gables* is to reconcile virtue, so conceived, with material comfort (narrowly) and appetite (broadly): Hawthorne genders these categories partly so that he can effect their reconciliation in a heterosexual marriage. But the success of this reconciliation is famously imperfect. Hawthorne had read Mandeville's *The Fable of the Bees* as well as one of the major eighteenth-century commentaries on it:[8] the flight of the protagonists to the Pyncheon estate recapitulates the flight of the newly moral bees from their corrupt hive to a pure one; the Pyncheon estate, however, is economically successful, and this controverts Mandeville's argument. For Mandeville, the bees flee from their opulent and "Spacious Hive" (1) when their new-found honesty leads to economic collapse: they are forced to take refuge in their spartan "hollow Tree" (407) because economic success is incompatible with virtue. For the more conventionally moral Hawthorne, this argument is unacceptable, and so he offers a flight from vice to virtue that in fact increases the characters' comfort.

He cannot easily effect this alteration of Mandeville: the romance's resolution, as a host of critics points out, does not persuasively create a foundation for a new moral world. In their acquisition of the Pyncheon country house the protagonists benefit from Judge Pyncheon's corrupt capitalist practices in spite of his absence. The pretense that they escape from his corruptive influence solely by dint of his death seems as sophistical as Hawthorne supposed the figure of the invisible hand to be.

In treating Fourierism and capitalism as comparable licentious systems against which the Pyncheon estate offers a bulwark, however, *The House of the Seven Gables* does more than merely offer a false remedy. It mystifies the conditions of the domestic sphere and conceals that portion of the Fourierist critique that foregrounds the links between domesticity and capitalism. Faithful in the main to separate-spheres ideology, the novel supposes that a private realm can avoid market forces: in leaving the cent-shop behind, the novel presumes that its protagonists have likewise escaped the cent-shop's sullying influence. It insinuates, too, that the Fourierist community in which Holgrave spent "some months" (*CE* 2:176) cannot afford refuge from the market, being ideologically of a piece with it. (Indeed, the catalogue of Holgrave's history that discloses his tenure with Fourierists lists, in the main, his previous employment, implying that living there was only one more in a series of jobs (*CE* 2:176).) But this reduction of Fourierism to its validation of appetite ignores or denies the Fourierist social critique altogether. This critique would note that the domestic sphere and the market are mutually constitutive: as John Humphrey Noyes states in a particularly Fourierist phrase, marriage is an "egotism for two" (quoted in *ACU* 257). Holgrave abandons the "community-men and come-outers" (*CE* 2:84) with whom he has been a fellow traveler. But in keeping with the Fourierist critique of the "isolated home," and far from agreeing with Hawthorne that rural domesticity and capitalism are fundamentally different, one might just as well say that Holgrave and the Pyncheons flee only from one manifestation of the market to another.

III. *THE BLITHEDALE ROMANCE*

In *The House of the Seven Gables* Hawthorne attempts to posit a social order in which virtue and material wealth can be reconciled, and predicates this on Holgrave's suppression of his appetite for "acquiring empire over the human spirit" (*CE* 2:212). In *The Blithedale Romance* Hawthorne takes the more pessimistic position that such appetites are not easily circumvented, and that society is therefore not susceptible to renovation. In Hawthorne's view, it is fallacious to assume as Fourierist theory does that society's translation from capitalism to communitarian socialism would effect an ideological inversion, translating the subject's identification with her own interests into an identification with the interest of the community. According to Fourier, this inversion will recover the "true" character corrupted by "Civilization." Hawthorne suggests that the inversion assumes that character is "but hot wax [. . .]; and guilt, or virtue, only the forms into which [one] should see fit to mould it," in the words of one of the patrons of the lyceum-stage (*CE* 3:198).[9] Whether this assumption is valid Hawthorne does not say: Coverdale rejects it on principle.[10] Westervelt's power over Priscilla—the romance's preëminent demonstration of characterological plasticity—is broken, but her escape may not derive from the power of "the true heart-throb of a woman's affection" to overcome "jugglery" (*CE* 3:203), as Coverdale affirms. Rather, it may derive from Hollingsworth's own "magnetism" (*CE* 3:134), brought to bear when Hollingsworth challenges Westervelt: it might, that is, entail no more than a competition between mesmerists. Nevertheless, Hawthorne argues that the attempts at socialist confraternity and sorority are naïve to assume themselves capable of effecting their own ideological transformation, and still more naïve to suppose that their example alone might spontaneously effect a social transformation. Absent this transformation, Blithedale is not categorically different from the lyceum-hall in which Westervelt treats his audiences to utopian visions. Blithedale's presumption that it is among the "harbingers [. . .] of a golden era" (*CE* 2:179) (to borrow a phrase from *The House of the Seven Gables*) finds an uncanny echo in Westervelt's disquisitions on "a new era that [is] dawning upon the world; an era that [will] link soul to soul, and the present life to what we call futurity, with a closeness that [shall] finally convert both worlds into one great, mutually conscious brotherhood" (*CE* 3:200). Westervelt mixes Emersonian Oversoul and Fourierist prophecy into a utopian melange that is nevertheless entirely cynical, designed for the emolument only of Westervelt (and dependent upon the enslavement of Priscilla). The rhetoric of reform has been wholly coöpted on the lyceum-stage by the spirit of capitalism. But Hawthorne implies that this is the tendency of reform projects that insufficiently displace the ego.

    The Blithedale Romance criticizes Fourier's conviction that something like Unityism could ever evolve from egotism or the gratification of individual appetite, no matter how one rearranges the social context. Coverdale's narrative does not assert this directly, however, unequivocally demonstrating its protagonists' betrayals of collective trust. Rather, it proceeds by insinuation. Characters cannot fully know the motives, actions, or commitment of others: the persistent representation of veils serves to foreground the opacity of the other. The first-person narration only compounds this, since, radically limited in his perspective, both Coverdale and his readers are barred from omniscience. Coverdale continually suspects, but cannot prove, that his companions in the communitarian experiment are more committed to personal than to collective benefit; the suspicion alone is enough to cast a pall over their actions. Fourier often quoted

Voltaire's lament on the limitations of science—"In how thick night nature remains veiled!" (quoted in *TFM* 19)—in order to argue that he himself had lifted the veil through his social science. Coverdale's narrative takes a less sanguine position: not only does nature remain veiled, but so do other people. As such, collective action will always fracture on the problem of mutual confidence: unable to repose perfect confidence in others' motives, one returns to self-reliance in a bid for an ideological center; the failure of confidence atomizes the social body into mutually distrustful units.

Coverdale's various representations of Hollingsworth are the most pressing example of this. Rudolph Von Abele long ago wrote that "[i]n the case of both [Hollingsworth's] initial commitment to Zenobia and his later courting of Priscilla, Hawthorne suggests that his motive is purely economic; he is chasing Old Moodie's brother's fortune from one inheritrix to another" (Von Abele 76). Such a suggestion must be attributed not to Hawthorne but to Coverdale, and the problem is that it tells us more about Coverdale's representations of Hollingsworth than about the "real" Hollingsworth, who is perpetually inaccessible to Coverdale's readers. Coverdale's representations of Hollingsworth are skeptical from the first. Almost as soon as he introduces Hollingsworth directly into the narrative, Coverdale begins to interrogate his commitment to Blithedale: "[h]is heart," Coverdale imagines as he describes their first evening at Blithedale, "was never really interested in our socialist scheme, but was forever busy with his strange, and, as most people thought it, impracticable plan for the reformation of criminals, through an appeal to their higher instincts" (*CE* 3:36). After Hollingsworth has nursed Coverdale back to health with "devoted care," Coverdale questions his motives, admitting the "horrible suspicion" that Hollingsworth "watched by my bed-side [. . .] only for the ulterior purpose of making me a proselyte to his views!" (*CE* 3:57). Such suspicions have considerable rhetorical power. To that point Coverdale has offered no reason for his "horrible suspicion"; given Hollingsworth's "more than brotherly attendance" (*CE* 3:41), such doubts are particularly ungenerous. Nevertheless, they influence the interpretation of Hollingsworth's subsequent actions. To attribute selflessness to Hollingsworth one must fight against the tendency of Coverdale's narrative.

The pall of suspicion that Coverdale casts over Hollingsworth's motives becomes more powerful still when Zenobia adds her testimony. She, too, accuses Hollingsworth of egotism, and her characterization of his motives is of such force that it persuades even him, so that in response he seeks to "lean on an affection" (*CE* 3:219), the perfect confidence of Priscilla. To his demand that Zenobia produce evidence of "one selfish end, in all I ever aimed at" (*CE* 3:218), she replies with her oft-quoted philippic that

[i]t is all self! [. . .] Nothing else; nothing but self, self, self! [. . .] I am
awake, disenchanted, disenthralled! Self, self, self! You have embodied
yourself in a project. [. . .] First, you aimed a death-blow, and a treach-
erous one, at this scheme of a purer and higher life, which so many
noble spirits had wrought out. Then, because Coverdale could not be
quite your slave, you threw him ruthlessly away. And you took me, too,
into your plan, as long as there was hope of my being available, and now
fling me aside again, a broken tool! But, foremost, and blackest of your
sins, you stifled down your inmost consciousness!—you did a deadly
wrong to your own heart!—you were ready to sacrifice this girl, whom,
if God ever visibly showed a purpose, He put into your charge, and
through whom He was striving to redeem you! (*CE* 3:218)

Hollingsworth tries to rebut this attack by resorting to his characteristic
misogyny, asserting that Zenobia's accusation "is a woman's view" (*CE*
3:218) and hence wrong, but his pallor suggests that he recognizes his eva-
sion to be feeble. And indeed, although all of Zenobia's representations are
subject to interrogation, both in terms of their substance (does her claim that
Hollingsworth was ready to sacrifice Priscilla mean that he consented to her
restoration to Westervelt, or might it mean that he was prepared, in spite of
preferring the seamstress, to marry Zenobia?) and in terms of their justice (is
it fair to characterize his break with Coverdale as one-sided and ruthless?),
nevertheless she persuades, because she directs her attack against his professed altruism. Both she and Coverdale critique Hollingsworth by aligning
him with the society they reject: predicated on self-fulfilment, capitalist theory from Adam Smith forward has had difficulty understanding altruism.[11]
But still more, by imputing egotism to Hollingsworth, they enlist in a
rhetorical tradition that denies altruistic motives to reformers.[12] By derogat-
ing Hollingsworth as self-interested, they are in effect performing a profoundly conservative rhetorical move, and as such, they do more than merely
align Hollingsworth with the society they reject; they use the rhetorical
strategies of that society themselves.

For his part, Coverdale does not restrict such characterizations to
Hollingsworth: he also readily applies them to Zenobia, who, he imagines,
"promise[s] liberal pecuniary aid" to Blithedale "[p]artly in earnest" and, "as
was her disposition, half in a proud jest" (*CE* 3:190), belittling her commitment and hence insinuating that her propensity to make Blithedale "show like
an illusion, a masquerade, a pastoral, a counterfeit Arcadia" (*CE* 3:21) is a
deliberate subversion. Similarly, he suggests that Zenobia's feminism springs
not from principled conviction but from a personal injury, an aspersion he

directs at all feminist reformers (and which recalls Holgrave's comments on the unhappiness of the reformer (*CE* 2:306–7)):

> women, however intellectually superior, [. . .] seldom disquiet them-
> selves about the rights or wrongs of their sex, unless their own individ-
> ual affections chance to lie in idleness, or to be ill at ease. They are not
> natural reformers, but become such by the pressure of exceptional mis-
> fortune. (*CE* 3:121)

It is possible that he adopts such a skeptical stance when it suits his rhetorical ends. He calls Zenobia's commitment to Blithedale into question mere moments before he presents two possible ways in which Priscilla may have returned to Westervelt: the "poor, pallid flower," Coverdale writes, "was either snatched from Zenobia's hand, or flung wilfully away!" (*CE* 3:193). Having cast doubt on Zenobia's integrity moments before, he implicitly makes more credible his insinuation that Zenobia plays the procuress for Westervelt.

In other words, one may reasonably call into question the extent to which Coverdale's critiques of his fellow communitarians are disinterested attempts to explicate character and to what extent they are deliberate calum-nies. One might readily imagine that Coverdale projects his own doubts about the viability of Blithedale's reform project onto others: the "worldly tone" he adopts when he returns to Boston and his readiness to speak "of the recent phase of my life as indeed fair matter for a jest" (*CE* 3:195), for instance, seem to echo his imputation to Zenobia of joining Blithedale as a "proud jest" (*CE* 3:190), an accusation that might, therefore, be properly understood to be self-directed. His attacks may also stem from a desire for his own narrative to be credited, or to vindicate his conduct, or to disguise his personal disappointment; they may, that is, be conscious rhetorical strate-gies veiling a will to power, both over his subject and over his readers.

The necessity of guessing Coverdale's motives reflects that the same relationship exists between reader and narrative as exists between Coverdale and his subjects. This may be the point of his famous unreliability: in attempting to determine how Coverdale's account distorts the object of his attention, one adopts a Coverdale-like position with respect to him. Coverdale's name is that of an early translator of the Bible into English; the incomplete character of his narration forces his readers to become translators as well. Coverdale's various attempts to "read" his communitarian colleagues allegorize the reading experience. Coverdale brings his ideological assump-tions to bear on his colleagues just as readers of *The Blithedale Romance* bring theirs to bear on the text. But in dramatizing the reading experience, Hawthorne suggests that an altruistic reading is extraordinarily difficult. When Coverdale rebukes Zenobia for lowering her curtain in the boarding-house and thereby preempting his spying, he states that

> It is really impossible to hide anything, in this world, to say nothing of the next. All that we ought to ask, therefore, is, that the witnesses of our conduct, and the speculators on our motives, should be capable of tak-ing the highest view which the circumstances of the case should admit. So much being secured, I, for one, would be most happy in feeling myself followed, everywhere, by an indefatigable human sympathy. (*CE* 3:163)

Zenobia responds to this brazen defence of peeping by stating: "We must trust for our intelligent sympathy to our guardian angels [. . .]. So long as the only spectator of my poor tragedy is a young man, at the window of his hotel, I must still claim the liberty to drop the curtain" (*CE* 3:163). Coverdale gets the worse of this argument, since the implications of Zeno-bia's characterization of him (that he is incapable of angelic sympathy and that his observation is merely voyeuristic) seems only too accurate: certainly, few readers have taken Coverdale as representing "indefatigable human sym-pathy," while articles about his scopophilia abound. In effect, Zenobia is say-ing to Coverdale that she reserves the right to conceal herself because she cannot trust in his motives. But to accept Zenobia's logic raises the question of where one might find a representative of "indefatigable human sympathy." What kind of reader would be capable of "taking the highest view which the circumstances of the case would admit"? In its narrative techniques, the novel illuminates the difficulty of maintaining confidence in others in the absence of guarantees of their virtue. But in the absence of such confidence, society will necessarily break down into mutually distrustful units: to submit the characters to a critique that attributes malice or perversity to them is therefore to participate in the capitalist structures of thought the communi-tarians have attempted to reject.

Zenobia, to all appearances guilty herself of betraying her political and biological sister, elaborates on the consequences of the failure of the capitalist imagination in her legend, "The Silvery Veil." Whatever other readings this complex interpolation into Coverdale's narrative can sustain, the context of its telling in a community of socialists suggests that we should also read it as a gloss on socialist theory. Zenobia bases her story on gossip about the iden-tity of the lyceum-hall's Veiled Lady. Theodore, the story's protagonist, makes a wager with his companions "of considerable amount" that he can learn the "mystery of the Veiled Lady" (*CE* 3:110), and for this reason invades her "private withdrawing-room" (*CE* 3:110–111). Detecting his presence, the Veiled Lady offers an alternative wager, in which, rather than lift the veil, he must kiss her through it, whereupon, she tells him, "all the felicity of earth and of the future world shall be thine and mine together," and there will be "never more a veil between us" (*CE* 3:113). The trusting kiss is, in other words, an erotic exchange that will inaugurate a utopia of perfect mutual knowledge. For Theodore, however, "whose natural tendency [is] towards skepticism" (*CE* 3:113), it is a contract with potentially injurious consequences: he takes "into view the probability," Zenobia says,

> that her face was none of the most bewitching. A delightful idea, truly, that he should salute the lips of a dead girl, or the jaws of a skeleton, or the grinning cavity of a monster's mouth! Even should she prove a comely maiden enough, in other respects, the odds were ten to one that her teeth were defective; a terrible drawback on the delectableness of a kiss! (*CE* 3:113)

For the misogynistic and skeptical Theodore, in other words, the Veiled Lady's offer is implicitly not only self-serving, but is predicated on deceiving him. Where the Veiled Lady attempts to inaugurate an economy predicated on mutual trust, Theodore reflexively remains wedded to a theory of exchange whereby appeals to trust are implicit deceptions. The result is, within the logic of the story, preordained, as the Veiled Lady attempts to explain: if Theodore lifts the veil without a concomitant gesture of trust, he forecloses any possibility of utopian fulfilment. "[F]rom that instant," the Veiled Lady warns him, "I am doomed to be thy evil fate, nor wilt thou ever taste another breath of happiness" (*CE* 3:113). In effect, by refusing to demonstrate trust, Theodore will guarantee the loss of his New Jerusalem, and, left "alone" (*CE* 3:114), will remain conscripted in the machinery of capitalism, in which desire is perpetually aroused and fulfilment perpetually deferred. This proves to be the case: Theodore declines the Veiled Lady's offer and pines "forever and ever, for another sight of that dim, mournful face— which might have been his life-long household fireside joy—to desire, and waste life in a feverish quest, and never meet it more!" (*CE* 3:114).

Zenobia suggests that Theodore's "contemptuous interpretation of [the Veiled Lady's] offer" amounts to a "wrong done to womanhood" (*CE* 3:114), and assenting to this characterization, Manfred Mackenzie has called Theodore a "misogynist hero" (Mackenzie 511). But the logic of the novel as a whole suggests that Theodore's dismissal of the Veiled Lady's offer reflects economic ideology as well. The Veiled Lady's offer depends upon Theodore accepting the purity of the Veiled Lady's motives—depends, that is, on suspending the ethic of competition. As such, it flies in the face of the logic of capitalism.

Theodore's refusal to kiss the Veiled Lady without first seeing her face is analogous to Coverdale's apparent inability to imagine unalloyed commitment. Like Theodore, he is doomed as a result to perpetual frustration, discovering an affection for Priscilla which he cannot consummate because she falls in love with Hollingsworth. Because the earnest and principled reformer is inconceivable to him, Coverdale dooms the new moral world to failure.

But, although the similarity between Coverdale and Theodore suggests that Zenobia is conscious of Coverdale's failings, satirizing him for them or warning him against them, "The Silvery Veil" is more than a coded critique of Coverdale alone. It follows immediately upon Zenobia's exchange with Westervelt and repeats Westervelt's affirmation that Priscilla will "plague" Zenobia (*CE* 3:104). From the moment that Zenobia has the Veiled Lady reappear as "a maiden, pale and shadowy, [who rises] up amid a knot of visionary people" (*CE* 3:114), "The Silvery Veil" is a thinly disguised portrait of Blithedale. In its conclusion, in which the "pale, mysterious girl" (*CE* 3:114) is restored to the "Magician" (*CE* 3:115) it prefigures Zenobia's apparent betrayal of Priscilla to Westervelt, and as such amounts to Zenobia's declaration of war. Even so, the communitarian section of "The Silvery Veil" resumes the theme of trust central to the first part of the story.

The communitarian section in fact offers an alternative explanation for the failure of trust. In her portrait of Theodore, Zenobia argues that his repudiation of the Veiled Lady's utopian contract is a moral failure. By contrast, in her account of the woman who restores the girl to the "Magician," Zenobia argues that the betrayal is a necessary reaction to the hostility of "the fates," which "have so ordained it," the Magician states, "that, whether by her own will, or no, this stranger [the maiden] is your deadliest enemy. In love, in worldly fortune, in all your pursuit of happiness, she is doomed to fling a blight over your prospects" (*CE* 3:115). Zenobia's legend attempts proleptically to justify her betrayal of Priscilla by displacing responsibility for it to a metaphysical domain: at Eliot's Pulpit she repeats her explanation, calling Priscilla her "evil fate" and affirming that "I never wished you harm" (*CE* 3:220). This explanation is clearly self-serving. But in suggesting that egotism is a response to transcendent forces colluding against one's best intentions and not a moral failing, Zenobia may be more accurate than she is in her representations of Theodore's immorality. Zenobia later laments to

integrity"
the moral
on which
, Zenobia
ative mar-
age in *The*
t it does in
e Romance
gotism can

ne changes
ist alterna-
myth; *The*
arlet Letter,
eversing the
of authorial
n is to some
of the Seven
and natural
presumably,
be a matter

tique of the
in *The House*
urierists, wh
e argues t
have ar
nconce
rom
car
d

e universe, her own sex and yours, and Providence, e common cause against the woman who swerves he beaten track" (*CE* 3:224).[13] Whether this tran- ized as Providence, Destiny, fate, or ideology, it ns, the conscious power of the subject to resist it: he only strategy one can adopt in response. "The maiden's resumption of the veil and the restora- llegory of the failure of altruism, the story's end- f Blithedale itself.

ance Hawthorne thus repeats the pessimism he st" (1844), a story equally skeptical about the Short of divine intervention, Hawthorne sug- rrupt. And even granting the rare possibility of e whole universe" will conspire against success- an respond in only so many ways: one can, like bmit oneself to "spiritual discipline" in order iple" (*CE* 3:53); or one can, like Coverdale, *status quo,* abandon reform and a belief in ugh" (*CE* 3:246) in a state of quietist dissipa- however, does Coverdale endorse. Instead, he to his days of communitarian folly, writing thedale. An anti-Fourier, he lives a comparable urier continued proselytizing until his death, s and the prospect of social reform, caught on private and public interest which Fourier like

t
H
Th
wou
The
Veile
fireside
Hollin
love is a
gious dec

Gables, Hawthorne attempted to provide an alterna- ems of capitalism and Fourierism in the marriage of ere *The Blithedale Romance* to repeat the themes of *Gables,* the marriage of Priscilla and Hollingsworth the foundation for a new moral economy. To be sure, e gestures in this direction. In Zenobia's legend, the contract holds out the promise of "life-long, household, :114), clearly a vision of domestic monogamy. Priscilla from her bondage, suggesting once again that istic relation that can supersede egotism. Coverdale's reli- faith in Priscilla's "virgin reserve and sanctity of soul" (CE

3:203) echoes the narrator's declaration of confidence in Holgrave's
in *The House of the Seven Gables* (*CE* 2:212), seemingly guaranteeing
wholeness of the marriage (virginity, once again, being the base
virtue is founded). But in casting doubt on Hollingsworth's motive
and Coverdale cast doubt on the moral purity of the novel's represen
riage. Stained by the imputation of Hollingsworth's egotism, marri
Blithedale Romance has none of the culturally redemptive power tha
The House of the Seven Gables. In other words, *The Blithedal*
acknowledges what *The House of the Seven Gables* denies, that e
infuse the domestic sphere as well as the market.

This is not, as I argue in the next chapter, because Hawtho
his mind about the domestic sphere or the merits of the Fourie
tive. The conclusion of *The House of the Seven Gables* is a utopian
Blithedale Romance is in the same anti-utopian mode as *The Sc*
and hence takes a less sanguine position about the possibility of r
effects of the Fall. The difference, that is, is one of genre, not
attitude. Which genre is more reflective of Hawthorne's position
extent moot; he himself states that in its utopianism *The House*
Gables was "more characteristic of my mind, and more proper
for me to write" (*CE* 16:461) than *The Scarlet Letter,* and hence,
also more characteristic than *The Blithedale Romance.* This may
of self-delusion, however.

Still, it is clear that Hawthorne articulates a serious cri
domestic sphere in *The Blithedale Romance* and does not do so
of the Seven Gables. This critique is influenced by that of the Fou
denied that marriage was extrinsic to the market. Hawthorn
they themselves will fail to translate egotism into Unityism; as I
Coverdale's narrative asserts that such a translation is all but i
But neither does Hawthorne exempt the domestic sphere f
making altruism all the more utopian, in the sense that it
nowhere. A defining part of the anti-utopianism of *The Blithe*
then, is that it accepts the Fourierist critique of contemporary
Fourierism's remedies, and lacks the conviction to install a ut
tive of its own. In a weak echo of Hester's prophecy of a new
"some brighter period" (*CE* 1:263), Coverdale desultorily
"[p]osterity may dig [Blithedale] up, and profit by it" (*CE* 3:2
like Blithedale's communitarianism provides the basis for uto
the interim, the only viable social model is one predicated on
riage. But since marriage may be simply one more "licentious
far from a ringing endorsement.

Chapter Four

Free Love and its Specters in the American Romances

I.

Determining the political tendencies of the American romances is a long-standing critical enterprise. Modern readers tend to find Hawthorne intensely conservative. But for certain of his contemporaries, Hawthorne was far from conservative enough; critics in the conservative religious presses even accused him of radical tendencies. Orestes Brownson said that *The Scarlet Letter* was emblematic of modern depravity:

> There is an unsound state of public morals [he wrote] when the novelist is permitted, without a scorching rebuke, to select such crimes [as adultery], and invest them with all the fascinations of a highly polished style. In a moral community such crimes are spoken of as rarely as possible, and when spoken of at all, it is always in terms which render them loathsome, and repel the imagination. (*CR* 143)

And Arthur Cleveland Coxe, reviewing *The Scarlet Letter* in *Church Review and Ecclesiastical Register,* warned that Hawthorne was threatening to become like George Sand and Eugène Sue, canonized as socialist (at least in sympathy) by Fourierists and others:

> We protest against any toleration to a popular and gifted writer, when he perpetrates bad morals. Let his brokerage of lust be put down at the very beginning. Already, among the million, we have imitations enough of George Sand and Eugene Sue; and if as yet there be no reputable name, involved in the manufacture of a Brothel Library, we congratulate the

country that we are yet in time to save such a reputation as that of
Hawthorne. (*CR* 146)

Lamenting that Hester should speak of her affair with Dimmesdale as having
"a consecration of its own" (*CE* 1:195), Coxe writes that "[w]e suppose this
sentiment must be charged to the doctrines enforced at 'Brook-farm'" (*CR*
151).[1] Hester's representation of her affair with Dimmesdale is, Coxe says,
"the essential morality of the work" (*CR* 151); in Coxe's view, therefore, Hester's capitulation to the Law in her resumption of the letter does not mitigate
what he takes to be the novel's radicalism. No matter how conservative the
ending, by giving voice to Hester's conviction that her affair was self-consecrating Hawthorne threatens to make *The Scarlet Letter* part of a "Brothel
Library." This is worth keeping in mind while reading Sacvan Bercovitch's
insistence on Hawthorne's aesthetics of accommodation and compromise.

Complaints against Hawthorne's political tendencies were not confined
to the right. If Coxe read *The Scarlet Letter* as an endorsement of what he
takes to be Brook Farm's doctrines (presumably the Fourierist critique of
marriage), socialists read *The Blithedale Romance* as a personal attack. Con-
flating Coverdale and Hawthorne, an anonymous reviewer in *The Circular*
(the propaganda journal of John Humphrey Noyes's Perfectionist community at Oneida) complains that Hawthorne

> writes [. . .] quite like a man of the world and ridicules in a quiet way
> the former enthusiasm of himself and his companions to realize 'the bet-
> ter life.' It was a beautiful dream—very amiable and romantic; he wishes
> he could still believe in such things, but somehow he can't, and he is
> doubtful if he ever did. [. . .] Hawthorne seems to have adopted the
> wisdom of universal doubt. He is ready to imagine and describe beauti-
> fully everything, but you have a painful doubt that he does not believe
> anything. Perhaps this combination of ideality and skepticism is a natu-
> ral one in charcter [*sic*], but to us it is a very disagreeable one. We prefer
> any amount of verdancy to the wisdom that comes by being burnt all
> over brown with experience of disappointment. (*Circular* 1:38 150)

The logic of the Oneida reviewer is similar to that of Coxe: the text implicitly endorses the perspective critical of reform.

That *The Scarlet Letter* was excoriated by the right for radicalism and
The Blithedale Romance by the left for conservatism does not imply that
Hawthorne underwent a momentous ideological shift: there is no evidence
of such in Hawthorne's biography—witness his sustained affiliation with the

Democratic Party—or in the novels themselves. The romances are ideologically more or less consistent and occupy politically a middle ground, alienating progressives and conservatives alike.

In broad strokes Hawthorne is ideologically consistent not only throughout the romances, but throughout his writing life. His attitude towards reform is a particularly useful barometer of this consistency. This attitude is predicated on a fundamental, apparently unresolveable, tension. On the one hand, he acknowledges that conditions are bad enough to warrant the reform impulse; on the other, he invariably denounces reform projects. In *The Scarlet Letter,* for instance, Hawthorne both critiques marriage and affirms the necessity of acquiescing to its current forms. Hawthorne's portrait of Hester suggests his intense imaginative sympathy for those who suffer, and one recalls, in reading it, portraits of masculine domestic tyranny in stories from the 1840s like "The Birth-Mark" and "Rappaccini's Daughter." But having proffered this sympathy, *The Scarlet Letter* argues that women ought to accept their existing situation and leave change to divine intervention. In what Sacvan Bercovitch has rightly called one of the crucial passages of the book, Hawthorne writes:

> the same dark question often rose into [Hester's] mind, with reference to the whole race of womanhood. Was existence worth accepting, even to the happiest among them? As concerned her own individual existence, she had long ago decided in the negative, and dismissed the whole point as settled. A tendency to speculation, though it may keep woman quiet, as it does man, yet makes her sad. She discerns, it may be, such a hopeless task before her. As a first step, the whole system of society is to be torn down, and built up anew. Then, the very nature of the opposite sex, or its long hereditary habit, which has become like nature, is to be essentially modified, before woman can be allowed to assume what seems a fair and suitable position. Finally, all other difficulties being obviated, woman cannot take advantage of these preliminary reforms, until she herself shall have undergone a still mightier change; in which, perhaps, the ethereal essence, wherein she has her truest life, will be found to have evaporated. (*CE* 1:166)

While the *status quo* threatens to make existence not worth accepting, nevertheless reform followed to its logical end is so wholly destabilizing as to change "natures" and "essences"—or the second nature of "long hereditary habit." The prospect ("it may be") of such antifoundationalism dismays him.[2] Instead he advocates quietism and a resignation to divine will: "at some brighter period," Hester ultimately prophesies, "when the world should have grown ripe for it, in Heaven's own time, a new truth [will] be revealed, in order to establish the whole relation between man and woman on a surer ground of mutual happiness" (*CE* 1:263). Until then, Hawthorne suggests, in spite of pervasive unhappiness, it is better to wait.

As Bercovitch notes, this is the same argument that Hawthorne applies to the problem of slavery in his 1852 campaign biography of Franklin Pierce, and it seems to be Hawthorne's general counsel to reformers—that it is better to endure a known disease than risk worse ills through blind attempts at a cure. Linking Providence to the American constitution, he writes that "merely human wisdom and human efforts cannot subvert [slavery], except by tearing to pieces the Constitution, breaking the pledges which it sanctions, and severing into distracted fragments that common country, which Providence brought into one nation through a continued miracle of almost two hundred years" (*CE* 23:350–1). He adds that

> Slavery [is] one of those evils, which Divine Providence does not leave
> to be remedied by human contrivances, but which, in its own good
> time, by some means impossible to be anticipated, but of the simplest
> and easiest operation, when all its uses shall have been fulfilled, it causes
> to vanish like a dream. There is no instance, in all history, of the human
> will and intellect having perfected any great moral reform by methods
> which it adapted to that end; but the progress of the world, at every
> step, leaves some evil or wrong on the path behind it, which the wisest
> of mankind, of their own set purpose, could never have found the way
> to rectify. (*CE* 23:352)

In a letter to Elizabeth Palmer Peabody in 1857, Hawthorne responds with irritation to her persistent attempts to interest him and Sophia in abolition, and apostrophizes against the "wretched things [which] are perpetuated under the notion of doing good!" "I presume you think," he adds,

> the abolition of flogging was a vast boon to sea-men. I see, on the con-
> trary, with perfect distinctness, that many murders and an immense
> mass of unpunishable cruelty—a thousand blows, at least, for every one
> that the cat-of-nine-tails would have inflicted—have resulted from that
> very thing. There is a moral in this fact, which I leave you to deduce.
> God's ways are in nothing more mysterious than in this matter of trying
> to do good. (*CE* 23:465)

And in "Chiefly About War Matters," an article Hawthorne published in *The Atlantic Monthly* during the Civil War, he writes that "[n]o human effort, on a grand scale, has ever yet resulted according to the purpose of its projectors. The advantages are always incidental. Man's accidents are God's purposes. We miss the good we sought, and do the good we little cared for" (*CE* 23:431).

"Man's accidents are God's purposes" was a claim dear to the Hawthornes' hearts: Sophia etched it onto the glass pane of a window in the Old Manse, where it still remains. Hawthorne's gradualism was obviously both deeply felt and, within the limits of its Providential faith, carefully theorized, and there is no reason to suppose that it implies an endorsement of the *status quo*: Sophia Hawthorne wrote to her sister Elizabeth Palmer Peabody that in spite of her and Nathaniel's resistance to abolition, they both "hate[d] the evil" (*CE* 23:466n2) of slavery. But the flaws of gradualism are obvious enough in hindsight, as they were to contemporaries like Elizabeth Palmer Peabody: to declare one's detestation of an iniquity is well and good, but not if in the same breath one declares the sublunary impossibility of overturning that iniquity—and, even worse, if one intimates that the iniquity might have its inscrutable "uses." Hawthorne's assurances that at some unspecified point God would intervene in human affairs and miraculously set all things right would be cold comfort to, say, a parent losing custody of her child in a slave market (to use a recurring image from the literature of abolition that Hawthorne appropriates in *The Scarlet Letter*[3]). Seen in its worst light, such gradualism tacitly assents to the evil it purports to decry, so that Hawthorne's antiabolitionism seems like simple racism and his antifeminism, misogyny.[4] Even seen in its best light, Hawthorne's gradualism is, in retrospect, a hopelessly inadequate response to the problems of antebellum America.

Still, to characterize Hawthorne as unremittingly conservative is simply false: to do so makes no allowance for the subtlety of his positions, nor even for their broad strokes. Those who understand Hawthorne as conservative have extreme difficulty with, for instance, his participation in Brook Farm. And they ignore various moments in the American romances that articulate a critique of antebellum America. Neither the critique of capitalism that emerges in Hawthorne's portrait of Jaffrey Pyncheon nor the corollary indictment of a political system beholden to a money power for "steal[ing] from the people, without its knowledge, the power of choosing its own rulers" (*CE* 2:274) reflects a conservative position. In many ways Hawthorne was, as T. Walter Herbert notes, a traitor to his class, in that "his social origins aligned him with the old elite class [. . .], yet he made an early, ardent commitment to the Jacksonians" (Herbert 89). This ardency has to be taken seriously.

One way to understand the tensions in Hawthorne's attitude towards reform is to see a conflict between his Whiggish social origins and his adult commitment to Jacksonian democracy. As Daniel Walker Howe notes, the Whigs "were apprehensive regarding social and moral development" (Howe 300) and their "personality ideal emphasized self-development but not self-indulgence" (Howe 301), attitudes more or less consistent with Hawthorne's own. On the other hand, Hawthorne's Jacksonian commitments reflected sympathy for the working classes and suspicion of the "money power." Charles Sellers has characterized America during the market revolution as engaged in "a *Kulturkampf*" waged between what he calls middle-class arminianism, which "sanctioned competitive individualism and the market's rewards of wealth and status," and working-class antinomianism, "rural America's communal egalitarianism" (Sellers 31), associated in Hawthorne's lifetime with the party of Andrew Jackson. This nineteenth-century culture war, Sellers argues, was fought "on the private battlegrounds of every human relationship" (31). Hawthorne fought this war internally, and it plays out in his ambivalence about reform.

The differences between the American romances in their treatment of reform do not derive from an evolving perspective. Rather, the differences derive from generic choices. As I suggested in Chapter Two, when Hawthorne writes about marriage (a synecdoche for society more generally), he tends to start from one of two basic positions. Either the marriage is utopian, in which case the domestic sphere is a kind of neo-Eden, or it is anti- or post-utopian, in which case the moral corruption of one of the participants—generally the husband—sullies the domestic sphere. Of the American romances, *The House of the Seven Gables* is in the utopian mode; *The Scarlet Letter* and *The Blithedale Romance* are post-utopian. As such, neither *The Scarlet Letter* nor *The Blithedale Romance* pretends to offer an immediate solution to social woes, and thus each critiques immediatist reformers as engaged in hopeless fools' errands. The utopianism of *The House of the Seven Gables*, by contrast, attempts to supplant reform by resolving conflicts both of gender and of class through marriage.[5] Although it attempts to effect its resolution by purifying and sacralizing those so-called "institutions that [have] grown out of the heart of mankind" (*CE* 10:26), the novel nevertheless cannot easily condemn immediatist reformers, at least not on the grounds of their immediatism. Instead, it appropriates their utopian claims and installs them at the heart of a reinvigorated domestic sphere.

Most critics suppose that *The House of the Seven Gables* is so different in tone from *The Scarlet Letter* because Hawthorne was trying in one way or another to court readers. Both William Charvat and Michael Gilmore have suggested that Hawthorne was intent on writing a happy ending to accommodate, in Charvat's words, the "world's wish that in stories everything should turn out well" (*CE* 2:xxi). Moreover, conscious of his image in an era both when celebrity culture was in its infancy[6] and what Allon White has called "symptomatic reading" was burgeoning,[7] Hawthorne may have wanted to follow the gloom of *The Scarlet Letter* with a work "more characteristic of my mind, and more proper and natural for me to write" (*CE* 16:461), as he put it in a letter to Horatio Bridge. He was sensitive about the public's perception of him, as one instance shows in particular. Shortly after the publication of *The House of the Seven Gables* in 1851, Allen Putnam, author of an account of the Salem witch-trials that read them in light of spiritualism, invited Hawthorne to act as his editor. Hawthorne wrote a letter declining Putnam's invitation, with the following explanation: although, he states, "your account of Salem Witchcraft is the most lucid and satisfactory that I have seen,"

> I must acknowledge a reluctance to connect myself with a work of the mystic character of the one proposed. My reputation (what little there is of it) has already too much fog and mist diffused through it, and if the public find me setting myself up as a sponsor for other people's books of dreamcraft and witchery, I shall get a very bad name. (*CE* 16:496)

As Jane Tompkins has shown, Hawthorne was as careful an architect of his literary reputation as were those, like James T. Fields and Evert Duyckinck, who championed him. His letters refer often to his bid to draw readers ("the great gull whom we are endeavouring to circumvent," as he put it in a letter to James Fields on the eve of *The Scarlet Letter*'s publication (*CE* 16:308)).[8] Given the unambiguous desire to "circumvent" his readership, it makes sense that to some extent he would sculpt the content of his books to gratify their expectations.

If such theories explain the turn from *The Scarlet Letter* to *The House of the Seven Gables,* they cannot in themselves account for Hawthorne's turn from *The House of the Seven Gables* to *The Blithedale Romance.* Hawthorne himself, in a letter to Horatio Bridge composed the week before he borrowed Caroline Tappan's volumes of Fourier (that is, on July 22, 1851), stated that "[s]hould it be a romance [that I write next], I mean to put an extra touch of the devil in it; for I doubt whether the public will stand two quiet books in a succession, without my losing ground" (*CE* 16:462). What Hawthorne means by an "extra touch of the devil" is not entirely clear. But whether or not he satisfied his own ambition to write a diabolic book, he was to be disappointed in the public response: *The Blithedale Romance* sold poorly, and Fields was to write (in personal correspondence to Mary Russell Mitford) that "I hope Hawthorne will give us no more Blithedales" (quoted in Mellow 403).

I account for the shift between *The House of the Seven Gables* and *The Blithedale Romance* by disagreeing with Hawthorne's conviction that the former was "more characteristic of [his] mind." In my view Hawthorne had difficulty sustaining the sentimental mode of *The House of the Seven Gables*, because he had difficulty embracing its values unreservedly. Even as he wrote the novel, he found, as he wrote in a letter to James Fields, that "[i]t darkens damnably towards the close" and that it took effort to "pour some setting sunshine on it" (*CE* 16:376). Although, as Tompkins has observed, Hawthorne was understood by many of his contemporaries as a sentimental novelist,[9] I tend (like most contemporary critics) to follow Melville, who wrote that "the world is mistaken in this Hawthorne" (*CR* 108), and who said that Hawthorne's "great power of blackness derives its force from its appeals to that Calvinistic sense of Innate Depravity and Original Sin, from whose visitations, in some shape or other, no deeply thinking mind is always and wholly free" (*CR* 107).[10] *The House of the Seven Gables* tries to dispel the complex problems of modernity by staging a retreat to rural domesticity. Whether you call the conclusion an exercise in Democratic myth-making or the enshrinement of a superseded culture as an eternal value (as Herbert and Alan Trachtenberg do, respectively[11]), the fact remains that the ending smacks of escapism rather than solution. Not having escaped the eyes of Hawthorne's critics, the logical problems of the ending are unlikely to have escaped those of Hawthorne, either. His recourse to an *ad captandam* topos as justification for writing a novel with "an extra touch of the devil" in it strikes me as a rationalization for abandoning the constrictions of a form in which, to repeat Charvat, "everything should turn out well."

One way of describing the differences between the American romances is to note that the conclusion of *The House of the Seven Gables* appears to resolve the tension internal to Hawthorne; it seemingly abandons the critique of the *status quo,* leaving only a muted hostility towards reformers' methods. Hawthorne's ambivalence about the legitimacy of the *status quo* is sublimated in the utopian marriage of Holgrave and Phoebe. Given the purifying power of her "example of feminine grace" (*CE* 2:80), the novel appears to argue, the reformers' critique is superfluous. This claim marks the fundamental difference between *The House of the Seven Gables* and the other two American romances, neither of which is entirely at peace with the *status quo* that each nevertheless restores.

In certain respects, the utopianism of *The House of the Seven Gables* is not wholly unrelated to the anti-utopianism of *The Blithedale Romance* and *The Scarlet Letter.* All three novels conclude by reaffirming marriage as the necessary foundation to society. In this sense particularly, *The Scarlet Letter* and *The Blithedale Romance* are as committed to the *status quo* as is *The House of the Seven Gables*. But *The House of the Seven Gables* enthusiastically endorses the *status quo,* while *The Scarlet Letter* and *The Blithedale Romance* are resigned to it. This difference becomes most clear in the novels' treatment of marriage: only *The House of the Seven Gables* entirely repudiates the radical critique of marriage (a repudiation signaled by Holgrave's abandonment of Fourierism for the new Eden of matrimony).

This chapter examines the American romances—in particular, *The House of the Seven Gables* and *The Blithedale Romance*—in light of the critiques of marriage originating among the Fourierists. These were far from the only critiques of marriage in antebellum America, of course, but where most critics advocated liberalizing divorce or increasing the economic autonomy of women within a marriage, the Fourierists, at their most searching, attacked marriage as a core manifestation of capitalism's tendency to atomize society, and, at their most radical, proposed its wholesale abandonment in favour of free love. As Amy Dru Stanley has noted, the specter of free love was one that haunted moderate marriage reformers in the nineteenth century.[12] It is fair to say that the Fourierists,[13] and more particularly their inheritors at Modern Times and the Oneida colony,[14] were the most radical critics of marriage in their day insofar as they argued for its fundamental transformation, or speculated about its wholesale abandonment. Such far-reaching critiques have a palpable influence on the American romances. The American romances do not, contrary to Arthur Cleveland Coxe's fears, advocate the realization of free love in the present. By and large, the American romances are a bulwark against challenges to the institution of marriage. But, especially in *The Blithedale Romance,* where he is protected behind the veil of his narrator Coverdale, Hawthorne suggests that the psychic stresses of marriage nevertheless outweigh its social utility, and acknowledges the allure of Fourierist alternatives. The novel installs these alternatives as a utopian value even as it so contains them as to make them impossible to realize.

II.

At least one of Hawthorne's contemporaries recognized the ideological function of marriage in the American romances. In a long review of *The Scarlet Letter,* George Bailey Loring wrote that

> In any form of society hitherto known, the sanctity of the devoted relation between the sexes has constituted the most certain foundation of all purity and all social safety. Imperfect as this great law has been in most of its development, founded upon and founding the rights of property,

instead of positively recognizing the delicacy of abstract virtue, and having become, of necessity, in the present organization, a bulwark of hereditary rights, and a bond for a deed of conveyance, it nevertheless appeals
to the highest sense of virtue and honor which a man finds in his breast.
[. . .] It was as heir of these virtues, and impressed with this education,
that Arthur Dimmesdale [. . .] found himself criminal. (*CR* 136)

Implicitly, in Loring's reading, Hester and Dimmesdale transgress not only
against the laws of marriage. Because those laws both found and are founded
upon the "rights of property," their adultery also implicitly transgresses
against property.

Equating marriage and the exchange of property ultimately supposes that
women and property are coextensive; as Gayle Rubin has suggested, patriarchal
models of sexual exchange imply a political economy in which women circu-
late as objects of exchange.[15] Adultery thus threatens to ambiguate title. This is
the logic of classic adultery narratives, as critics such as Richard Helgerson and
Jo Labanyi have shown.[16] None of the American romances fundamentally
challenge this logic; rather, they depend upon it for their aesthetic coherence.
But this reliance is something few critics have noted.[17]

Following Loring and reading property and marriage as intimately
related provides a key to the American romances, since all of them involve
transgressions either against marriage or against property. *The Blithedale
Romance* is perhaps the only one of the three in which this is not immediately
obvious, but much of the novel's tension derives from the question of whether
or not Zenobia has been previously married—whether, in Coverdale's words,
she is contemplating a "perilous and dreadful wrong [. . .] towards herself
and Hollingsworth" (*CE* 3:127) in taking him (according to the gossip of the
community) as a lover. Blithedale is an appropriate staging ground for this
drama because, as a socialist community, it seems to be predicated to some
extent on community of property.[18] The American romances all document
the condition of society when these twin foundations of "all purity and all
social safety," in Loring's words, are violated.

What distinguishes Hawthorne from other writers representing crimes
against marriage or property—what makes the American romances interesting—is that in all cases, these transgressions occur in the anterior action of
the novels: Hester's adultery, Pyncheon's theft, Zenobia's mysterious history,
all take place before the principal action begins. In *The Scarlet Letter,* Hester's
crime in fact specifically stands for the fall from utopian grace: alongside the
cemetery, the prison stands for the "the earliest practical necessit[y]" vitiating
the Utopian aspirations of "[t]he founders of [any] new colony" (*CE* 1:47),

and Hester's adultery is the emblematic crime dramatizing the truth of this apophthegm. Thus the societies represented in the American romances are implicitly already corrupted; *The Scarlet Letter* and *The Blithedale Romance* attempt to contend with a degraded reality, while *The House of the Seven Gables,* as a measure of its utopianism, tries to restore prelapsarian purity.[19]

Because socialists were widely held to favor community both of property and of women, Hawthorne's frequent reference to Fourierists throughout *The House of the Seven Gables* and *The Blithedale Romance* is consistent with his symbolic aims. Fourierist communities raise the specter of a world of ambiguated property and marriage, and thus they represent in an aggravated form the ambiguation of title and paternity that the inaugural crimes of adultery and property theft produce. In some respects, Hawthorne's use of Fourierism is eccentric, because conservatives attacking Fourierism for ambiguating property and marriage would hardly accept Hawthorne's intimation that such ambiguity was merely an exaggeration of what already obtained, and that Fourierism was the mirror image of the *status quo.* Nevertheless, in other respects, Hawthorne's representation of Fourierism is a common enough one among middle-class writers: whatever the nuances of the Fourierists' actual position with respect to property and marriage, they were routinely accused—and with some justice—of promulgating theories validating free love and community of property.

Thus in *Cannibals All!, Or, Slaves Without Masters* (1857), the slavery apologist George Fitzhugh attacks Horace Greeley's Fourierism, arguing that "in a few generations" of living in phalansteries "all the distinctions of separate property, and of separate wives and children, would be obliterated and lost, and society would gradually and gently be fused and crystallized into a system of perfect Communism" (Fitzhugh 139). By the time that Fitzhugh wrote *Cannibals All!,* invoking the specter of a world of ambiguated marriage and property was already a cliché among enemies of socialists. *The Communist Manifesto* even includes a procatalepsis against it:

> But you intend introducing a community of women, shrieks the whole Middle-class like a tragic chorus.
>
> [. . .]
>
> [. . .] [N]othing can be more ludicrous [. . .]. We do not require to introduce community of women, it has always existed. Your Middle-class gentry are not satisfied with having the wives and daughters of their Wage-slaves at their disposal,—not to mention the innumerable public prostitutes,—but they take a particular pleasure in seducing each

other's wives. Middle-class marriage is in reality a community of wives. At the most, then, we could only be reproached for wishing to substitute an open, above-board community of women, for the present mean, hypocritical, sneaking kind of community. But it is evident enough that with the disappearance of the present conditions of production, the community of women occasioned by them,—namely, official and non-official prostitution will also disappear. (Marx and Engels 148)[20]

Among socialists, the communitarian Owenists and Fourierists were the principal targets of such accusations.

Fitzhugh's accusation that property and paternity would become ambiguated in the phalanx does not represent Fourierist theory accurately, however. In the competition for adherents among the communitarian-minded left, the Fourierists tried to stake out a relatively conservative ground on property; in their papers and journals they continually distinguished themselves from other communitarians by pointing to Fourier's defense of private property. Albert Brisbane's *Social Destiny of Man* is typical of Fourierist literature, asking its readers

not to confound the system of Association which we shall propose, with those [. . .] trials which have been attempted or executed by Mr. Owen, the Rappites, Shakers, and others. Although well intended, [. . .] the absence of individual property (the greatest guarantee of individual liberty) which characterize[s] them, [has] excited a distrust on the part of the public against Association. (Brisbane 29)

One of the chapters in *Social Destiny of Man* has, among several other epigraphs, the statement that "[a]ll community of property is the grave of individual liberty" (quoted in Brisbane 26).

This is not to say that Fourierists disavowed all community of property: rather, they imagined a productive tension between collective and individual ownership. As Beecher states, Fourier "did not plan to abolish all forms of private property in the Phalanx. Rather, he insisted that the rights of individual ownership should never be allowed to take precedence over the interests of the community as a whole" (*UV* 298n2).[21] An essay in *The Harbinger* reprinted from *La Phalange* defended individual property against the attacks of "communists" while also allowing for a degree of communal ownership, stating that

in Harmony [. . .] the savans will be continually occupied with seeking delicate combinations to balance the universal and enthusiastic action of Unityism [collective property] by the action of favoritism [individual property] [. . .]. (*Harbinger* 4:234)

But such defences were often, as above, both vague and imperfectly theorized; although the phalanxes were typically joint-stock plans protective of individual investment, and in spite of the Fourierists' protestations, critics can be forgiven for supposing that the distinction between communists and Fourierists was rather fine.

Just as the Fourierists officially took, among socialists, a relatively conservative position in the debate on property, they were officially reluctant to broaden the range of "legitimate" sexual relationships, at least in the present. Already in *The Theory of the Four Movements* Fourier argued for "the necessity of [marriage] in Civilization" (*TFM* 109). When Fourierists confronted allegations that they meant to dismantle the institution of marriage, they emphasized Fourier's deferral of change, professing a wait-and-see attitude about the forms marriage might take in a future social order.

Nevertheless, Fourierists also spoke of marriage's tendency to be legal prostitution or *de facto* adultery, because the motive to marry was so often economic. The wife in "Civilization" was tantamount to a slave: "Is a young woman," Fourier fulminates,

> not a piece of merchandise offered for sale to whoever wants to negotiate her acquisition and exclusive ownership? Is not the consent she gives to the marriage bond derisory and enforced upon her by the tyranny of all the prejudices which have beset her since childhood? People try to persuade her that her chains are merely garlands of flowers: but can she really be under any illusion about her degradation [. . .]? (*TFM* 129–130)

Robert Gladish notes that in the Fourier-inflected view of Henry James, Sr., "any relationship of men and women that was of body and not of heart was adulterous, and this whether the couple was married or not" (Gladish 110). A relation devoid of emotional attachment debased marriage by making it only a matter of property ownership: as James puts it in his preface to Hennequin's *Love in the Phalanstery,*

> [t]he present law of the sexual relations clearly demands revision. By giving its subject an absolute property in the affections of another—a property based not upon his own worthiness, but upon a liability in the other to public ignominy and suffering, it not only too commonly

engenders a purely material relation among those who observe it, but
directly instigates deception, adultery, domestic tyranny, and dissension
throughout the land. (quoted in Stoehr [1979] 27)

Where marriage was concerned, both Fourier and many Fourierists thought
that relations between the sexes would take forms other than marriage in
future phalanxes. Fourier's suppressed work on the erotic life in "Harmony,"
Le Nouveau Monde Amoureux, imagines a vastly different array of legitimate
sexual practices where polygamy is the norm and monogamy is only a toler-
ated eccentricity: "all men," Fourier writes, "have a penchant for polygamy"
and "[t]he behavior of civilized ladies shows that they have the same penchant" (*UV* 334). An exclusive and unvarying attachment is, he argues, in
conflict with the human passion for variety. Since the passions cannot be
repressed, this unnatural relation produces hypocrisy and erotic intrigue:
"could anything better than the isolated household and permanent marriage
have been invented," Fourier asks, "to introduce dullness, venality, and
treachery into relations of love and pleasure?" (*TFM* 111).

Although *Le Nouveau Monde Amoureux* remained unpublished in the
nineteenth century (suppressed by Fourierists wary of scandal), other texts,
including *The Theory of the Four Movements,* were forthright enough in their
treatment of utopian eroticism that conservative critics of Fourierism could
with some justice accuse Fourierists of practicing, as Donald M'Laren put it
in his 1844 jeremiad *Boa Constrictor, or Fourier Association Self-Exposed,*
"base duplicity in their profession of adherence to the marriage institution of
civilized society" (M'Laren 23). Henry James, Sr., translated Victor Hennequin's *Les Amours au Phalanstère* in 1849, a text which articulated some of
Fourier's theories on sexuality, and thus gave further fuel to Fourierism's critics (James, as his 1852 debates on marriage with Stephen Pearl Andrews and
Horace Greeley show, did not advocate the abandonment of marriage, urg-
ing instead liberalization of divorce laws—but this was a distinction lost on
his critics on the right). James's translation provoked dissension among the
Fourierists as well: when the Fourierist journal *The Harbinger* folded in February 1849, it was "in the midst of wrangling over sexual reforms" (*UA* 355).

It is important to insist, however, that Fourierists in the phalanxes did
not engage in erotic experimentation. As Guarneri notes, the Brook Farmers
were careful to preëmpt scandal by carefully monitoring their own conduct
(*UA* 198). Enemies of the Ceresco Phalanx in Wisconsin accused it of practicing free love, but there is no evidence to support these accusations; typically, rumours of sexual impropriety were fostered by Fourierists' enemies in
an attempt to discredit the communities.[22]

Still, Fourierists were clearly susceptible to accusations that they favored sexual communitarianism and the erosion of individual property. That Brisbane tried to preëmpt the latter accusation in his first American publication shows how vulnerable the Fourierists were to such misunderstanding, and that Fitzhugh seventeen years later could make his attack so desultorily suggests how comprehensively they had failed in articulating their position. Therefore, when in *The House of the Seven Gables* Hawthorne associates Holgrave both with the abolition of private property and Fourierism, it is not clear whether Hawthorne is deliberately tarring Fourierism with the imputation of Proudhonism, or is using Fourierism as a metonym for all varieties of socialism, or is simply confused. But it appears that he would not have believed the Fourierist claim to respect individual property as "the greatest guarantee of personal liberty."

III. *THE HOUSE OF THE SEVEN GABLES*

The close relationship between property and sexuality in *The House of the Seven Gables* becomes clear when one considers that the novel begins with a seeming crime against property and ends with a conciliating marriage. The alleged property theft marks a fall from utopian grace in that it casts the legitimacy of the Pyncheon property into lasting doubt; the marriage entails the restoration of Eden. If the feud between the Maules and the Pyncheons begins with the theft of Maule's land, it expresses itself subsequently through struggles over male control of women's bodies. Matthew Maule and Gervayse Pyncheon exchange Alice; the feud ends when Holgrave proposes to Phoebe and she accepts. In the symbolic logic of the romance, Phoebe's body stands for the stolen Maule property: when she marries Holgrave, the Pyncheons compensate for their earlier theft.

This substitution of women for property finesses the complexities of the inaugural theft. The alliance of Pyncheon and Maule symbolized in Holgrave's and Phoebe's marriage does nothing to solve the problem of property's legitimacy. To begin with, it ignores the profit that Jaffrey Pyncheon makes through his capitalist speculations, from which the reconciled Pyncheons and Maules ultimately benefit but which, the narrator intimates, depends upon the economic victimization of countless others. At a more fundamental level, as Robert Martin has noted, what Hawthorne configures as the inaugural theft of land—Jaffrey Pyncheon's appropriation of Maule's property during the witch trials—does not acknowledge the earlier appropriation of land from native Americans.[23] The problematics of the colonial acquisition of territory is gestured towards in "the hieroglyphics of several Indian sagamores" on the

Pyncheon deed to "a vast extent of territory at the eastward" (*CE* 2:316), insofar, at least, as it foregrounds the presence of "Indian sagamores" in colonial America. But the novel's solution to the Pyncheon-Maule feud does nothing to compensate for this foundational national crime. Thus, as countless critics have observed, the novel's conclusion does not adequately resolve the problematics of legitimate title articulated in the introduction.

Instead, it insists on the sexual purity of the participants in the marriage. For the substitution of marriage for property to cohere, it must guarantee the "legitimacy"—that is to say, the sexual innocence—of both Holgrave and Phoebe. *The House of the Seven Gables* thus takes special care to contain the specter of illicit sexuality. As I noted in the previous chapter, both Jaffrey Pyncheon and—in Holgrave's historical fiction—Matthew Maule are represented in terms of sexual excess. Pyncheon exhausts his wife, one assumes by dint of the "prominent" masculinity from which Phoebe retreats (*CE* 2:118). Matthew Maule, whose pocket ruler phallically "protrude[s]" from its "long pocket" (*CE* 2:201), becomes, as we shall see, a serial (mesmeric) rapist. The utopia that emerges at the end of the novel depends on the extirpation or containment of such sexuality.

This containment plays out in the novel principally in the relationships between men and Phoebe. Clifford disavows any sexual component whatsoever in the pleasure he derives from looking at Phoebe's body. Although staged in sexual terms—he takes "unfailing note of every charm that appertain[s] to her sex, and [sees] the ripeness of her lips, and the virginal development of her bosom" (*CE* 2:141)—Clifford's appreciation of Phoebe is, according to the narrator, rather "a perception, or a sympathy, than a sentiment belonging to himself as an individual. He read Phoebe, as he would a sweet and simple story [. . .]. She was not an actual fact for him but the interpretation of all that he had lacked on earth" (*CE* 2:142). Clifford's excitement is not possessively sexual, the romance insists, but disinterestedly aesthetic.

Various degrees of critical skepticism have greeted Hawthorne's attempt to forestall a sexual component in the friendship of Phoebe and Clifford. The romance's conclusion, however, would seem to require it. Undercurrents of erotic desire in Phoebe and Clifford's relationship would threaten the propriety of the Pyncheon estate. Nor is theirs the only relationship that requires such containment. Uncle Venner too has an infatuation with Phoebe: he states that "if I were a young man, I'd get one of Alice's Posies, and keep it in water [for] Phoebe" (*CE* 2:288). When Phoebe invites him to join the Pyncheons and Maules on their newly inherited estate, he says, "if you were to speak to a young man as you do to an old one, his chance of keeping his heart, another minute, would not be worth one of the buttons on my waistcoat" (*CE* 2:317). Venner's insistence on his age on both occasions is analogous to the narrator's containment of Clifford's desire: neither man is a potential erotic rival for Holgrave. The romance excludes sexuality from these men's appreciation of Phoebe so that, even if their living arrangements resemble socialism, their erotic relations remain conventional. It makes sense, then, that Jaffrey Pyncheon, the only character whose masculinity Phoebe notices (aside from Holgrave), is the one who dies.

If the narrative circumscribes and preempts the desires of men other than Holgrave for Phoebe, it seems to deny altogether the possibility that Phoebe might herself experience sexual desire. She recoils from the Judge's embrace because "the man, the sex, somehow or other, was entirely too prominent in the Judge's demonstrations of that sort. Phoebe's eyes sank, and, without knowing why, she felt herself blushing deeply under his look" (*CE* 2:118). Her sinking eyes in this instance anticipate her response to Holgrave's wooing, when she lets "her eyes droop" (*CE* 2:307). In these representations of Phoebe's averted gaze, as Shawn Michelle Smith has noted, Hawthorne develops a contrast between Phoebe and Alice Pyncheon, who gives Matthew Maule an "admiring glance" which "she [makes] no effort to conceal" when she sees "the remarkable comeliness, strength, and energy of Maule's figure" (*CE* 2:201) (and which he resents); "Phoebe's interiority," Smith writes, "her very essence, distinguishes her from the exterior display of the aristocratic woman, and her gendered submissiveness shields her from class pride" (Smith 27–8). The contrast between Phoebe and Alice shows itself, therefore, not merely in terms of class, but in terms of sexual experience. Alice Pyncheon is in a continuum with sexually unembarrassed women like Hester Prynne and Zenobia;[24] Phoebe, of course, is aligned with sexual innocents like Priscilla. This emphasis on Phoebe's innocence means that when she enters into the exchange system of marriage, she will be unsullied even by the imputation of experience (presumably her utopian marriage will so sanctify sexual exchange that experience will be indistinguishable from innocence). Because of the novel's equation between women and property, it needs to establish the sexual innocence of Phoebe: were she to experience sexual desire for men other than Holgrave, it would undermine the novel's attempts to establish purity of title.

No less potentially disruptive than Phoebe's sexuality, however, is Holgrave's. *The House of the Seven Gables* takes pains to indicate that Holgrave will remain faithful. The need to contain his sexuality is in certain respects greater than that of Phoebe because of the cavalier sexual mores conventionally imputed to socialist reformers. In *Eve and the New Jerusalem,* Barbara

Taylor cites a cautionary tale called "Moral Harmony" which circulated in a Manchester newspaper in 1840 and which perfectly demonstrates the sexual threat that Hawthorne has to contain in depicting a socialist man intent upon marrying an innocent young woman from the country. "Moral Harmony" depicts a young reformer who marries the daughter of a "rural cottager" only to rob and abandon her when she becomes pregnant (anon. in Taylor 187n). "Her career terminates," Taylor writes, "in a pauper's funeral, attended by many angry women, while her former lover dances the night away at a Social Festival" (Taylor 188n). The English reformer is startlingly similar to Holgrave: the reformer "wears the garb of a mechanic [. . .] converses about science and the march of intellect [. . .] declaims, fluently, concerning political rights and moral organization, and talks of signing the People's Charter" (anon. in Taylor 187n); Holgrave wears clothes "of the simplest kind" (*CE* 2:43) and his speech "at a meeting of his banditti-like associates" is "full of wild and disorganizing matter" (*CE* 2:84). The character type Hawthorne subtilizes in his portrait of Holgrave is one in whom political pretenses are hypocritical, and in whom affirmations of romantic love are a masque for erotic scoundrelism.

To keep Holgrave's radicalism from extending to the bedroom is one point of introducing his "Alice Pyncheon" into the text. In Holgrave's fiction, his ancestor Matthew Maule mesmerizes Alice and subsequently marries a "laborer's daughter" (*CE* 2:209): this amounts to a demonic vision of socialist sexual reform. Reading it in light of Holgrave's authorship suggests that "Alice Pyncheon" is Holgrave's attempt to translate appetite into art: in the same way that Clifford displaces a sexual attraction to Phoebe by reading her as a story (*CE* 2:142), Holgrave displaces radical sexuality into his own literary productions, where he anathematizes it.[25]

It is well known that Hawthorne interpreted mesmerism in sexual terms: prior to their marriage he wrote to Sophia protesting her plans to submit to mesmerism as therapy for her headaches: she had intended to turn to her friend (and former boarder at Brook Farm) Cornelia Park for mesmeric relief. Hawthorne was resolutely opposed: "There would be an intrusion," he wrote, "into thy holy of holies—and the intruder would not be thy husband! Canst thou think, without a shrinking of thy soul, of any human being coming into closer communion with thee than I may?" (*CE* 15:588). Although a woman, Park used an implicitly masculine force, according at least to Hawthorne's understanding, to penetrate into regions that should be explored exclusively within matrimonial bonds.

Thus Matthew Maule's mesmeric domination of Alice Pyncheon is implicitly sexual in nature. In effect, when Maule mesmerizes Alice in the presence of her father, he is staging a rape, one whose effects are repeated subsequently whenever his "will [. . .] constrain[s] her to do its grotesque and fantastic bidding" (*CE* 2:208) (they are repeated because Alice's iterated subjection implies that Maule's phallic "will" remains inside her "holy of holies"). The psychic sex into which Matthew conscripts Alice ironizes his own marriage, at the solemnization of which Maule forces Alice to attend: he "summoned proud Alice Pyncheon to wait upon his bride. And so she did; and when the twain were one, Alice woke out of her enchanted sleep" (*CE* 2:209). The spectacle of Maule's mesmeric sexual victim attending upon his bride is fraught with irony, since Holgrave suggests that what really is solemnized is a kind of polygamy. The kiss that Alice bestows upon Maule's wife recapitulates the kiss of bride and groom and thus consummates the erotic triangle which Maule has instigated through his enslavement of Alice. Just as Hester's adultery explodes monogamous desire and inaugurates an erotic triangle, so too does Maule's mesmerism inaugurate a three-way marriage.

That Holgrave finds himself in a position to mesmerize Phoebe immediately after finishing his recital of "Alice Pyncheon" draws a parallel between him and Maule that has escaped no one. Holgrave, of course, resists the temptation to "render [. . .] his spell over Phoebe indissoluble," and the narrator is quick to sermonize on his virtue: Holgrave has "the rare and high quality of reverence for another's individuality"; he has "integrity forever after to be confided in" (*CE* 2:212); and so on. Holgrave's integrity functions as a reassurance to the reader: it precludes the possibility of any socialistic sexual reforms insinuating themselves into the Pyncheon estate after the conclusion of the romance. The "succession of kaleidoscopic pictures, in which a gifted eye might [. . .] see [. . .] fore-shadowed the coming fortunes of [. . .] the descendant of the legendary wizard, and the village-maiden, over whom he had thrown love's web of sorcery" (*CE* 2:319) will not include anything so uncongenial to middle-class sensibility. Bourgeois monogamy will develop within the Pyncheon estate unscathed.

Whatever the virtues of this analysis, it does not explain why, if the point of *The House of the Seven Gables* is to represent a marriage that reconciles classes and legitimates property, Hawthorne opts to make one of the partners in the marriage someone so suspect in terms of his own sexual legitimacy. Why associate Holgrave with Fourierism, if, as I note above, typical representations of socialists in literature portrayed them as fornicating reprobates intent on ruining innocent young women? Why undertake the labor of domesticating a "wild reformer" (*CE* 2:313)? The answer has to do with Hawthorne's twin perspectives on reform—that its critiques were legitimate but that its solutions were unacceptable. In its portrait of Jaffrey Pyncheon, after all, *The House of the Seven*

Gables shares the revulsion of Fourierists at capitalist excess. But the novel attempts to show that its conservative solution—middle-class domesticity—is superior to the solutions tendered by Fourierists and others. By showing a Fourierist accepting the renovated Eden and hence forsaking the wilderness of reform, Hawthorne tries further to legitimate the middle-class utopia he tenders.

This explains, too, various correspondences between the Fourierist phalanx and Hawthorne's middle-class utopia: by appropriating various features of Fourierism Hawthorne's utopia shows that it has all the virtues of Fourierism with none of the social disruptions. In the Pyncheon estate, Hawthorne is not by any means representing a mystified Fourierist phalanx. Still, one can hear echoes of Fourierist doctrine throughout the novel. As Myra Jehlen has observed,[26] we know very little about the estate; nevertheless, we can infer what life there might resemble from Hawthorne's earlier depiction of the protagonists together in the garden of the House of the Seven Gables. Significantly, from the moment that Phoebe and Holgrave first meet there, it is associated with communitarianism. A postlapsarian Adam and Eve, Holgrave and Phoebe agree to tend the garden together, a collaboration that Holgrave characterizes as "somewhat on the community-system" (*CE* 2:93) (given what we know of Holgrave's own history in a "community of Fourierists" (*CE* 2:176) we can reasonably infer that the "community-system" he has in mind is by and large Fourierist). And the class reconciliation of the Pyncheon estate is emphasized by the inclusion of Venner, who forsakes the debased communitarianism of the work-house for a "cottage in [the] garden" (*CE* 2:317) of the Pyncheon estate. Fourierism promised a reconciliation of classes but the persistence of class difference (in fealty to Fourier's supposition that human beings craved variety); the Pyncheon estate promises a distorted form of this, including representatives of all three classes but distinctly tainted with class condescension (one cannot fail to note that Venner is a caricature of the sage rustic).[27]

Hawthorne similarly installs a recognizably Fourierist thesis at the symbolic center of his utopia. In his portrait of Phoebe, the angel of renovated middle-class domesticity around whom the members of the new estate constellate, Hawthorne borrows the Fourierist ideal of attractive industry. "Work," Fourier writes,

> is [. . .] a delight for many creatures such as the beavers, bees, wasps, and ants, who are perfectly free to lapse into a state of inertia. God has provided them with a social mechanism which attracts them to work

and makes it a source of happiness for them. Why should he have failed to grant us a benefit which he bestows upon the animals? (*UV* 144)

Fourier imagines "a system of industrial attraction [. . .] [that] will endow manufacturing and farming tasks with a host of charms" and make "work more alluring than are the festivities, balls, and spectacles of today" (*UV* 274). Phoebe's labor is comparable: "while she deal[s] with it," the narrator writes, it has "the easy and flexible charm of play" (*CE* 2:82). As Gillian Brown has trenchantly argued, Phoebe's ludic labor denies "the corporeality of women's work" (Brown 80), and *The House of the Seven Gables* therefore participates in the pastoralization of women's labor that undergirds the "cult of true womanhood." Because Phoebe's labor is not enervating, Brown notes, it goes against the grain of "the idea of work as damaging to the individual [that] pervades nineteenth-century thought" (Brown 81). As the quotations from Fourier show, the idea of work as damaging was pervasive, but not ubiquitous. Hawthorne appears to borrow Fourierist theses on attractive labor as a means to buttress middle-class ideology. What Fourier used to critique the monotony of domesticity, and which socialists imagined as justification for collaborative labor—it made work enjoyable—Hawthorne uses as justification for immuring Phoebe in the domestic sphere.

That the conservatism of *The House of the Seven Gables* incorporates such recognizably Fourierist elements suggests that Hawthorne is undertaking an ideological operation similar to what Bercovitch has identified as characteristic of Emersonian liberal individualism. Like Emerson, Hawthorne stages a "wholesale appropriation of utopia, all the hopes of reform and revolution nourished on both sides of the Atlantic by the turmoil of modernization, for the American way" (*RA* 335). In a novel where middle-class ideology legitimates property and conciliates classes while enshrining a happy homemaker at the symbolic center, Hawthorne borrows Fourierist utopianism, which thereby is so etiolated that it loses altogether its radical power and instead serves to buttress the *status quo*.

IV. *THE BLITHEDALE ROMANCE* AND *THE SCARLET LETTER*

Like *The House of the Seven Gables*, *The Blithedale Romance* ends with the evocation of a marriage in a rural cottage; unlike the narrator of *The House of the Seven Gables*, however, Coverdale is unable to invest this marriage with anything like utopianism. This may be because Coverdale is jealous of Hollingsworth (or, as various critics have suggested, of Priscilla): the ambivalence may reflect Coverdale's character, that is, rather than some postulated authorial or textual position. Certainly, reading only *The Blithedale Romance,* one cannot resolve the problem of the relation between Coverdale and author: Coverdale so thoroughly dominates the novel that other positions, especially including those of Hawthorne himself, are impossible to locate within the text itself. As Nina Baym has argued, "[t]he book's reality is Coverdale's world; ultimately he is its only character, and everything that happens in the novel must be understood in reference to him" (Baym 547).

One can critique Coverdale, that is, but one cannot see "through" him.[28] And the centrality of Coverdale's perspective means that *The Blithedale Romance* reproduces the middle-class ideology of *The House of the Seven Gables* but lacks the earlier novel's commitment. What results is a more complex novel, one whose attitude towards the *status quo* is far more ambivalent.

As I argue above, one can attribute the difference in tone to Hawthorne's temperamental discomfort with the simple happy ending of *The House of the Seven Gables.* The problems presented by Coverdale's narration are more difficult to resolve: the obscurity into which Coverdale's narrative casts Hawthorne himself is absolute. *The Blithedale Romance* is in this respect proto-modernist, and can be classed alongside the fiction of Meredith, Stevenson, Conrad, James, and others, all of whom were experimenting with what Allon White has called the uses of obscurity. As White states, "the mutual adoption of deflective strategy and enigmatic method by so many writers during this period, the exploratory use of secrecy, lying, obscurity, impression and withdrawal, form an interconnection of cultural concern and activity which became a generative complex of modernism" (White 54). Hawthorne may have been responding anxiously to the rise of symptomatic reading, the practice, as Wai-chee Dimock aptly characterizes it, of "focus[ing] on the character of the author as a mode of speculative diagnosis" (Dimock 174) (a mode of reading to which Hawthorne was subjected in his time,[29] and a mode in which my own appraisals of Hawthorne's temperament engage). But this seems more defensive than the playfulness of the preface to *The Blithedale Romance* would suggest. Hawthorne foregrounds the links between himself and Coverdale in the preface by acknowledging the novel's debt to his experiences at Brook Farm, but just as quickly distances himself from Coverdale by denigrating all of the principal characters, Coverdale included (*CE* 3:1–3). I read the obscurity in light of Hawthorne's declaration in "The Old Manse" that "[s]o far as I am a man of really individual attributes, I veil my face" (*CE* 10:33); one might think of Hawthorne's rhetorical operations in *The Blithedale Romance* as an extended variation on this declaration. Hawthorne's statement in "The Old Manse" was made as a prolepsis against accusations of egotism (*CE* 10:32). Here, in a novel so preoccupied with the problem of egotism, the self-veiling emphasizes the impossibility of perfectly knowing others.

One can nevertheless overstate the narratological problems that Coverdale's mediation presents. Read in isolation from the rest of Hawthorne's *oeuvre*, *The Blithedale Romance* is indeed an obscurity engine, the reveries of a capricious and deflective narrator. Read alongside other Hawthorne texts, however, various continuities come to the fore, allowing one to differentiate between positions that are unique to Coverdale and those so often articulated by Hawthorne as to be safely ascribable to him. One would hesitate to second Henry James, Jr., who said of Coverdale that "in so far as we may measure this lightly indicated identity of his, it has a great deal in common with that of his creator" (James 105). One needs, moreover, to emphasize the provisionality of one's conclusions. Nevertheless one can still speak about distinctively Hawthornean preoccupations in *The Blithedale Romance*.

Central among these is a concern with property and marriage: *The Blithedale Romance* propounds the necessity of their persistence, although without the optimism of *The House of the Seven Gables*. As in *The House of the Seven Gables*, property and marriage are intimately related. The plot of *The Blithedale Romance* revolves around two related questions: who will win Hollingsworth's affections? And who will inherit Moodie's estate? The answer to each question is, of course, Priscilla, which suggests that, as in *The House of the Seven Gables*, the property plot is the correlative of the love plot. But *The Blithedale Romance* complicates considerably both of these plots by introducing sexual rivalry: *The House of the Seven Gables* presents a relatively simple erotic narrative, where neither Holgrave and Phoebe has to compete for the other's affections. By contrast, in *The Blithedale Romance* there is a tangled skein of relationships that can reduce at best to a triangle; one should rather speak of an erotic network, allowing that Coverdale supposes himself to be attracted from one moment to the next to Zenobia, Hollingsworth, and Priscilla, and, more especially, given Westervelt's supposed history with Zenobia. *The Blithedale Romance* resembles *The House of the Seven Gables* insofar as the narrative culminates in a marriage, but because of the complex erotic rivalries from which this marriage emerges, the monogamous resolution remains imperfect. Two instances in the dénouement make this particularly clear: Coverdale represents Hollingsworth as haunted by the specter of Zenobia; and Coverdale confesses himself to have been in love with Priscilla. Where *The House of the Seven Gables* is a relatively simple narrative in which the legitimacy of title is restored—or is supposed to be restored—by marriage,

The Blithedale Romance presents a considerably more complex narrative in which desire is only imperfectly channeled into the dyad of marriage and in which the legitimacy of title cannot be guaranteed.

Blithedale is an appropriate setting for the love and inheritance plots to unfold because a socialist community would be susceptible to accusations that it favored the dissolution of marriage and individual title. Coverdale affirms early on that the system at Blithedale bears a distinct resemblance to that of Fourier, but then retreats: having noted the similarity, he says that "[t]here was far less resemblance [. . .] than the world chose to imagine; inasmuch as the two theories differed, as widely as the zenith from the nadir, in their main principles" (*CE* 3:53). As Lauren Berlant has noted, zenith and nadir here imply a spirit-flesh dyad: "[t]he 'zenith,'" Berlant writes, "is Hollingsworth's domain: the spirit, the heart. The 'nadir' of Fourier engages what Coverdale calls 'the promised delights of his system': the erogenous zones treated by Fourier's theories of the passions" (Berlant [1988] 40). At the end of his narrative Coverdale states, however, that Blithedale "proved long ago a failure, first lapsing into Fourierism, and dying, as it well deserved, for this infidelity to its own higher spirit" (*CE* 3:246). Because historically Brook Farm converted into Fourierism after Hawthorne had left, this passage has not received especial attention, read as a historically accurate detail and little else; given the spirit-flesh dyad earlier applied to the systems of Blithedale and Fourier, however, the passage suggests strongly that Blithedale becomes a free-love community before its "death."[30] Even without admitting this as a possibility, however, the fact remains that as a communitarian experiment, Blithedale would be *ipso facto* associated with free love. The novel's retrenchment to conservative monogamy and individual title thus takes place in a domain where these are especially embattled.

Blithedale is not the only place in the novel in which marriage and property are under attack, however. The tenement in which Moodie raises Priscilla is another site where, in Fitzhugh's words, "all the distinctions of separate property, and of separate wives and children" are at risk of being "obliterated and lost" (Fitzhugh 139). Formerly a "stately habitation" of a Puritan governor, the tenement now houses "[m]any families" (*CE* 3:184) with "innumerable progeny" (*CE* 3:187), none of whom Coverdale's narrative differentiates. The boarding house in which Coverdale sees Zenobia, Priscilla, and Westervelt is likewise associated with sexual license; as Luther Luedtke notes, it recalls a seraglio (Luedtke 202); Edwin Burrows and Mike Wallace have noted that boarding houses, with their centrally cooked and commonly eaten meals, threatened family integrity; wives might mingle promiscuously with others while husbands were off at work. Enforced intimacy mocked middle-class values of family privacy and the sanctity of the home. (Burrows and Wallace 971)

Implicitly, Blithedale and Boston are fundamentally akin, respectively a utopian and demonic vision of ambiguated property and paternity; in spite of the reformers' supposition that they are challenging the "false and cruel principles, on which human society has all along been based" (*CE* 3:19), they are instead reproducing it in an Arcadian guise—or so Coverdale's narrative suggests.

At its most simple, *The Blithedale Romance* is a competition between the apparently sexually innocent Priscilla and the apparently sexually experienced Zenobia for the affections of Hollingsworth. As in *The House of the Seven Gables,* sexual innocence and sexual experience are both freighted with symbolic value. Priscilla's virginity, like that of Phoebe, implies more than sexual innocence; it implies also purity of title. This purity is corroborated in the legitimacy of her wealth: the rural cottage she lives in with Hollingsworth at the end of the novel lacks the taint of illegitimacy that proves to hover around Zenobia's offers of "liberal pecuniary aid," first to Blithedale and then to Hollingsworth (*CE* 3:190). In contrast to Priscilla, Zenobia is doubly compromised. Her estate proves to belong legally to Moodie, and her life appears to be "hopelessly entangled with a villain's!" (*CE* 3:225). Because of Coverdale's inferences about her and the "whispers of an attachment, and even a secret marriage" (*CE* 3:189), this entanglement appears to be sexual: as Coverdale says in a misogynistic flurry, "[t]here is no folded petal, no latent dew-drop, in this perfectly developed rose!" (CE 3:47). In other words, not only is Zenobia's title to her wealth illegitimate, but, granted the validity of Coverdale's inferences, sexually she is "impure."

As Berlant notes,[31] the significance of virginity in the text is signaled partly through Coverdale's meditations on the Arcadian fantasies of the Blithedale communitarians: "Altogether," he writes,

by projecting our minds outward, we had imparted a show of novelty to existence, and contemplated it as hopefully as if the soil, beneath our feet, had not been fathom-deep with the dust of deluded generations, on every one of which, as on ourselves, the world had imposed itself as a hitherto unwedded bride. (*CE* 3:128)

The "world," in Coverdale's formulation, is a sexually experienced woman masquerading as a virgin. The similarity between this metaphor and Coverdale's version of Zenobia is clear enough, and underscored by the proximity of this passage to Coverdale's meditations on the "great wrong" he fears that Zenobia is contemplating "towards herself and Hollingsworth" (*CE* 3:127). According to Coverdale's logic, Zenobia imposes herself on Hollingsworth just as "the world" imposes itself on Blithedale, threatening to compromise him. Only by repudiating Zenobia and cleaving to the virginal Priscilla can Hollingsworth be spared.

Read this way, the novel documents the retreat of Hollingsworth from Blithedale and the world to the only guarantors of legitimacy, the "true woman" and the middle-class home. As such, it follows the logic of *The House of the Seven Gables*: Hollingsworth is another Holgrave, and Priscilla another Phoebe. But the narrative in various respects complicates and subverts this reading. To begin with, the accuracy of Coverdale's inferences about Zenobia's sexual history is never conclusively established; it is entirely possible, in other words, that she is in fact "a hitherto unwedded bride." Moreover, the integrity of Priscilla's "virgin reserve and sanctity of soul" in the wake of Westervelt's mesmeric manipulation of her can only be guaranteed by Coverdale's "religiously" believing it: it is explicitly a leap of faith (*CE* 3:203).[32] When one recalls Hawthorne's comparisons of mesmerism to sexual penetration, Coverdale's faith in Priscilla's "virgin reserve" seems forced, a self-conscious ideological move visibly under strain.

What this would imply is that the scapegoating of Zenobia and the enshrinement of Priscilla as a domestic ideal are both equally compromised: Priscilla does not necessarily guarantee the legitimacy of the rural cottage; and Zenobia may not deserve Coverdale's attacks for her supposed "impurity" (even were one to grant that sexual experience implies moral corruption). The entire opposition between the experienced world and innocent middle-class domesticity begins to totter, still standing only thanks to Coverdale's testimonials. This is scarcely a firm foundation on which to build middle-class authority: the rural cottage risks revealing itself as identical to the working-class tenement or the Fourierist phalanstery, accorded superior status owing more to the efforts of middle-class propagandists like Coverdale than to any essential difference.

Coverdale's observations of middle-class "nature" from the window of his hotel room underscore the artifice of his categories. The boarding-house opposite the hotel striates classes: Coverdale's gaze passes over it from top to bottom, and, in effect, he sees the antebellum North's class structure reproduced architecturally. "In one of the upper chambers," he writes,

> I saw a young man in a dressing-gown, standing before the glass and brushing his hair, for a quarter-of-an-hour together. He then spent an equal space of time in the elaborate arrangement of his cravat, and finally made his appearance in a dress-coat, which I suspected to be newly come from the tailor's, and now first put on for a dinner-party. (*CE* 3:150)

The young dandy's concern with his appearance recalls Westervelt, likewise characterized by his fashionable dress. In stark contrast with this privilege, Coverdale espies domestic servants on the main floor and in the "lower regions" (*CE* 3:151): housemaids, a cook, and "an Irish man-servant" (*CE* 3:151). These are engaged in labor, or, in the case of the man-servant, in a petty deception—he "[throws] away the fragments of a china dish, which, unquestionably, he had just broken" (*CE* 3:151)—that reflects his subjection to equally petty discipline.

Between these floors, Coverdale sees a domestic drama enacted; his response to the sentimental spectacle betrays his own middle-class affiliation. "At a window" in Coverdale's view,

> two children, prettily dressed, were looking out. By-and-by, a middle-aged gentleman came softly behind them, kissed the little girl, and play-fully pulled the little boy's ear. It was a papa, no doubt, just come in from his counting-room or office; and anon appeared mamma, stealing as softly behind papa, as he had stolen behind the children, and laying her hand on his shoulder to surprise him. There followed a kiss between papa and mamma, but a noiseless one; for the children did not turn their heads. (*CE* 3:150–151)

The artifice of the context in which this scene of middle-class domesticity is enacted ironizes Coverdale's enthusiastic declaration that "I have not seen a prettier bit of nature, in all my summer in the country" (*CE* 3:151). Everything about this "rather stylish boarding-house" (*CE* 3:151) emphasizes contingency, including the clothing of the children and the recent provenance of the children's "papa" from a "counting-room or office," all of which signal their class status. Coverdale's bid to naturalize this middle-class family romance is unpersuasive, confirming only that he ideologically identifies with the middle classes.

What undermines this naturalizing enterprise still more is Coverdale's momentary glimpse of the "respectable mistress of the boarding-house" (*CE* 3:151). This is "a lady, showily dressed, with a curling front of what must have been false hair, and reddish-brown, I suppose, in hue" (*CE* 3:151). Coverdale characteristically temporizes in this description, saying that his "remoteness allow[s] [him] only to guess at such particulars" (*CE* 3:151), but it nevertheless emphasizes once again the artifice of the building. Like the "gold band around the upper part of [Westervelt's] teeth" which suggests to Coverdale that "his wonderful beauty of face [. . .] might be removeable like a mask" (*CE* 3:95), the false hair of the boarding-house mistress signals the extent to which the building is a theatre comparable to the lyceum-hall.[33]

One might suppose that, having tendered the possibility that the middle-class home is as provisional as is Blithedale, *The Blithedale Romance* would retreat from the strong endorsement of marriage of *The House of the Seven Gables*. To some extent this is the case; as T. Walter Herbert has noted, the marriage depends upon the psychic prostration of Hollingsworth (Herbert 21–24): in spite of Priscilla's "veiled happiness" (*CE* 3:242), the marriage is an unromantic compromise. In Herbert's words, *The Blithedale Romance* concludes with "a radical criticism of the domestic ideal" (Herbert 18), a critique altogether absent from *The House of the Seven Gables*. And yet *The Blithedale Romance* offers nothing as a substitute for marriage: Coverdale lives as a bachelor, but his life "has come to rather an idle pass" (*CE* 3:247), as he puts it, and his confession of unrequited love (however one reads it) dramatically illustrates his unhappiness. Whatever alternative erotic and economic arrangements Blithedale might have provided are foreclosed, except, perhaps, for the benefit of a posterity ready to "dig [. . .] up" the community's lessons (*CE* 3:246).[34]

In articulating a critique of monogamy and then refusing to endorse alternatives, *The Blithedale Romance* recalls *The Scarlet Letter*'s counsel of patience after the fall of utopia. The Prynne marriage is compromised in the anterior action of the novel, suggesting that the world is always already adulterated. But the novel ambiguates the location of the original adultery. In legal terms, Hester commits adultery with Dimmesdale. But when Chillingworth refers to his marriage as a "false and unnatural relation" (*CE* 1:75),[35] he ambiguates the adultery by suggesting that the marriage itself was adulterous and implying that, although his cuckold "wronged" him (*CE* 1:75), Hester's extramarital liaison was nevertheless true and natural. Chillingworth's phraseology is comparable to that of Fourierists describing marriage in "Civilization." Marx Edgeworth Lazarus, for instance, attacked

> the evils now resulting from constraint in the relations of love, and [the] false dependence on pecuniary interest, the withering of true affections, the false and unhappy marriages, the adultery, the libertinism and the prostitution with which our civilized cities are rotten (quoted in Spurlock 68).

Henry James, Sr., characterized loveless marriage as adultery in his preface to *Love in the Phalanstery.* Alfred Habegger, the elder James's biographer, notes that Hester, in describing her love affair with Dimmesdale as having "a consecration of its own" (*CE* 1:195), uses the same argument as does James: "Hawthorne, too, it seemed," Habegger writes, "was absorbed in the marriage question" (Habegger 320). *The Scarlet Letter* is structured around a binary opposition between Law and Nature, and Chillingworth and Dimmesdale are, respectively, Hester's legal and natural husbands. The A on Hester's chest therefore refers to the "adulterous" marriage that she entered into with Roger Chillingworth just as much as it designates adultery more conventionally defined. As Herbert puts it, Hester "has two husbands" (186), and Dimmesdale and Chillingworth are "reciprocal cuckolds" (188).

But, as Bercovitch has noted, having articulated a critique of the *status quo, The Scarlet Letter* preaches accommodation, compromise, and patience. Although Hawthorne argues that in the practical as opposed to utopian society, marriage is always already broken, he nevertheless resists experiments seeking a remedy. He directs his concern instead towards inducting Pearl into the human community—towards containing the deleterious effects, that is, of a faulty social foundation. To do so, *The Scarlet Letter* concludes with two acknowledgements of paternity. On the scaffold, Dimmesdale declares that he was Hester's partner in adultery, an admission that allows Pearl to shed sentimental tears "upon her father's cheek" (*CE* 1:256). The second acknowledgement has attracted little critical notice, but it is equally important:

> At old Roger Chillingworth's decease (which took place within the year), and by his last will and testament, of which Governor Bellingham and the Reverend Mr. Wilson were executors, he bequeathed a very considerable amount of property, both here and in England, to little Pearl, the daughter of Hester Prynne. (*CE* 1:261).

In effect, just as Dimmesdale has declared himself to be the natural father of Pearl, Chillingworth declares himself to be her legal father. The narrator insists upon the legal process not only through the language of inheritance but also by noting that the magistracy—specifically, those two who earlier threatened to deprive Hester of custody—are the will's executors: Chillingworth's posthumous adoption of Pearl carries the weight of the legalistic Puritan community. All three partners in the triple marriage are Pearl's parents, allowing her to "grow up amid human sorrow, nor for ever do battle with the world, but be a woman in it" (*CE* 1:256). Such accommodation, Hawthorne suggests, is the best one can hope for in a fallen world.

Although *The Blithedale Romance* also preaches patience, it is more critical of the *status quo* than is *The Scarlet Letter,* both in its immediate portrait of the psychic costs of marriage, and in its portrait of society in general—the portrait of tenement life is as vivid as anything in a condition-of-England or city-mysteries novel.[36] And unlike *The Scarlet Letter,* there is no great sense of optimism in *The Blithedale Romance* for the future: where Hester believes "a new truth [will] be revealed, in order to establish the whole relation between man and woman on a surer ground of mutual happiness" (*CE* 1:263), Coverdale casts "a listless glance towards the future" (*CE* 3:247). Where Hester makes her prophecies from within her cottage, and thus implicitly identifies her utopianism with domesticity, Coverdale makes his own prophecy "standing by Zenobia's grave" (*CE* 3:243). Firm belief posed against listless glance; cottage posed against grave: Coverdale's ambivalence cannot match Hester's confident expectation. This pessimism may be a reflection of Coverdale's character, an Ecclesiastes-like disenchantment that Hawthorne means for his readers to critique. It may also reflect the "extra touch of the devil" (*CE* 16:462) that Hawthorne had resolved to put into his novel before even beginning to write it.

There is a third possibility, too: the repudiation of progress may operate alongside the ironization of the novel's narration to contain the utopian dispensation, in order to provide Hawthorne with a safe way to articulate it. Early in *The Blithedale Romance,* Coverdale celebrates Blithedale for "seeming to authorize any individual, of either sex, to fall in love with any other, regardless of what would elsewhere be judged suitable and prudent" (*CE* 3:72). This is a radical pronouncement in several respects, even with the qualification that its authorization is only "seeming." At the very least, Coverdale's pronouncement endorses love across class divisions, as Zenobia makes clear when she reminds Coverdale of Blithedale's utopian erotics: "I wonder," Zenobia states,

> in such Arcadian freedom of falling in love as we have lately enjoyed, it never occurred to you to fall in love with Priscilla! In society, indeed, a genuine American never dreams of stepping across the inappreciable airline which separates one class from another. But what was rank to the colonists of Blithedale? (*CE* 3:170)

In endorsing such cross-class love, Blithedale is, Zenobia suggests, unAmerican, where to be American implies to be a member of a society rigidly striated into mutually alienated classes.

Such love is already radical, but Blithedale implicitly endorses love in still more radical forms. As Robert Martin has noted,[37] Coverdale's phrasing allows one to read this erotic freedom to include same-sex love; in concert with Coverdale's longing for Hollingsworth the passage has led Benjamin Scott Grossberg to treat Blithedale as a "queer utopia."[38] T. Walter Herbert remarks that Hawthorne's representations of male-male desire are typically marked by a "homophobic vigilance" (262) consistent with the general polarizing of masculine erotic desire into "heterosexual" and "homosexual" categories in the nineteenth century. But Herbert also notes that the intensity of Hawthorne's vigilance must derive in part from guilty desire.[39] The containments of Blithedale as a locus of free love—interred for "infidelity to its own higher spirit" (*CE* 3:246), deferred to a remote future where it may or may not be recovered—as well as the power of disavowal Hawthorne arrogates to himself through the device of a first-person narrator allow him to validate alternative forms of desire from behind self-protecting veils. Blithedale's collapse coincides with the destruction of two intense same-sex friendships, one between Hollingsworth and Coverdale and another between Zenobia and Priscilla.[40] The destruction of these relationships anticipates the conclusion's half-hearted reassertion of bourgeois heterosexual monogamy. But the relationships also bespeak Hawthorne's muted longing for "more than brotherly" alternatives. Although the burden of Hawthorne's symbolism across *The Scarlet Letter* and *The Blithedale Romance* is that Fourierism is merely an exaggerated version of a corrupt *status quo,* in this respect Fourierism poses a genuine challenge. *The Blithedale Romance* is an anxious attempt both to give voice to and to contain Hawthorne's own radical speculations.

As Arthur Cleveland Coxe's scandalized response to Hawthorne's representation of adultery shows, mere mention of transgressive sexuality by a "popular and gifted writer" could cause that writer to be associated with "the doctrines enforced at 'Brook-farm'" (*CR* 151). How much more politically dangerous would Hawthorne appear to Coxe and Coxe's fellow travelers, then, after writing a novel in which the narrator—even an ironic one—appears to speak without revulsion about free love? Although in various ways Coverdale contains the radicalism that Blithedale authorizes, he persists in citing the community as the repository of a worthwhile truth. That is to say, just as Hester's and Dimmesdale's affair implicitly provides the affective model for Hester's new relation "between man and woman" (*CE* 1:263), free love remains entrenched as a utopian value at the novel's conclusion, more emphatically so, certainly, than the marriage of Priscilla and Hollingsworth. It is impossible to imagine Hawthorne sharing the reformatory zeal of the free-love anarchists at Modern Times, advocating a free-love community in the present: he was far from being a Mary Gove Nichols. And yet *The Blithedale Romance* testifies to the allure that free love, in all its permutations, had for him.

Conclusion

I.

Fourierism enjoyed its primary influence in the United States in the two decades between 1840, when Albert Brisbane published *Social Destiny of Man,* and 1860, when the approach of the Civil War made the Fourierist critique of wage labor appear seditious. Fourierism was at its most intense in the first of these two decades. In the 1840s the vast majority of the phalanxes boomed (and went bust); Horace Greeley's New York *Tribune* published its daily articles on Fourierism; Brook Farm converted to Fourierism before sliding into bankruptcy; and an international movement encompassing England, France, and the United States sought to implement Fourier's theories in a practical, albeit etiolated, form.

Fourierism's career thus overlaps with much of Hawthorne's career as a writer. Of the six principal works of fiction that he wrote for adults—*Twice-Told Tales, Mosses from an Old Manse, The Scarlet Letter, The House of the Seven Gables, The Blithedale Romance,* and *The Marble Faun*—only *Twice-Told Tales* and *The Marble Faun* were published outside of the Fourierist period. The remaining four, including the three American romances, were published between 1846 and 1852. It is thus not in the least surprising that Fourierism is among the subjects with which Hawthorne's fiction is preoccupied; the greater surprise, given the overlap of dates and especially his close ties to people prominent in New England reform, would be if he had shown no interest in Fourierism whatsoever.

Although Hawthorne is in the main critical of Fourierism, his engagements are not all hostile. If, as I have argued, "Fourierism" becomes a metonym for elements of reform that Hawthorne contains or repudiates, there are nevertheless distinctively Fourierist theses that Hawthorne seeks to absorb and claim. To argue that Hawthorne is opposed to all elements of

Fourierism is to accept that Fourierism is the sum of the parts Hawthorne rejects. In reading Hawthorne's fiction one must be alert to elements of Fourierism that reappear, *mutatis mutandis,* in contexts that Hawthorne takes to be ideologically acceptable.

The House of the Seven Gables is the most useful of the American romances in allowing us to determine what elements of Fourierism that Hawthorne might find attractive. Chief among these is the Fourierist tenet of attractive industry. That Hawthorne associates Phoebe's domestic labor with play is, to those familiar with Fourierist discourses on labor, unmistakably derivative. This is obviously not to say that Phoebe is some kind of Fourierist worker. Rather, Hawthorne appropriates one of the supposed benefits of Fourierist communal work in support of the domestic sphere that he is intent on fetishizing.

Hawthorne appropriates another tenet central to Fourierism in his portrait of class harmony at the Pyncheon estate. Fourier was eager to sustain class differences because he supposed that one of the fundamental human appetites was for variety; in his view, a varied social structure gratified the passions. But Fourier supposed that the economies of living communally would provide enough wealth for all members of the phalanx to live comfortably, with the poorest guaranteed what he called a "social minimum." Because of universal plenty, class difference would not produce conflict. This is, one recalls, the virtue of Typee society in Charles Dana's review of Melville's "peep" at Polynesian life: according to Dana, the Typee live in a social paradise because of "*abundance for every person*" (*Harbinger* 2:265; Dana's emphasis). Where Dana associates such abundance with a Fourierist world of federated labor, however, Hawthorne associates it with the domestic sphere, as his portrait of the fecund garden in "The Old Manse" suggests. In *The House of the Seven Gables,* the Pyncheon wealth means that there is no risk of privation, and within the confines of the estate, the members will enjoy class harmony. Hawthorne specifically includes not only members of the fading New England aristocracy (Clifford and Hepzibah) and members of the emergent middle classes (Holgrave and Phoebe), but also Uncle Venner, an abject figure who would otherwise find himself in the work house. Hawthorne absorbs the Fourierist claim to have resolved the problem of class conflict into a society organized not around the community but the family (significantly, as an "Uncle," Venner is granted the status of an honorary family member).[1]

In an etiolated way, Hawthorne even appropriates the Fourierist idea of communal labor. When Holgrave and Phoebe first meet in the Pyncheon garden, Holgrave proposes that they work together to restore the garden to health. Their initial collaboration in the garden anticipates their marriage, in which they transfigure "the earth, and [make] it Eden again" (*CE* 2:307); it is freighted with Miltonic associations. But Holgrave also specifically compares it to communitarian labor (*CE* 2:92). The gardening of Phoebe and Holgrave thus not only recalls that of Adam and Eve, it also borrows from socialist utopianism.

This is not to say that Hawthorne is tacitly socialist; to suppose so would be to confuse bathwater and baby. Instead, he adopts those Fourierist theses that are not threatening to middle-class values and incorporates them into his own bourgeois utopia. Hawthorne aims to co-opt the utopian power of Fourierist discourse without endorsing the socialist alternative to capitalism that Fourierism supposes itself to offer. Enshrining domesticity as utopian ideal in *The House of the Seven Gables,* Hawthorne's aim is specifically to show that domesticity offers Fourierism's virtues without the dislocations demanded by Fourierism.

If there are certain qualities of Fourierism that Hawthorne admires, he is nevertheless profoundly uncomfortable with many of its arguments and assumptions. He is skeptical of Fourierism's validation of libidinal impulses, one predicated on the theory that human nature is fundamentally good. Hawthorne shows his debt to the Puritan sense of innate depravity and his commitment to self-discipline in his condemnation of the Blithedale colonists. He also opposes, it is true, absolute repression—his fictions involving Puritanism and Shaker communitarianism intimate that strict repression is really perverted license—but these are ultimately preferable to places like Merry Mount or Blithedale. The example of "The May-Pole of Merry Mount," first published in 1836, shows that Hawthorne's hostility to license is not restricted to Fourierism, for here his target is the undisciplined pre-bourgeois subject. But in "The May-Pole of Merry Mount" Hawthorne turns to remote history and distorts his source material; Fourierism provides him with a contemporary repudiation of self-discipline. Hawthorne need not distort Fourierist theory in order to use it as a metonym for anti-disciplinarity. Hollingsworth and Endicott are figures of exaggerated discipline, and their denunciations of the anti-disciplinary utopias are shrill, but as disciplinarians they approach more nearly than their libidinous enemies do to what Hawthorne takes to be both socially desirable and socially necessary. Endicott inducts Edith and Edgar into the Pilgrim utopia, and a chastened Hollingsworth moves with his new wife Priscilla into a rural cottage, that synecdoche of the *status quo,* while both Merry Mount and Blithedale are dispersed.

Hawthorne also repudiates Fourierist claims to provide an alternative to capitalism. As a system that bases social harmony on individual self-indulgence, Fourierism is not, as he sees it, categorically different from capitalism.

In "Egotism; or, the Bosom-Serpent," the restoration of Roderick's sanity depends on his forgetting himself "in the idea of another" (*CE* 10:283). But neither capitalism nor Fourierism can foster this forgetting. In Hawthorne's view, both Fourierism and capitalism foster egotism, and Fourierist and capitalist alike seek to gain influence over others, an operation that Hawthorne likens to imperialism. Thus the Fourierist Holgrave must overcome an impulse to "acquir[e] empire over the human spirit" (*CE* 2:212); the capitalist Jaffrey Pyncheon's dominance over his cousin Clifford justifies his exclusion from the concluding utopia. Holgrave's repudiation of Fourierism means for Hawthorne that he learns to manage his appetites, and thus, as an appropriately self-disciplining subject, deserves trust and admiration.[2]

Fourierist and other critiques of contemporary society demanded reforms whose scope terrified Hawthorne. Hester's meditation on the prerequisites of successful reform—wholesale dismantling of everything, including at the level of selfhood—is, I think, Hawthorne's own. Fourier's radical interpretation of society treats as contingent things that Hawthorne badly wants to regard as intrinsic and eternal, such as gender difference. For Hawthorne, modernity in general seems to entail an assault on foundations: witness the treatment of the antifoundational tendencies of modernity in the chapter of *The Blithedale Romance* set in the lyceum-hall. But if this is a general characteristic of modernity, Fourierism emblematizes it. Fleeing from Blithedale, Coverdale complains that "[i]t was impossible, situated as we were, not to imbibe the idea that everything in nature and human existence was fluid, or fast becoming so" (*CE* 3:140). Fourierism stands for a fearful provisionality.

Hawthorne finds Fourierism objectionable chiefly, however, for its attitude towards the domestic sphere. Hawthorne freights the domestic sphere with profound ideological significance. He posits monogamous marriage as the middle path between excesses of discipline and indulgence; in keeping with separate-spheres ideology, domesticity is also the appropriate corrective to market egotism. Nevertheless, the domestic relation is not one that Hawthorne sets at odds with society; unlike Fourierism, it is not oppositional. As Hawthorne puts it in "The Old Manse," the domestic sphere is an institution "that [has] grown out of the heart of mankind" (*CE* 10:26). Because Fourier challenges monogamy and sees it as a synecdoche of capitalist society he is unacceptable to Hawthorne. Worse, when Fourier is at his most provocative, he anticipates the eventual dissolution of marriage in favor of alternative economic and sexual relations among the members of an entire community. Assuming that property and marriage are at the root of all social stability, Hawthorne cannot reconcile Fourier's validation of such community with order.

Fourier's critique of the *status quo* shook Hawthorne's confidence in the stable foundations of American society. The American romances all demonstrate profound anxiety about the legitimacy of title and the stability of monogamy. Only *The House of the Seven Gables* concludes with these twin foundations reëstablished; the novel pretends at a minimum that a "pure" marriage is possible, and, by supposing that Phoebe's marriage to Holgrave compensates for the Pyncheons' theft of property, it strongly implies that such a marriage can restore legitimacy to title. Neither *The Blithedale Romance* nor *The Scarlet Letter* adopts this view: in both, the world is always already illegitimate and impure, always already in the same condition, that is, as the Fourierist phalanx in the nightmares of the right. Fourier would say that, since such uncertainty is inevitable, one might as well "widen the scope of legitimate [. . .] relationships" (*UV* 172). Hawthorne takes a different view: rather than adjust social structures to accord with a reality of ambiguated title and paternity, he affirms that it is all the more necessary to reaffirm their legitimacy or to find ways to compensate for the lack of clarity. This is manifestly a declaration of faith: in spite of evidence to the contrary, Coverdale affirms "religiously" that Priscilla has retained her "virgin reserve and sanctity of soul" (*CE* 3:203). Seeking to install her as the domestic ideal, Coverdale can afford to impute to her neither a lack of virgin reserve nor "profaneness" of soul. Since Hawthorne's fiction always validates the domestic sphere, one can credibly characterize Coverdale in this instance as Hawthorne's mouthpiece. Yet Hawthorne ironizes Coverdale's religious affirmations by providing textual details that have led various critics to note links between Priscilla and prostitution. Given the sexual connotations that mesmerism carries for Hawthorne elsewhere (as, for instance, in *The House of the Seven Gables*), Coverdale's claim that Priscilla emerges from her experience as the Veiled Lady with "sanctity of soul" intact seems unlikely, a nervous attempt to sustain a compromised system. *The Blithedale Romance* ends with this paradox: the society that requires such anxious buttressing does not have particularly solid foundations, but no acceptable alternative to it exists.

In an attempt to resolve this paradox, Hawthorne turns to a redemptive but perpetually deferred future. In what I have called the two anti-utopian novels (and paradoxically in light of Hawthorne's defence of monogamy), this redemption involves free love. When Hester imagines a "new truth" establishing harmony between the sexes, the affective model in the novel for this relation is her self-consecrating love affair—so objectionable to conservative readers—with Dimmesdale. In *The Blithedale Romance* Coverdale imagines a posterity that will "profit" from the "truth" that Blithedale discovered (*CE* 3:246). This truth entails communitarianism and "spiritualized" labor, but also, overridingly, what Zenobia calls an "Arcadian freedom of falling in love" (*CE* 3:170). This freedom, Coverdale states, consists of "fall[ing] in love with any other, regardless of what would elsewhere be judged suitable and prudent" (*CE* 3:72). Zenobia characterizes such polymorphous love as un-American (*CE* 3:170); nevertheless, such love is implicitly among the lessons that Blithedale promises to teach posterity. In both novels, Hawthorne distances himself from these concluding utopian visions by having characters articulate them. And the potentially endless deferral of utopian fulfillment saps the radical force from these visions: in obvious ways, their containment only serves to buttress the *status quo*. Still, it is fascinating that Hawthorne opts to conclude both *The Scarlet Letter* and *The Blithedale Romance* in this manner. When the antinomies of Law and Nature achieve dialectical synthesis, Hawthorne suggests, free love will not be a social danger. Hawthorne is not able to conceive of such a society: neither Hester nor Coverdale presumes to describe the utopias that each envisions. Nevertheless, free love—love in accordance with nature—is implicitly what defines the "surer ground of mutual happiness" (*CE* 1:263) that the future promises.

These stringently contained visions of free love testify ultimately to the power that Fourierism exercised over Hawthorne's imagination. It is likely that this accounts for Hawthorne's urgency in containing so many elements of Fourierism; no doubt, too, it accounts for his direct engagement with Fourier in both of the American novels set in the present, and his oblique engagement with it in *The Scarlet Letter*. In its visions of a garden of earthly delights, Fourierism was both alluring and, for that very reason, dangerous.

II.

In the past fifteen years, criticism has been keenly interested in the ways in which Hawthorne reflected and produced ideologies of gender and class. Using *The House of the Seven Gables* as her principal text, Gillian Brown has demonstrated how Hawthorne participated in the fetishization of the domestic sphere and the domestic woman's body at a moment when separate-spheres ideology was consolidating itself in America. Joel Pfister has read Hawthorne's fiction in terms of ideologies of class and gender, relating Hawthorne's distinctively psychological themes, which led Frederick Crews and others to see Hawthorne as adumbrative of Freud, to the emergence of the middle classes. A brilliant study by T. Walter Herbert shows how tensions between the ideology of domesticity and the lived experience of the Hawthornes in their marriage manifest themselves in Hawthornes' novels.

For all of these critics, Hawthorne is a key figure in the history of the middle-class domestic sphere.

Reading Hawthorne in light of Fourierism shows how this domestic sphere came to constitute itself in part through a confrontation with its most radical critics. Like the Fourierist critique of wage labor, which in Guarneri's view led the North to consolidate its defence of free labor in the years before the Civil War (*UA* 382), the Fourierist critique of marriage and private life led the middle classes to refine their defence of domesticity. To read Hawthorne's fiction of the 1840s and 1850s without attending to contemporary Fourierist debates is to suppose that the domestic ideal arises more or less spontaneously, or out of the wreckage of already superseded social forms (as when the aging Pyncheon aristocrats give way to the middle-class Holgrave and Phoebe). My reading in Hawthorne's fiction suggests that domesticity develops partly in response to the communitarian challenge. It is not coincidental that Hawthorne's fetishization of the domestic ideal begins to sharpen with *Mosses from an Old Manse,* written at the height of Fourierist influence in the States.

Studying Hawthorne's engagement with Fourier shows, too, how the concerns of the American romances—in sequence, with adultery, with property theft, and with communitarianism—are all interrelated. Each of the romances is preoccupied with finding firm foundations for property and especially for marriage, which Loring called "the most certain foundation of all purity and all social safety" (*CR* 136). This in turn suggests a way to reconcile critics interested in Hawthorne's role in the history of gender with critics like Lauren Berlant who are interested in national themes in Hawthorne. At the moment, there is little interaction between these two schools of criticism; reading Hawthorne in light of the socialist critique of marriage and property shows how large political themes develop in the American romances through the most intimate exchanges.

Studying the representation of Fourierism in Hawthorne has ramifications for students of American Fourierism, as well. In *The Utopian Alternative,* Carl Guarneri shows that American Fourierists "failed to create a distinctively Fourierist high culture" (*UA* 215). Although they tried to establish a socialist canon by enlisting sympathetic authors like Eugène Sue and George Sand—*The Harbinger* serialized Sand's *Consuelo* in translation—their attempts to cultivate an original art were frustrated by the reluctance of artists who were declared fellow travelers to produce work on utopian themes. And although writers like George Foster and George Lippard created Fourier-inflected literary works in the city-mysteries genre, these were popular productions rather than the hieratic art that would allow Fourierists to claim aesthetic legitimacy.

The example of Hawthorne suggests that, instead of inspiring a utopian literature demonstrative of Fourierist "truths," Fourierist discourse provided "serious" artists with a body of images and themes that they could appropriate and impress into the service of their own aesthetic ends. David S. Reynolds has shown that the canonized authors of antebellum American literature—Emerson, Dickinson, Hawthorne, Melville, Poe, Thoreau, Whitman—all borrowed popular imagery, in the interest of domesticating it. "[T]he literary text," Reynolds writes, "is a rich compound of socioliterary strands, each of which stems from a tremendous body of submerged writings" (10). The so-called major writers of the American Renaissance "sought [. . .] to incorporate as many different popular images as possible and to reconstruct these images by imbuing them with a depth and control they lacked in their crude native state" (10). Although one might contest Reynolds's assumption that these popular discourses were "crude" and lacked "depth and control," Hawthorne's use of Fourierist discourse nevertheless reinforces Reynolds's essential point.[3] Fourierism becomes, at least in part, a resource for Hawthorne to plunder as he develops his novels and stories.

Reynolds, however, shies away from emphasizing the political project undergirding these middle-class appropriations. Ironically, given his project, he assumes throughout *Beneath the American Renaissance* that notions of aesthetic quality are apolitical rather than inflected by gender, race, and class. Hawthorne's appropriations of Fourierism are useful in part because they are largely political and thus show in a particularly stark way how politically oriented such appropriations are in general. Like the work of other middle-class writers of the 1840s and 1850s, Hawthorne's art is clearly not ideologically neutral.

Hawthorne's appropriations of Fourierism suggest, however, what was stake in the Fourierists' attempts to create a socialist art. When Hawthorne published *The Blithedale Romance,* it was clear to readers with socialist sympathies that they were under attack, notwithstanding Hawthorne's claims in the preface that "he [did not] put forward the slightest pretensions to illustrate a theory, or illustrate a conclusion, favorable or otherwise, in respect to Socialism" (*CE* 3:1). The anonymous reviewer in John Humphrey Noyes's Oneida *Circular* rejected this claim out of hand, and argued that "if the Brook Farm society is to have a resurrection now in literature, and become a topic of historical criticism, we may have something to say about it" (*Circular* 1:38 150). Recognizing historical criticism as politically contested, that is, the reviewer announced the Perfectionists' intention to take an active part in creating it. But until 1874, when Marie Howland wrote *Papa's Own Girl,* no novels of any moment were published to contest Hawthorne's interpretation of Fourierism. Quickly embraced into the heart of the emergent American literary canon, Hawthorne had—and continues to have—a profound influence on the historical understanding of Fourierism.

Notes

NOTES TO CHAPTER ONE

1. Throughout this study I refer to American Fourierists; in fact, these reformers described themselves as "Associationists" as a way to distance themselves from some of Fourier's more provocative—or outrageous—theories, and to show that they were not beholden to a single theorist. It was the Associationists' enemies who persisted in characterizing Association as Fourierism. But the Associationists' claims of independence, while not phantasmal, are nevertheless misleading. Fourier was overwhelmingly the major influence on the Associationists, as the title of their principal journal, *The Harbinger,* suggests: "harbinger" is, as Alfred Habegger notes in his biography of the elder Henry James (248), a bilingual pun playing on Fourier's name ("harbinger" translates into French as "un fourrier"). I have opted to call them Fourierists for the sake of simplicity.

2. The most powerful of these is Lauren Berlant, "Fantasies of Utopia in *The Blithedale Romance,*" *American Literary History* 1:1 (Spring 1989): 30–62. Berlant's article, however, precedes the publication in 1991 of Carl Guarneri's history of American Fourierism, and hence cannot profit from his insights. Moreover, she makes no linkages between Fourierism as represented in the novel and Fourierism as practiced by Hawthorne's contemporaries—she makes no reference, for instance, to the free-love movement and its debt to Fourier, even though Coverdale's inclination to reduce interpersonal and political relations to a love plot is one of her concerns. There is, in other words, ample room in which to develop and challenge Berlant's insights. For other important treatments of Hawthorne and Fourier, see Taylor Stoehr, *Hawthorne's Mad Scientists: Pseudoscience and Social Science in Nineteenth-Century Life and Letters* (Hampden: Archon Books, 1978); Gerard Nawrocki, "*The Blithedale Romance* and Charles Fourier," *Studia Anglica Posnaniensia: An International Review of English Studies* 29 (1994): 199–209; Arthur Sherbo, "Albert Brisbane and Hawthorne's Holgrave and

Hollingsworth," *NEQ* 27 (December 1954): 531–534, and the final chapter of William Hall Brock, *Phalanx on a Hill: Responses to Fourierism in the Transcendentalist Circle,* diss. Loyola U, 1995. Robert K. Martin has also written on *The Blithedale Romance* and Fourier, in an unpublished article, "Fourier in America," he was generous enough to allow me to consult.

3. For Fourier's presence in *The House of the Seven Gables,* see the references to Fourier in Joel Pfister, *The Production of Personal Life* (Stanford: Stanford UP, 1991) 158–160, and Sherbo, 531–4. Various critics make passing reference to Holgrave's Fourierism; few treat it as crucial to the novel.

4. I intend the term "communitarianism" to include both secular and pietistic communitarian experiments: Arthur Bestor coined the term and applied it exclusively to secular experiments, but I use the term more catholically. To distinguish between secular and pietistic communities, as Guarneri has suggested, is an exaggerated and belated opposition.

5. Carl J. Guarneri's *The Utopian Alternative: Fourierism in Nineteenth-Century America* (Ithaca: Cornell UP, 1991) is the central text in recent work. Other work includes Christopher Clark, *The Communitarian Moment: The Radical Challenge of the Northampton Association* (Ithaca: Cornell UP, 1995); Richard Francis, *Transcendentalist Utopias: Individual and Community at Brook Farm, Fruitlands, and Walden* (Ithaca: Cornell UP, 1997); Carl J. Guarneri, "The Americanization of Utopia: Fourierism and the Dilemma of Utopian Dissent in the United States," *Utopian Studies* 5.1 (1994): 72–88; Carl J. Guarneri, "Reconstructing the Antebellum Communitarian Movement: Oneida and Fourierism," *Journal of the Early Republic* 16 (Fall 1996): 463–485; Andrew E. Hunt, "The Wisconsin Phalanx: A Forgotten Success Story," *Canadian Review of American Studies* 28:2 (1998): 119–143; Donald E. Pitzer, ed., *America's Communal Utopias* (Chapel Hill: U of North Carolina P, 1997); Roland Schaer, Gregory Claeys, and Lyman Tower Sargent, eds., *Utopia: The Search for the Ideal Society in the Western World* (New York: The New York Public Library/Oxford UP, 2000); Kathryn Manson Tomasek, *"The Pivot of the Mechanism": Women, Gender, and Discourse in Fourierism and the Antebellum United States,* diss., U of Wisconsin-Madison, 1995.

6. For a discussion of the relations between spiritualism and Fourierism, see *UA* 349–353.

7. This is one of my complaints of William Hall Brock's otherwise intriguing reading of the Fourier of *The Blithedale Romance* in light of the Marx of Derrida's *Specters of Marx.* By accepting Hawthorne's spectralization of Fourier as analogous to the contemporary spectralization of Marx, Brock assumes that Fourierism as a social force, if not as a critique, was dead. This was not the case: when Hawthorne composed *The Blithedale Romance,* the North American Phalanx in New Jersey was still operative, and would be until 1855. Even if this were not so, Fourierism was still a social force: as

Guarneri writes, "[d]espite the phalanxes' failure, Fourierism lingered in radical circles during the 1850s and inspired new plans and organizations" (*UA* 348), most obviously those of Mary Gove and Thomas Low Nichols.

8. Guarneri makes a strong case for the historical significance of Fourierism and for its wide influence in the 1840s and 1850s. As Guarneri notes, Fourierism had its "greatest practical impact" in the United States (*UA* 2). In addition to the twenty-nine Fourierist phalanxes of the early- to mid-1840s,

> [n]ondenominational utopian socialist churches were established in Boston, Philadelphia, and Cincinnati. New England and New York Fourierists allied themselves with the emerging labor movement of the 1840s to promote producer and consumer cooperatives. In more than two dozen cities and towns "unions" or clubs gathered utopian socialists to hear lectures, discuss Fourier's ideas, and plan scaled-down Fourierist projects such as cooperative stores and urban communes. (*UA* 3)

From March 1842 until April 1843, Horace Greeley's *New York Tribune* published Albert Brisbane's daily column of Fourierist propaganda on the front page, and Fourierists published various journals of their own, most notably Brook Farm's *The Harbinger*. When Brisbane published *A Concise Exposition of the Practical Part of Fourier's Social Science* (1844), it sold 10,000 copies. According to Guarneri, in its American incarnation Fourierism "enlist[ed] as many as 100,000 supporters" (*UA* 3). Such impressive figures may be misleading: of the 10,000 copies of Brisbane's *Concise Exposition,* few may have been read, and fewer taken seriously. And of the 100,000 "supporters" (a number that Guarneri does not appear to substantiate), many if not most may have offered no more than passive support. Still, such statistics at least show that Fourierism captured widespread attention As Guarneri writes elsewhere, "[a]t least 15,000 Americans became personally involved at one time or another in the Fourierist movement" (*ACU* 167). However short-lived, American Fourierism was hardly a marginal communitarian phenomenon along the lines of John Humphrey Noyes's Perfectionist community at Oneida.

9. This study focuses on Hawthorne's representations of Fourierism, and makes only limited reference to other authors of the period addressing it. This requires some justification, since Hawthorne is neither emblematic of his time, nor a uniquely subtle reader of Fourier. Claims for Hawthorne's aesthetic exemplarity, as a generation of criticism has shown, are so provisional as to be less than useful as justification: no one can any longer be content to second Herman Melville's affirmation that Hawthorne was a literary genius, and to leave it at that. But an exclusive focus on Hawthorne is defensible on at least one ground. To a significant extent *The Blithedale Romance* has coded the critical response to Fourierism. That is, as Hawthorne became the gravitational centre of the American canon, his

representations of Fourierism gained considerable power. My own acquaintance with Fourierism began with *The Blithedale Romance,* and in spite of changes in the discipline this remains, it is reasonable to say, the experience of almost all literary critics (Elizabeth Barrett Browning's reëmergence may come to give *Aurora Leigh* similar status). To determine the cultural work of Hawthorne's representations of Fourier is thus to determine the unacknowledged provisionality of our own understanding of Fourierism. The logical next step is a reconstructive one, to place Hawthorne's Fourier alongside those of other, less central and perhaps more sympathetic writers, in the hope of achieving a more nuanced portrait of nineteenth-century literary representations of Fourierism than has hitherto obtained. But, especially given the complexity of Hawthorne's work, this is beyond the purview of a single study.

10.   Works by others evincing a concern with Fourierism include the anonymous *Henry Russell* (1847), Sophia Appleton's *Sequel to the Vision of Bangor in the Twentieth Century* (1848), Orestes Brownson's *The Spirit-Rapper* (1854), James Fenimore Cooper's *The Crater* (1848), Marie Howland's *Papa's Own Girl* (1874), and George Lippard's *The Quaker City* (1846) in the United States; Elizabeth Barrett Browning's *Aurora Leigh* (1856) and Benjamin Disraeli's *Sybil* (1846) in England; a multitude of works in France, including Gustave Flaubert's *Bouvard et Pecuchet* (1880) and Emile Zola's *Travail* (1901); and, in Russia, Fyodor Dostoyevsky's *Crime and Punishment* (1865–6) (Raskolnikov is modeled on one of Dostoyevsky's Fourierist acquaintances in the Petrashevski circle). And this is only to attend to fiction. Recent work has been done reading Emily Dickinson's poetry for its communitarian resonances; the works of Walt Whitman also demand such attention, as does the anti-marriage poem *Husband vs. Wife* (1858) of Henry Clapp, Jr. On Dickinson, see Stephen Noyes Orton, *Banning the Tribes: Emily Dickinson and the Communitarian Movement,* diss., U of North Carolina, 1998). For some gestures towards a reading of Whitman and Fourierism, see David S. Reynolds, *Walt Whitman's America: A Cultural Biography* (New York: Vintage, 1995), especially 222–226. The influence on Whitman's poetry of New York's literary bohemians—especially Henry Clapp, Jr.—and their reading in Fourier merits further attention. Aside from writing *Husband vs. Wife* (1858), Henry Clapp, Jr., also translated Fourier's *Théorie des Quatre Mouvements* into English in an 1857 edition, with a long preface by Albert Brisbane. Clapp's was the only complete translation of this work until Ian Patterson's 1996 translation for Cambridge Texts in the History of Political Thought.

11.   It is possible that Pellarin's biography was one of the volumes that Hawthorne borrowed from Caroline Tappan. I think this is unlikely to be the case, however: Tappan also lent volumes of Fourier to Emerson in 1845, almost certainly the same ones; the Pellarin biography is not mentioned

among these. William Hall Brock tentatively identifies these volumes as *Théorie des Quatre Mouvements* and *Théorie de l'unité universelle*. See Brock 189–194. This does not exclude the further possibility that Hawthorne knew certain details of Fourier's biography from elsewhere, although the possibility that he would know of Gengembre seems to me slim.

12. *UA* 79–80.

13. For a detailed study of Considérant's transformation of Fourierism into a mass movement, see Jonathan Beecher, *Victor Considérant and the Rise and Fall of French Romantic Socialism* (Berkeley: U of California P, 2001).

14. See, for instance, Catherine Francblin, "Le Feminisme Utopique de Ch. Fourier," *Tel Quel* 62 (1975): 44–69; Leslie F. Goldstein, "Early Feminist Themes in French Utopian Socialism: the St.-Simonians and Fourier," *Journal of the History of Ideas* 43:1 (Jan.-Mar. 1982): 91–103. See also Tomasek 91–145. As Tomasek persuasively argues, Fourier's "vision of an ideal future remained limited by his androcentric perspective. When Fourier wrote about women and sexuality in Harmony, he betrayed his inability to envision an ideal society without gender inequality" (91).

15. Fourier subscribed to what Anne McClintock has characterized as the ideology of anachronistic space, where the further from the imperial center, the more "primitive" the culture.

16. Jonathan Beecher, *Charles Fourier: The Visionary and His World* (Berkeley: U of California P, 1986) 299–300.

17. As Gillian Brown notes,

> the idea of work as damaging pervades nineteenth-century thought; it recurs not only in Marx's exposition of the alienated worker but also in [Catherine] Beecher's worries about the health of housekeepers, in factory novels' descriptions of injured and deformed laborers, and in medical admonitions about the perils of overwork. (81)

The Fourierist idea is an exception, as is that associated with the "cult of true womanhood" (the focus of Brown's reading of *The House of the Seven Gables*). I return to the convergence of Fourier and theorists of true womanhood in my treatment of Phoebe, in Chapter Four.

18. Beecher [1986] 294. The relevant passage in *The German Ideology* reads

> in communist society, [. . .] nobody has one exclusive sphere of activity but each can become accomplished in any branch he wishes, [for] society regulates the general production and thus makes it possible for me to do one thing today and another tomorrow, to hunt in the morning, fish in the afternoon, rear cattle in the evening, criticise after dinner, just as I have a mind, without ever becoming hunter, fisherman, shepherd or critic. (Marx and Engels 160)

19. *UA* 354–363.

20. *TFM* 47.
21. Quoted in Beecher [1986] 340–341. The archibras was one of the features of Fourierism most susceptible to caricature: see, for instance, plates 27, 28 in Beecher.
22. *TFM* 49–51n.
23. In a letter to her mother, Sophia critiques Fourier and others. See Mellow 249, and my discussion below.
24. *UA* 358.
25. The logic of the Centenary editors seems to have struck James R. Mellow as similarly problematic, although he does not explicitly challenge it. In his biography of Hawthorne he states that "[d]uring the summer of 1844, [Hawthorne] had been reading up on Fourier's philosophy" (Mellow 248) before making reference to it in the notebooks.
26. Foucault develops this term in "Of Other Spaces: Utopias and Hetero-topias," *Rethinking Architecture: a Reader in Cultural Theory,* ed. Neil Leach (New York: Routledge 1997): 350–356.
27. Francis 146.
28. This claim needs qualification: Fourier first published in 1808, some time after the Revolution, and published the majority of his work after Waterloo. Nevertheless, Fourier was profoundly influenced by the Revolution: it eroded his confidence in Enlightenment rationalism, which led him in turn to adopt his theory of passions as the motivators of human action.
29. Martin, "Fourier in America."
30. T. Walter Herbert, *Dearest Beloved: The Hawthornes and the Making of the Middle-Class Family* (Berkeley: U of California P, 1993) 138–142.
31. Both the date of the letter's composition and its recipient are unknown. The Centenary editors suggest that Bridge was the recipient; Mellow suggests Frank Farley. Mellow also suggests that a later composition date is possible, and that Hawthorne wrote this letter in the wake of the phalanstery fire.
32. See Lyndsay Swift, *Brook Farm: Its Members, Scholars, and Visitors* (Secaucus: Citadel Press, 1973) 24–25.
33. Marianne Dwight Orvis, *Letters from Brook Farm* (Philadelphia: Porcupine Press, Inc., 1972) 145–150.
34. Swift 26. Hawthorne was therefore being reportorial when in his conclusion to *The Blithedale Romance,* he represented Blithedale after its death as being a place where "the town-paupers [. . .] creep sluggishly a-field (*CE* 3:246).
35. Elsewhere I have argued that what the painter reads as a propensity in Walter to domestic abuse is rather a propensity towards revolutionary violence.
36. *UA* 336–342.
37. Arthur Cleveland Coxe makes this claim in his review of *The Scarlet Letter* in *Church Review and Ecclesiastical Register;* of Hester's declaration that her affair with Dimmesdale "had a consecration of its own" (*CE* 1:195), Coxe

sniffs, "We suppose this sort of sentiment must be charged to the doctrines enforced at 'Brook-farm'" (*CR* 151).

38. Given that Hawthorne himself spent "some months" in a utopian community (albeit one that became Fourierist only after he had left), but then returned to conservative respectability by marrying Sophia, his representation of Holgrave is clearly at one level a self-portrait. Holgrave's repudiation of Fourierism is (probably) also Hawthorne's.

39. *UA* 197–203. That this was nevertheless a standard charge against Fourierist communities is suggested by the experience of the Wisconsin Phalanx, which, in spite of conservative bylaws governing behaviour faced accusations that it promoted free love. See Hunt 131, 137.

40. George Sand was the author with whom Fourierists most identified. Although Guarneri writes that the American Associationists were generally frustrated in their attempts to create a Fourierist art, they nevertheless claimed certain authors as articulating Fourierist doctrine. Predictably, George Sand and Eugène Sue were preëminent among these: the inaugural issue of *The Harbinger* featured on its first page a translation of Sand's *Consuelo* by Francis G. Shaw.

41. Orvis 122–125.

42. My reasoning here implies my disagreement with Sacvan Bercovitch's representation of Hawthorne's romances following *The Scarlet Letter.* In his view, only *The Scarlet Letter* successfully articulates a gradualist message. By contrast with Hester's resumption of her letter, "Holgrave's strained conversion, Coverdale's problematic confession, [and the] [. . .] homecoming of Hilda" (*OSL* 104) reflect Hawthorne's post-Hester failure to imagine the terms upon which he might persuasively articulate compromise. And those who see ambivalence or ambiguity in Hawthorne's representations of Holgrave, Coverdale, and Hilda are mistaking "narrative weaknesses" for "authorial strengths," wrongly reading Hawthorne's imaginative failures as evidence of deconstructive clues "by which [Hawthorne] meant for us to demystify cultural myths" (*OSL* 104n). Any departure from the strictest terms of Bercovitch's thesis, in other words, constitutes Hawthorne's failure as an artist. But there is reason to suppose, particularly in *The Blithedale Romance,* that Hawthorne *is* ambivalent about the "benefits of gradualism" (*OSL* 87). The novel's portraits of Irish tenement dwellers, of paupers in the fields of Blithedale, of Coverdale's apathy, of Zenobia's despair, and of Hollingsworth's penitence all suggest that the costs of gradualism, both psychic and material, outweigh the benefits.

NOTES TO CHAPTER TWO

1. Images of economic hardship would have extra force in 1838, in the wake of the crisis of 1837.

2. See especially Rosabeth Moss Kanter, *Commitment and Community: Communes and Utopias in Sociological Perspective* (Cambridge: Harvard UP,

1972). Kanter divides communes into three classes, religious, politico-economic, and psychosocial, of which the first two categories are particularly relevant to the nineteenth century.

3. Nathaniel Morton's text transcribes William Bradford's *Of Plymouth Plantation* almost verbatim.

4. One effect of this fictional strategy might be, as Colacurcio has suggested, to arouse readers' historical suspicions and lead them back to the source material with a deconstructive skepticism. But Hawthorne's historical revisions might equally serve to lead a reader back to the primary sources with a moral already in hand and to view Merry Mount as a carnival justly requiring Puritan containment, however much one might shudder at the excess of the fictional Endicott's enthusiasm. If Colacurcio's interpretive method has a fault, it is that it gives Hawthorne too much credit for anticipating Colacurcio: it painstakingly develops a portrait of Hawthorne's historiographical elisions, insertions, and manipulations, and then argues that the discovery of these is what Hawthorne's fiction seeks to elicit from its readers, so that critical method and authorial intention collapse into one another.

5. See, for instance, William Carlos Williams, *In the American Grain* (New York: Albert and Charles Boni, 1925).

6. This description of the world's condition, however, occurs at the end of the story, and seemingly contradicts an earlier claim about the contest between Merry Mount and the Puritans. In his recital of "authentic passages from history" (*CE* 9:62), the narrator affirms that

    the future complexion of New England was involved in this important quarrel. Should the grisly saints establish their jurisdiction over the gay sinners, then would their spirits darken all the clime, and make it a land of clouded visages, of hard toil, of sermon and psalm, forever. But should the banner-staff of Merry Mount be fortunate, sunshine would break upon the hills, and flowers would beautify the forest, and late posterity do homage to the May-Pole! (*CE* 9:62)

    This is a statement freighted with metahistorical irony, since here the narrator entangles himself in his subject, acknowledging that the outcome of the Plymouth-Merry Mount contest will fundamentally influence his account: he does not stand outside New England's history, but within it. And so his perspective is limited by the Puritan victory; ideologically constituted after Puritanism has achieved hegemony, he cannot fail to naturalize the conflict. His concluding vision of the world as one steeped in moral gloom is not an objective characterization from an external perspective but precisely the result of the gloomy Puritan's victory.

7. The passage in "The May-Pole of Merry Mount" which elicits this observation is as follows: "'I thought not to repent me of cutting down a May-Pole,' replied Endicott, 'yet now I could find in my heart to plant it again, and

give each of these bestial pagans one other dance round their idol. It would have served rarely for a whipping post!'" (*CE* 9:64): given the already established phallic connotations of the May-Pole, critics have justly perceived in this statement Hawthorne's intimation that Puritan sexuality stands to Merry Mount sexuality as sadism does to hedonism.

8. As such, Hawthorne mythologizes separate-spheres ideology. Two decades of criticism has submitted this ideology to critique, showing that the distinction between (masculine) public and (feminine) private spheres arose alongside the entrenchment of capitalism. The supposition that the domestic sphere offered men a refuge from capitalist processes is of course spurious: relations of economic domination persisted in the domestic sphere. The foundational studies of separate spheres are Nancy F. Cott, *The Bonds of Womanhood: 'Woman's Sphere' in New England, 1780–1835* (New Haven: Yale UP, 1977) and Mary P. Ryan, *Cradle of the Middle Class: The Family in Oneida County, New York, 1790–1865* (New York: Cambridge UP, 1981). For a recent summary of subsequent scholarship that has qualified and challenged Cott's and Ryan's basic insights, see Amy Dru Stanley, "Home Life and the Morality of the Market," *The Market Revolution in America: Social, Political, and Religious Expressions, 1800–1880*, eds. Melvyn Stokes and Stephen Conway (Charlottesville: UP of Virginia, 1996) 74–96.

9. *CE* 23:624–632.

10. It is possible that Hawthorne is honestly struggling to remember the term "phalanstery" in this passage. But he uses a comparable formulation in *The Blithedale Romance:* when Coverdale discusses Blithedale's "permanent plans," he says that "[o]ne of our purposes was to erect a Phalanstery (as I think we called it, after Fourier; but the phraseology of those days is not very fresh in my remembrance)" (*CE* 3:128). I suspect that Hawthorne is being coy in these instances, feigning ignorance so as to distance himself (or his narrator) from Fourierism.

11. The timing of the publication of Dana's review on April 4, 1846, and Hawthorne's composition of "The Old Manse" is nearly perfect: Hawthorne sent it to Evert Duyckinck on April 15, 1846, writing that

> I send you ["The Old Manse"], promised so many thousand years ago. The delay has really not been my fault—only my misfortune. Nothing that I tried to write would flow out of my pen, till a very little while ago—when forth came this sketch, of its own accord, and much unlike what I had purposed. (*CE* 16:152)

As recently as February 22, 1846, Hawthorne had not written the sketch, as Sophia states in a letter to her mother. Hawthorne, she writes, "has not long enough dreamed over the new tale or essay which is to commence the first volume" of *Mosses* (*CE* 16:146n1).

12. Inspired by *Typee,* Marx Edgeworth Lazarus's *The Solar Ray* (1851) would go so far as to suggest that a phalanx be established in the tropics. See *UA,*

137, 450–51n64. No such venture was attempted, but Lazarus's exhortation indicates the influence that Melville's representation of the South Pacific had on Fourierists.

13. Sacvan Bercovitch, *The Rites of Assent: Transformations in the Symbolic Construction of America* (New York: Routledge, 1993) 307–352.

14. For the first article to see Roderick Elliston as a portrait of Jones Very, see Robert D. Arner, "Hawthorne and Jones Very," *NEQ* 42 (1967): 267–275. Arner's thesis, which reduces "Egotism; or, the Bosom-Serpent" to veiled biography, has been widely accepted. In *The Province of Piety*, for instance, Michael Colacurcio takes it as a given.

15. There is a biographical element in this preoccupation: in a short essay published in the *National Magazine* in January 1853, Hawthorne wrote of his mother's ancestral home in Salem that by 1853 it was "the residence of half a dozen Irish families" (*CE* 23:380). This is a revealing gloss on *The Blithedale Romance*'s representation of the Puritan governor's mansion, formerly "a stately habitation" (*CE* 3:184) but now degenerated into a "dusky house" (*CE* 3:187) filled with "big, red, Irish matrons" and their "innumerable progeny" (*CE* 3:187).

16. As Stephen Knadler has observed, Roderick first feels "at his bosom [. . .] the sickening motion of a thing alive" only after the quack has brought his diagnosis "into public view" (*CE* 10:272). For Knadler, the diagnosis is performative, emblematic of the nineteenth-century psychiatric community's role in "simultaneously creating the inner depth of the modern psychological man and turning all into spectators of this secret private life" (Knadler 286). I see the quack's performative diagnosis not only as reflective of the "nineteenth-century psychiatric community" but also as emblematic of all exchanges in the market: only once the subject stops projecting his or her own preoccupations onto others and becomes self-forgetting can mental and social health return.

17. Herkimer's diagnosis finds no support elsewhere in the story. This undermines his moral, as does the possibility that he is recapitulating the processes that have had such a disastrous effect on Roderick. Hawthorne, it may be, is subverting the utopian conclusion of his story. Certainly, Rosina's confidence that "[t]he past, dismal as it seems, shall fling no gloom upon the future" (*CE* 10:283) is at odds with Hawthorne's concern with history's persistence elsewhere in his oeuvre.

18. Fourierist theory influenced Frederick Law Olmsted in his designs of urban parks like Central Park in New York and Boston's emerald necklace. See *UA* 399–400 and Albert Fein, "Fourierism in Nineteenth-Century America: A Social and Environmental Perspective," *France and North America: Utopias and Utopians*, ed. Mathé Allain (Lafayette: University of Southwestern Louisiana, 1978) 133–148.

19. This resembles T. Walter Herbert's argument about *The Blithedale Romance* in *Dearest Beloved: The Hawthornes and the Making of the Middle-Class Family* (Los Angeles: U California P, 1993) 3–30.

20. See Mellow's discussion, 259–271.

21. Both "Egotism; or, the Bosom-Serpent" and its companion story, "The Christmas Banquet" (in which Roderick, Rosina, and Herkimer also appear), were originally planned as part of a story cycle, "Allegories of the Heart." Given the symbolic significance accorded the heart in *Mosses*, it seems likely that these stories would in the aggregate anatomize marriage—and the society for which it stands—from both utopian and anti-utopian perspectives.

NOTES TO CHAPTER THREE

1. In *Conquest of Bread*, Kropotkin writes, "From the outset socialism took three independent lines of development, which found their expression in Saint-Simon, Fourier, and Robert Owen. Saint-Simonism has developed into social democracy, and Fourierism into anarchism; while Owenism is developing, in England and America, into trade-unionism, coöperation, and the so-called municipal socialism, and remains hostile to social democratic state socialism, while it has many points of contact with anarchism" (404–5).

2. Beecher [1986] 498.

3. *UA* 174–177. The similarity between Fourierist and capitalist theory is somewhat more than a general validation of individual potential. That is to say, all nineteenth-century socialists championed "individuality"—in Sacvan Bercovitch's words, "the belief in the absolute integrity, spiritual primacy, and inviolable sanctity of the self" (*RA* 314)—but sought to realize it in some social arrangement other than the isolating structures of capitalism. Although Fourier denounced *laissez-faire* and capitalist atomization with a fervor that matched other socialist writers, the centrality of individual appetite in Fourierism distinguishes it from its socialist cousins.

4. See, for instance, T. Walter Herbert, *Dearest Beloved: The Hawthornes and the Making of the Middle-Class Family* (Berkeley: U of California P, 1995) 88–106, and Robert K. Martin, "Haunted by Jim Crow," *American Gothic: New Interventions in a Nationalist Narrative*, eds. Robert K Martin and Eric Savoy (Iowa City: U of Iowa P, 1998) 129–142.

5. Hawthorne's portrait of the organ grinder derives from his notebooks (Clifford is modelled on Una Hawthorne, who also cried as a result of the spectacle): see *CE* 8:271. His original notes make no reference to the Italian provenance of the street musician, however, and the performer is an adult, not a child. Italian street musicians were, indeed, becoming a "modern feature of

[American] streets;" they became the object of philanthropic intervention in the 1870s, as concern for the living conditions of the children combined with nativist distaste for their *padrones.* See John E. Zucchi, *The Little Slaves of the Harp: Italian Child Street Musicians in Nineteenth-Century Paris, London, and New York* (Kingston: McGill-Queen's UP, 1992).

6. See Robert K. Martin, "Haunted by Jim Crow," 135.

7. There is an ample literature on the gender politics of Hawthorne's portrait of Phoebe, but see especially Gillian Brown, *Domestic Individualism: Imagining Individualism in Nineteenth-Century America* (Berkeley: U of California P, 1990) 63–95, Teresa Goddu, "The Circulation of Women in *The House of the Seven Gables,*" *Studies in the Novel* 23:1 (Spring 1991): 119–127, Shawn Michelle Smith, *American Archives: Gender, Race, and Class in Visual Culture* (Princeton: Princeton UP, 1999) 11–28. Hawthorne's exemplar of middle-class femininity (and his compliment to Sophia, whose nickname was Phoebe), Phoebe reflects Hawthorne's commitment to the cult of domesticity and his ties with theorists like Sarah Hale.

8. Evidence for Hawthorne's familiarity with Mandeville can be found in Marion Kesselring's record of Hawthorne's borrowings from the Salem Athenaeum. Hawthorne borrowed the first volume of Mandeville on June 2, 1828, and the second on June 3, and borrowed *The True Meaning of The Fable of the Bees: in a Letter to the Author of a Book intitled "An Enquiry whether a General Practice of Virtue tends to the Wealth or Poverty, Benefit or Disadvantage of a People?"* on December 3, 1831. Marion Kesselring, *Hawthorne's Reading, 1828–1850: A Transcription and Identification of Titles Recorded in the Charge-Books of the Salem Athenaeum* (New York: New York Public Library, 1949) 56, 63.

9. Compare this comment with the Fourierist Romney Leigh's rueful admission in the dénouement of *Aurora Leigh* that his "men and women of disordered lives,/[. . .]/Broke up those waxen masks I made them wear,/With fierce contortions of the natural face" (Barrett Browning 8:890–893).

10. Coverdale states that

> if these things were to be believed, the individual soul was virtually annihilated, and all that is sweet and pure, in our present life, debased, and [. . .] the idea of man's eternal responsibility was made ridiculous, and immortality rendered, at once, impossible, and not worth acceptance. But I would have perished on the spot, sooner than believe it. (*CE* 3:198)

This passage does not imply refutation (an impossible task) of the "cold and dead materialism" of Westervelt and the lyceum-hall (*CE* 3:200), but rather a retreat on religious grounds. As I read it, however, Coverdale's statement reflects his—and Hawthorne's—anxious suspicion that the "pale man in blue spectacles" (*CE* 3:198) may be right. Part and parcel with his refutation of the lyceum-hall's materialism, Coverdale's belief in Priscilla's purity, as I argue in the next chapter, protests too much, but it is necessary to shore up his faith in "man's eternal responsibility."

11. Such difficulty is evident in *Wealth of Nations.* Smith states that "I have never known much good done by those who affected to trade for the public good" (Smith i.478): such merchants are *ipso facto* guilty of an affectation; at the very level of diction, Smith denies the possibility that those who profess to trade for the public good might be in earnest. Perhaps this skepticism is healthy. Nevertheless, it reflects a general inability to imagine a system predicated on something other than the self.

12. This tradition develops in the American context into portraits of what David Reynolds has called "the immoral reformer" (Reynolds 87), pious hypocrites of whom Hollingsworth is a type (provided we accept Coverdale's representation of him).

13. Given the circumstances, Zenobia's gender specificity is entirely understandable, but it holds true for the Blithedale experimenters as well: Zenobia's lament recalls Coverdale's early insight that, "as regarded society at large, we [communitarians] stood in a position of new hostility, rather than new brotherhood. [. . .] [W]e were inevitably estranged from the rest of mankind" (*CE* 3:20–21).

NOTES TO CHAPTER FOUR

1. Edgar Allan Poe, faulting Hawthorne's reliance on allegory, also blamed Fourierism (used metonymically for Transcendentalism): in his review of Hawthorne's short fiction, Poe states that Hawthorne's "spirit of 'metaphor run-mad' is clearly imbibed from the phalanx and phalanstery atmosphere in which he has been so long struggling for breath." Poe's advice: "Let him mend his pen, get a bottle of visible ink, come out from the Old Manse, cut Mr. Alcott, hang (if possible) the editor of *The Dial*, and throw out of the window to the pigs all his odd numbers of *The North American Review*" (*CR* 104). Since Hawthorne was writing allegory throughout the 1830s, Poe's inferences about Transcendentalism's influence on Hawthorne are misplaced. Nevertheless, the passage shows that the religious presses were not alone in perceiving some relation between Hawthorne and Fourierism.

2. In part, I suspect, because he fears that this antifoundationalism may be true. In the chapter of *The Blithedale Romance* set in the village-hall, Coverdale describes modernity as "the epoch of annihilated space" (*CE* 3:195), meaning that modern technology has collapsed the time it takes to travel great distances. But he also means that space has collapsed—the village hall houses "the choir of Ethiopian melodists, [. . .] the diorama of Moscow or Bunker Hill, or the moving panorama of the Chinese wall [. . .] wax figures [of the] Pope and the Mormon Prophet" (*CE* 3:196). Alongside the annihilation of distances, Coverdale fears an assault on essences: when

"a pale man in blue spectacles" tells him that "human character [is] but soft wax," Coverdale responds with "unutterable [. . .] horror and disgust" because, he says, he sees that

> if these things were to be believed, the individual soul was virtually *annihilated,* and all that is sweet and pure, in our present life, debased, and that the idea of man's eternal responsibility was made ridiculous, and immortality rendered, at once, impossible, and not worth acceptance. (*CE* 3:198, emphasis added)

But, he adds, "I would have perished on the spot, sooner than believe it" (*CE* 3:198). When Westervelt (part and parcel of the village-hall's antifoundationalism) stages his exhibition of the Veiled Lady, Coverdale writes that the presentation "was ingenious, eloquent, plausible, with a delusive show of spirituality, yet really imbued throughout with a cold and dead materialism" (*CE* 3:200). The kind of ontological vertigo that Coverdale experiences in the village-hall also afflicts him at Blithedale: "it was impossible [. . .] not to imbibe the idea," he states,

> that everything in nature and human existence was fluid, or fast becoming so; that the crust of the Earth, in many places, was broken, and its whole surface portentously upheaving; that it was a day of crisis, and that we ourselves were in the critical vortex. Our great globe floated in the atmosphere of infinite space like an unsubstantial bubble. (*CE* 3:140)

Against this erosion of eternal verities, Coverdale places the "true woman": Priscilla's flight from Westervelt to Hollingsworth is sacralized by Coverdale's narrative. As I argue below, however, it is possible that Coverdale protests too much.

3. Leland S. Person, "The Dark Labyrinth of Mind: Hawthorne, Hester, and the Ironies of Racial Mothering," *Studies in American Fiction* 29:1 (Spring 2001): 33–48.

4. My intent here is not to deny that Hawthorne was both racist and misogynist, a denial that would fly in the face of a great deal of evidence; as I shall argue below, the misogyny of the American romances reveals itself in the symbolic logic informing the relationship between property and marriage.

5. As Shawn Michelle Smith notes, *The House of the Seven Gables* resolves class conflict by shifting it into the idiom of gender relations, and then implying that the only "natural" social structure is one in which women can be deferent. The tragedy of Maule and Alice Pyncheon is that the class position of each disrupts gender "laws," allowing Alice to suppose—delusively—that she can withstand Maule's mesmeric power because of her class superiority; Holgrave and Phoebe "restore" feminine deference to masculinity in marrying, and simultaneously right the wrong done to the Maules by the Pyncheons. The novel thus "denies the significance of class hierarchies by masking them in

a culture of gender" (Smith 28). It is significant, given the fact that the novel resolves class conflict in this way, that no character is a feminist reformer: to include one would have disrupted the logic of the reconciliation by raising the possibility that hierarchies of gender are no more natural than those of class.

6. For the relation of Hawthorne to the emergent phenomenon of celebrity culture, see Michael T. Gilmore, "Hidden in Plain Sight: The Scarlet Letter and American Legibility," *Studies in American Fiction* 29:1 (Spring 2001): 121–8.

7. On the rise of symptomatic reading, see Allon White, *The Uses of Obscurity: the Fiction of Early Modernism* (London: Routledge and Kegan Paul, 1981).

8. Most of the letters in which Hawthorne makes brazenly commercial statements such as this one, however, occur in letters to James T. Fields, and it is possible that Hawthorne was exaggerating his interest in marketing to appeal to a publisher with a genius for marketing. That is, as much as they may reflect Hawthorne's genuine attention to the "great gull," they may also be part of a performance for the benefit of a smaller, more proximate gull.

9. As Tompkins writes,

> To critics who took for granted the moral purity of children, the holiness of the heart's affections, the divinity of nature, and the sanctity of the home, and who conceived of the poet as a prophet who could elevate the soul by "revealing the hidden harmonies of common things," sketches like "Sunday at Home," "Sights from a Steeple," "A Rill from the Town Pump," and novels like *The House of the Seven Gables* and [Susan Warner's] *The Wide, Wide World* formed a perfect continuum; it is not that these critics couldn't see the difference between Warner's work and Hawthorne's, but that, given their way of seeing, there was no difference. (Tompkins 18)

10. I admit that this model of Hawthorne is a retrospective invention and hence contingent. Nevertheless, it is the one that structures my interpretation of Hawthorne's works.

11. T. Walter Herbert, *Dearest Beloved: The Hawthornes and the Making of the Middle-Class Family* (Berkeley: U of California P, 1993) 88–106; Alan Trachtenberg, "Seeing and Believing: Hawthorne's Reflections on the Daguerreotype in *The House of the Seven Gables*," *American Literary History* 9:3 (Fall 1997): 460–81.

12. Stanley writes that

> Among the demands of the First National Rights Convention held in 1850 was amending the property laws affecting husband and wife. [Elizabeth Cady] Stanton relentlessly called for more than property reforms, claiming that the question of marriage itself lay at the heart of woman's enfranchisement; but others feared that such arguments might appear to promote "free love." (Stanley 176–7)

One recalls that Henry James, Sr., had translated and published Victor Hennequin's *Les Amours au phalanstère* in 1848, and thus "free love" in the above instance almost certainly implies Fourierism.

13.   By no means were all Fourierists critics of *status quo* marriage, a point I shall emphasize below. American phalanxes were careful to avoid giving the impression that they were free lovers; most Fourierists seem to have been in the American mainstream in their attitudes towards marriage. Nevertheless, Fourierism in the public eye seems to have been associated with sexual as well as social communalism, and there were various Fourierists who did, in fact, advocate free love. In his own writing, Fourier argued that marriage would in the course of societal evolution be abandoned, but he maintained that for the present, marriage ought to remain in place.

14.   In arguing that the Perfectionist communitarians at Oneida were the inheritors of Fourier's free-love theories, I am in effect accepting Guarneri's provocative thesis to this effect. Carl J. Guarneri, "Reconstructing the Antebellum Communitarian Movement: Oneida and Fourierism," *Journal of the Early Republic* 16 (Fall 1996): 463–485.

15.   Gayle Rubin, "The Traffic in Women: Notes on the 'Political Economy of Sex,'" in *Toward an Anthropology of Women*, ed. Rayna Reiter (New York: Monthly Review P, 1975), 157–210.

16.   *Adulterous Alliances*, Richard Helgerson's study of early modern adultery narratives, engages with this relationship throughout his study, which in broad outline shows how adultery represented threats to an emerging domestic middle class from forces of the state. Jo Labanyi's studies of the classic realist novels of adultery, all of which were written in the nineteenth century, show how adultery reflects the increasing economic autonomy of women, configured as a violation of the marriage contract.

17.   The critic who most nearly has broached this issue, to my knowledge, is Teresa Goddu, who has read *The House of the Seven Gables* in light of Gayle Rubin's critiques of the political economy of sex. Goddu notes that "[b]esides a healthy circulation of property, the novel's democratic model [. . .] depends upon the proper circulation of women within society" (Goddu 119). Goddu's diction in this sentence is misleading: the logic of her own reading suggests that she should write something like "alongside" or "standing for" rather than "besides." In Goddu's reading, as in mine, women symbolize, or in effect are, property.

18.   I say "seems to be" because this is not absolutely clear in Coverdale's narrative. Brook Farm was a joint-stock community rather than a communally owned one, and the Fourierists, as we shall see, represented themselves as defenders of private property. Coverdale describes his hermitage as his "one exclusive possession" (*CE* 3:99) while at Blithedale, suggesting that at least informally a general community of property obtains. On the other hand, both he and Zenobia retain property that neither adds to the communal resources.

19. Hawthorne does not use "utopian" and "Edenic" interchangeably: when he writes of Holgrave and Phoebe that by falling in love "[t]hey transfigured the earth, and made it Eden again, and themselves the two first dwellers in it" (*CE* 2:307), he is giving them his ideological endorsement. When he refers to utopia or utopianism, he signals an ideological critique: the Puritans in *The Scarlet Letter* who project a "Utopia of human virtue and happiness" (*CE* 1:47) have already, in his view, failed. My use of "utopian" to describe the aspirations of *The House of the Seven Gables* is essentially taking the same attitude to Hawthorne's renovated Eden that he takes towards colonial Boston.

20. I quote from Helen Macfarlane's translation of *The Communist Manifesto,* the first in English, which appeared in November 1850. The 1848 German original reads as follows:

> Aber Ihr Kommunisten wollt die Weibergemeinschaft einfürhren, schreit uns die ganze Bourgeoisie im Chor entgegen.
> [...]
> [...] [N]ichts [ist] lächerlicher als das hochmoralische Entsetzen unsrer Bourgeois über die angebliche officielle Webergemeinschaft der Kommunisten. Die Kommunisten brauchen die Weibergemein-schaft nicht einzuführen, sie hat fast immer existirt.
>
> Unsre Bourgeois nicht zufrieden damit, daß ihnen die Weiber und Töchter ihrer Proletarier zur Verfügung stehen, von der officiellen Prostitution gar nicht zu sprechen, finden ein Hauptvergnügen darin ihre Ehefrauen wechselseitig zu verführen.
>
> Die Bürgerliche Ehe ist in Wirklichkeit die Gemeinschaft der Ehe-frauen. Man könnte höchstens den Kommunisten vorwerfen, daß sie an der Stelle einer heuchlerisch versteckten, eine officielle, offenherzige Weibergemeinschaft einführeu wollen. Es versteht sich übrigens von selbst, daß mit Aufhebung der jetzigen Produktions-Verhältnisse auch die aus ihnen hervorgehende Weigergemeinschaft, d. h. die officielle und nicht officielle Prostitution verschwindet. (Marx and Engels 148)

21. Fourier on property is far from unambiguous: in *Théorie de l'unité universelle* he writes that

> l'esprit de PROPRIÉTÉ SIMPLE [...] domine en civilisation. Il n'y règne aucun principe sur la PROPRIÉTÉ COMPOSÉE, ou assujet-tissement des possessions individuelles aux besoins de la masse. On sait fort bien reconnaître ce principe en cas de guerre: on n'hesite pas à raser, incendier tout ce qui gène la défense; on ne donne pas 24 heures de répit, et on y est bien fondé, parce qu'il s'agit de l'utilité générale devant laquelle doivent tomber les prétensions de l'égoïsme et de la propriété simple, vraiment illibérale.
> Les coutumes civilisées n'admettent plus ce principe, lorsqu'il s'agit de garanties autres que celles de guerre ou de routes et canaux. Chacun

oppose son caprice au bien général; et là-dessus interviennent les philosophes, *qui soutiennent les libertés individuelles aux dépens des collectives,* et prétendent qu'un citoyen a des droits imprescriptible au mauvais goût, à la violation des convenances publiques.

Tel est le principe de la PROPRIÉTÉ SIMPLE, *droit de gêner arbitrairement les intérêts généraux pour satisfaire les fantaisies individuelles.* Aussi voit-on pleine licence accordée aux vandales qui prennent fantaisie de compromettre la salubrité et l'embellissement, par des constructions grotesques, des caricatures, quelquefois plus coûteuses qu'un beau et un bon bâtiment. Souvent ces vandales, par une avarice meurtrière, construisent des maisons malsaines et privées d'air, où ils entassent économiquement des fourmillières de populace; et l'on décore du nom de liberté ces spéculations assassines. Autant vaudrait autoriser les charlatans qui, abusant de la crédulité du peuple, exercent la médecine sans aucune connaissance. Ils peuvent dire aussi qu'ils font valoir leur industrie, qu'ils usent *des droits imprescriptibles.*

On a reconnu la nécessité de limiter ces prétendus droits en médecine comme en fortification, de les subordonner aux convenances générales; ainsi, le principe de propriété composée, déjà introduit dans le regime des monnaies, est de même établi en constructions militaires et administratives (routes, canaux et fortifications). Si on l'eût étendu aux constructions civiles et particulières, c'en était fait de la civilisation; elle serait tombée en un demi-siècle, et le genre humain se serait élevé au garantisme par la seule impulsion de ce luxe que réprouve la malencontreuse philosophie, ce luxe qui pourtant est 1er. foyer d'attraction. (*UU* 308–9, Fourier's emphasis) the spirit of SIMPLE PROPERTY [. . .] dominates in Civilization. There rules no principle whatsoever with respect to COMPLEX PROPERTY, or the subjection of individual possessions to the needs of the many. In war this principle is very well recognized: one does not hesitate to raze or burn anything that compromises defence; not 24 hours of warning are given, and this is fully justified, because it concerns the public good, before which must fall the pretensions of egotism and simple—in fact illiberal—property.

Civilized custom no longer admits this principle once one turns to circumstances other than those of war or of roads and canals. Each opposes his own whims to the general good; and on that subject philosophers intervene, *who uphold individual above collective liberties,* and who pretend that a citizen has imprescriptible rights to bad taste, in violation of public convenience.

Such is the principle of SIMPLE PROPERTY, *the right arbitrarily to hamper the interests of the public to gratify individual fantasies.* Therefore one sees full licence granted to vandals who take it as their whim to compromise health and beauty, through grotesque buildings, caricatures, at times more expensive than a handsome and sturdy building. Often these vandals, with murderous greed, construct unhealthy and poorly ventilated buildings, where they economically entomb veritable anthills of people; and the murderous speculations are ennobled with the name of liberty. Just as well might one authorize those charlatans who, abusing popular credulity, practice medicine without any knowledge. They can also say that their industry is justified, and that they exercise imprescriptible rights.

As in the building of fortifications, we have recognized the necessity of limiting the pretended rights in medicine, of subordinating them to the general good; thus the principle of complex property, already introduced in the monetary system, is also established in military and administrative construction (roads, canals, and fortifications). If one extended complex property to civil and individual construction, that would be it for Civilization; it would have fallen within fifty years, and the human race would elevate itself to guaranteeism by the single impulsion of that luxury which is condemned by unfortunate philosophy, that luxury which nevertheless is the first principle of attraction. (My translation, Fourier's emphasis)

Critics could legitimately discern in such a passage a will to abrogate altogether the rights of the individual property-owner.

22. See Andrew E. Hunt, "The Wisconsin Phalanx: A Forgotten Success Story" in *Canadian Review of American Studies* 28:2 (1998), 131.

23. See Robert K. Martin, "Haunted by Jim Crow: Gothic Fictions by Hawthorne and Faulkner," *American Gothic: New Interventions in a National Narrative,* eds. Robert K. Martin and Eric Savoy (Iowa City: Iowa UP, 1998), 132.

24. Such sexually frank women are recurring figures in Hawthorne's fiction. In addition to Alice, Hester, and Zenobia, one could mention Lady Eleanore, Miriam, and Beatrice Rappaccini. All of these women are at once sexually alluring and sexually intimidating; all of them receive a brutal comeuppance for their sexuality. Lady Eleanore contracts smallpox and is disfigured, Alice is forced to endure serial rape, Beatrice and Zenobia commit suicide, Miriam and Hester both impose penitential regimes upon themselves that robs them of their sexuality. Those who survive are chastened into etiolated figures of conventional, deferent womanhood: Eleanore, for instance, begs Jervase Helwyse to look not upon the woman you once loved! The curse of Heaven hath stricken me, because I would not call man my brother, nor woman sister. I wrapt myself in PRIDE as in a MANTLE, and scorned the sympathies of nature; and therefore has nature made this wretched body the medium of a dreadful sympathy. You are avenged—they are all avenged—Nature is avenged—for I am Eleanore Rochcliffe! (*CE* 9:287)

Before Alice Pyncheon dies, she demonstrates that she is "penitent of her one earthly sin, and proud no more!" (*CE* 2:210), a circumstance that

Holgrave applauds. As Hawthorne's apologists note, Hawthorne's men are subject to critique on the basis of how they respond to such women; nevertheless, in subjecting powerful women to humiliation, there is a degree of sadistic fervor which is deeply problematic.

25. Hawthorne leaves ambiguous whether Holgrave is recalling an event that happened in the fictional world of *The House of the Seven Gables,* or if the story of Alice Pyncheon and Matthew Maule is altogether his own invention. For my purposes, the distinction is less important than establishing that Holgrave is drawn to the subject because of the threat he himself poses as a latter-day Matthew Maule. In this light, his much lauded "reverence" for Phoebe's "individuality" (*CE* 2:212) may derive from his displacement of sexual appetite into fiction.

26. In a paper delivered at the June 2000 meeting of the Hawthorne Society in Boston, MA.

27. It is perhaps reflective of the resistance to complexity in *The House of the Seven Gables* that, in contrast to the class condescension of the Pyncheons and Holgrave to Venner, the class condescension of the middle-class Blithedale experimenters is something which Hawthorne, through Coverdale, critiques: on the occasion of the first meal at Blithedale,

> We all sat down—grisly Silas Foster, his rotund helpmate, and the two bouncing handmaidens, included—and looked at one another in a friendly, but rather awkward way. It was the first trial of our theories of equal brotherhood and sisterhood; and we people of superior cultivation and refinement (for as such, I presume, we unhestitatingly reckoned ourselves) felt as if something were already accomplished towards the millennium of love. The truth is, however, that the laboring oar was with our unpolished companions; it being far easier to condescend, than to accept of condescension. (*CE* 3:24)

Unlike these "unpolished companions," Coverdale notes, the monied communitarians have the resources to leave. "The poor, proud man," he concludes, "should look at both sides of sympathy like this" (*CE* 3:25). Neither the Pyncheons nor Holgrave evince a similar self-awareness as they condescend to Venner.

28. A more recent expression of Baym's basic narratological position is that of Hillis Miller, whose reading of "The Minister's Black Veil" argues that one cannot hope to perceive what informs Parson Hooper's assumption of the veil. Critics who suppose that they have determined Hooper's motives are self-deluding: "[t]he veil," Miller writes, "is an enigmatic sign that appears to give access to what it stands for while forbidding the one who confronts it to move behind it by any effort of hermeneutic interpretation" (Miller 94).

29. See, for instance, Edwin Percy Whipple's reviews of the American romances (*CR* 123–5, 168–71, 199–203). It is significant, however, that Hawthorne

liked Whipple's reviews: of Whipple's review of *The House of the Seven Gables,* he writes, "Whipple's notices have done more than please me; for they have helped me to see my book" (*CE* 16:435).

30. There is good reason to suppose that this was the younger Henry James's understanding; in *The Bostonians,* his reinscription of *The Blithedale Romance,* the equivalent of Blithedale is Cayuga (a mixture, presumably, of Brook Farm and Oneida), and is explicitly a free-love community.

31. See Lauren Berlant, "Fantasies of Utopia in *The Blithedale Romance,*" *American Literary History* 1:1 (1988): 30–62, especially 32–4.

32. A leap of faith that many readers have not been prepared to make along with Coverdale. In *Studies in Classic American Literature,* D. H. Lawrence characterizes Priscilla as a "little psychic prostitute" (Lawrence 115). And in an influential article now almost forty years old, Alan and Barbara Lefcowitz argue that both Zenobia and Coverdale assume, when Hollingsworth first brings Priscilla to Blithedale, she is a prostitute on whose behalf he has intervened. See Alan and Barbara Lefcowitz, "Some Rents in the Veil: New Light on Priscilla and Zenobia in *The Blithedale Romance,*" *Nineteenth-Century Fiction* 21 (1966), 263–275. The possibility that nineteenth-century readers may have drawn the same conclusion is suggested by Elizabeth Barrett Browning's feminist reinscription of *The Blithedale Romance, Aurora Leigh.* The Priscilla-figure in *Aurora Leigh,* Marian Erle, is explicitly betrayed into prostitution by Lady Waldemar, a Zenobia-like rival for the affections of Romney Leigh.

33. Given the moral critique so often implied in Hawthorne's representations of disguised characters (Westervelt is the immediate example, but see also the deacon's unwittingly ironic remarks to Dimmesdale with respect to gloves and purity (*CE* 1:158)), the false hair of the boarding-house mistress seems to signal some sort of corruption. Luther Luedtke has likened Zenobia's room in the boarding-house to a seraglio or harem (Luedtke 202). Coverdale's emphasis on the showy dress of the boarding-house mistress and especially her false hair contribute to these intimations—there seems to be the faintest suggestion that the mistress is a madam. This in turn would suggest that the boarding-house replicates *in urbe* the phalanstery as a (supposed) site of sexual license.

34. Because Coverdale describes Blithedale's collapse as a death, his suggestion that posterity dig up and profit from the truth of Blithedale suggests an exhumation or tomb-robbing. Such rhetoric is especially gruesome in light of the connection between Zenobia and Blithedale (she is buried in its pasture).

35. His diction anticipates that of Coverdale, who says of the Blithedale experimenters that they meant to show "mankind the example of a life governed by other than the *false and cruel principles,* on which human society has all along been based" (*CE* 3:19, emphasis added). This foregrounds once again the symbolic importance of marriage and adultery: the former represents the base of human society; the latter, a threat to its stability.

36. The tenement scene, in which a spectacle of working-class squalor circum-scribes a locus of purity, recalls a number of condition-of-England novels: it is Hawthorne's version of a realist commonplace. It bears an especially close resemblance to a scene in Charles Kingsley's *Alton Locke* (1850), in which a tenement—described as a "phalanstery of all the fiends"—formerly "wit-nessed the luxury, and rung to the laugher of some one great fashionable family, alone in their glory" (Kingsley 33). *The Blithedale Romance* likewise contrasts a scene of present poverty with a festive past.

37. Robert K. Martin, "Fourier in America."

38. Benjamin Scott Grossberg, "'The Tender Passion was Very Rife among Us': Coverdale's Queer Utopia and *The Blithedale Romance*," *Studies in American Fiction* 28:1 (Spring 2000): 3–25. For another treatment of Blithedale through the prism of queer theory, see Monika Mueller's *This Infinite Fraternity of Feel-ing: Gender, Genre, and Homoerotic Crisis in Hawthorne's The Blithedale Romance and Melville's Pierre* (Madison: Fairleigh Dickinson UP: 1996). Com-menting on the eroticized diction of the scene in which Hollingsworth and Coverdale part company, Mueller writes, "[t]he peculiar phrasing used by Coverdale [. . .] suggests that there [is] a whole lot more at stake than social reform" (Mueller 50). But Blithedale's links to Fourierism suggest that social reform and questions of erotic attachment are interrelated; the failure of the more than brotherly friendship between Coverdale and Hollingsworth antici-pates and predicts the failure of Blithedale itself.

39. Literary criticism attending to same-sex anxieties in Hawthorne's biography typically points to two relationships: that between Hawthorne and Melville and especially that between Hawthorne and his uncle, Robert Manning, with whom he shared a bed until he was fifteen. James Mellow, in the endnotes to his biography of Hawthorne, speculates that Hawthorne was abused by his uncle, an abuse that led to the various portraits of overbearing and vicious older men in Hawthorne's fiction (portraits that often end in these men's humiliation) (Mellow 610–611). Gloria Erlich rejects the possibility of direct abuse, which "would probably have left Hawthorne more retributive, less con-flicted, perhaps less seriously affected, than a subtle aura of seduction of which the source, whether self or other was uncertain" (Erlich 118–9). Instead, Erlich suggests "a continuing reciprocal homosexual relationship, one or more overt acts provoked by the nephew rather than the uncle, and so forth" (119). Her-bert tentatively accepts the possibility of abuse, but follows Erlich in suggesting that Hawthorne may also have felt a guilty attraction for his uncle, and likewise floating the possibility that Hawthorne initiated sexual contact with his uncle himself: "Did Nathaniel guiltily seek physical comfort from Uncle Robert as they slept together? Did he feel trapped by the allure of a defiling solace?" (Herbert 262–263). One might think of Blithedale in its utopian erotics as representative of such allure, in which the possibilities of "defilement" are carefully preëmpted through Hawthorne's careful efforts at containment.

40. The relationship between Hollingsworth and Coverdale is usually cited in queer readings of *The Blithedale Romance*. Less often is the relationship between Zenobia and Priscilla queered. The relationship that Coverdale describes, however, is filled with the same intensity as the Hollingsworth-Coverdale friendship, and one should not discount the possibility that there is a homoerotic component to their relationship as well. One needs to proceed cautiously in articulating such a reading: as Carroll Smith-Rosenberg has shown, the anachronistic dyad opposing "heterosexuality" and "homosexuality" is incapable of accounting adequately for nineteenth-century relationships among women, which, "[p]aradoxically to twentieth-century minds, [often appear] to have been both sensual and platonic" (Smith-Rosenberg 55). The point of Smith-Rosenberg's study, of course, is not to deny the existence of homoerotic relationships among women but rather the insufficiency of modern binary oppositions to understand nineteenth-century relationships among women. She affirms that between what we would call "committed heterosexuality" and "uncompromising homosexuality" there exists "a wide latitude of emotions and sexual feelings," and that in the nineteenth century, there was a cultural environment "permit[ting] individuals a great deal of freedom in moving across this spectrum" (76). Where Priscilla's and Zenobia's relationship is located in this spectrum cannot be easily fixed. Nor can the relationship be disentangled from Coverdale's representations of it; it is possible that these representations reflect on Coverdale's scopophilic fantasy life more than they shed light on the "true" nature of the Zenobia-Priscilla relationship. But Coverdale calls attention to the intensity of Priscilla's affection for Zenobia (*CE* 3:32–3), and shows that Priscilla responds to Zenobia's physical contact (*CE* 3:35), which suggests that the relationship, perhaps unconsciously, participates in the (Fourierist) freedom of love to which Coverdale and Zenobia both refer. It is evident, at any rate, that the failure of philanthropy at Blithedale is dramatized in the collapse of the brotherly relationship of Hollingsworth and Coverdale and the sisterly relationship of Zenobia and Priscilla; Zenobia's betrayal of Priscilla is more political than familial, since she is still ignorant of their biological relation.

NOTES TO THE CONCLUSION

1. The portrait of Venner is nevertheless a familiar caricature of the non-threatening working-class man, brimming with homilies and "feelosofy." Silas Foster in *The Blithedale Romance* is a comparable type. A demonic image of the working classes appears in *The House of the Seven Gables* in the form of one of Hepzibah's cent-shop patrons (*CE* 2:53). To say that Hawthorne appropriates the utopian claims of the Fourierists is not to say that he escapes class biases.

2. Often Hawthorne symbolizes such excessive selfhood in images of hypersexuality and so represents attempts to dominate others psychically using the imagery of sexual assault. But he does not necessarily do so, as the non-sexual conflict between Jaffrey and Clifford Pyncheon shows. That is, Hawthorne's objection to Fourierism is partly because of Fourier's theories on sex, but it is not reducible to these theories.

3. Reynolds's project is principally concerned with appropriation in a single direction: *Beneath the American Renaissance* is a study in how "high art" appropriated the forms and concerns of "low art." Although the latter obviously exceeded the former in terms of sheer volume, it is nevertheless unlikely that the flow of influence was so one-sided. Instead, it is probable that influence worked both ways.

Bibliography

Armstrong, Nancy. *Desire and Domestic Fiction: A Political History of the Novel.* Oxford: Oxford UP, 1987.

Arner, Robert D. "Hawthorne and Jones Very: Two Dimensions of Satire in 'Egotism; or, The Bosom Serpent.'" *NEQ* 42 (1967): 267–75.

Bales, Kent. "The Blithedale Romance: Coverdale's Mean and Subversive Egotism." *Bucknell Review* 21:2–3 (Fall-Winter 1973): 60–82.

Barrett Browning, Elizabeth. *Aurora Leigh.* Ed. Margaret Reynolds. Norton Critical Edition. New York: W. W. Norton and Company, 1996.

Baym, Nina. "*The Blithedale Romance:* A Radical Reading." *Journal of English and Germanic Philology.* 67 (1968): 545–69.

Beecher, Jonathan. *Charles Fourier: The Visionary and His World.* Berkeley: U of California P, 1986.

———. "Parody and Liberation in *The New Amorous World* of Charles Fourier. *History Workshop Journal* 20 (1985): 125–34.

———. *Victor Considérant and the Rise and Fall of French Romantic Socialism.* Berkeley: U of California P, 2001.

Bercovitch, Sacvan. *The Office of The Scarlet Letter.* Baltimore: Johns Hopkins UP, 1991.

———. *The Rites of Assent: Transformations in the Symbolic Construction of America.* New York: Routledge, 1993.

Berlant, Lauren. *The Anatomy of National Fantasy: Hawthorne, Utopia, and Everyday Life.* Chicago: U of Chicago P, 1991.

———. "Fantasies of Utopia in *The Blithedale Romance.*" *American Literary History* 1:1 (1988): 30–62.

Bridge, Horatio. *Journal of an African Cruiser.* Ed. Nathaniel Hawthorne. New York: Wiley and Putnam, 1845.

Brisbane, Albert. *Social Destiny of Man, or, Association and Reorganization of Society.* 1840. Reprints of Economic Classics. New York: Augustus M. Kelley, 1969.

Brock, William Hall. *Phalanx on a Hill: Responses to Fourierism in the Transcendentalist Circle.* Diss. Loyola U, 1995.

Brodhead, Richard H. *The School of Hawthorne.* Oxford: Oxford UP, 1986.

Brown, Gillian. *Domestic Individualism: Imagining Self in Nineteenth-Century America.* Berkeley: U of California P, 1990.

Bumas, E. Shaksan. "Fictions of the Panopticon: Prison, Utopia, and the Out-Penitent in the Works of Nathaniel Hawthorne." *American Literature* 73 (2001): 121–145.

Burrows, Edwin G. and Wallace, Mike. *Gotham: A History of New York City to 1898.* Oxford: Oxford UP, 1999.

The Circular. Brooklyn and Oneida: 1851–64.

Clark, Christopher. *The Communitarian Moment: The Radical Challenge of the Northampton Association.* Ithaca: Cornell UP, 1995.

Colacurcio, Michael J. *The Province of Piety: Moral History in Hawthorne's Early Tales.* 1984. Durham: Duke UP, 1995.

Cott, Nancy F. *The Bonds of Womanhood: 'Woman's Sphere' in New England, 1780–1835.* New Haven: Yale UP, 1977.

Crews, Frederick. *The Sins of the Fathers: Hawthorne's Psychological Themes.* 1966. 1st California pbk. Berkeley: U of California P, 1989.

Davis, Andrew Jackson. *The Principles of Nature, Her Divine Revelations, and A Voice to Mankind.* New York: S. S. Lyon and William Fishbough, 1847.

Delano, Sterling. *Brook Farm: The Dark Side of Utopia.* Cambridge, MA: Harvard UP, 2004.

——. *The Harbinger and New England Transcendentalism: A Portrait of Associationism in America.* Madison: Fairleigh Dickinson UP, 1983.

Dimock, Wai-Chee. *Empire for Liberty: Melville and the Poetics of Individualism.* Princeton: Princeton UP, 1989.

Eagleton, Terry. *The Ideology of the Aesthetic.* Oxford: Basil Blackwell, 1990.

Elbert, Monika M. "Hawthorne's Reconceptualization of Transcendentalist Charity." *ATQ* 11:3 (Sept. 1997): 213–232.

Erlich, Gloria C. *Family Themes and Hawthorne's Fiction: The Tenacious Web.* New Brunswick: Rutgers UP, 1984.

Fein, Albert. "Fourierism in Nineteenth-Century America: A Social and Environmental Perspective." *France and North America: Utopias and Utopians.* Ed. Mathé Allain. Lafayette: University of Southwestern Louisiana, 1978. 133–148.

Fitzhugh, George. *Cannibals All! Or, Slaves Without Masters.* 1857. Ed. Natalia Smith and Kathleen Feeney. 1st ed. 1998. Documenting the American South, or, The Southern Experience in 19th-century America, University of North Carolina at Chapel Hill <http://docsouth.unc.edu/fitzhughcan/fitzhugh.html>.

Foster, Lawrence. *Women, Family, and Utopia: Communal Experiments of the Shakers, the Oneida Community, and the Mormons.* Syracuse: Syracuse UP, 1991.

Foucault, Michel. *Discipline and Punish.* New York: Vintage, 1979.

———. "Of Other Spaces: Utopias and Heterotopias." *Rethinking Architecture: A reader in cultural theory.* Ed. Leach, Neal. New York: Routledge, 1997. 350–6.

Fourier, François Marie Charles. *The Theory of the Four Movements.* Eds. and Trans. Gareth Stedman Jones and Ian Paterson. Cambridge Texts in the History of Political Thought. Cambridge: Cambridge UP, 1996.

———. *Théorie de l'unité universelle.* 1841. Oeuvres Complètes de Charles Fourier. Tome Quatrième. Reimpression anastaltique. Paris: éditions anthropos, 1966.

———. *The Utopian Vision of Charles Fourier: Selected Texts on Work, Love, and Passionate Attraction.* Eds. and Trans. Jonathan Beecher and Richard Bienvenu. Columbia: U of Missouri P, 1983.

Francblin, Catherine. "Le Féminisme Utopique de Ch. Fourier." *Tel Quel* 62 (1975): 44–69.

Francis, Richard. *Transcendental Utopias: Individual and Community at Brook Farm, Fruitlands, and Walden.* Ithaca: Cornell UP, 1997.

Frank, Joseph. *Dostoevsky: The Seeds of Revolt, 1821–1849.* Princeton: Princeton UP, 1976.

Gilmore, Michael T. *American Romanticism and the Marketplace.* Chicago: U of Chicago P, 1985.

———. "Hidden in Plain Sight: The Scarlet Letter and American Legibility." *Studies in American Fiction* 29:1 (Spring 2001): 121–8.

Gladish, Robert W. *Swedenborg, Fourier, and the American of the 1840s.* Bryn Athyn: Swedenborg Scientific Association, 1983.

Goddu, Teresa. "The Circulation of Women in *The House of the Seven Gables.*" *Studies in the Novel* 23:1 (Spring 1991): 119–27.

Goldstein, Leslie F. "Early Feminist Themes in French Utopian Socialism: The St.-Simonians and Fourier." *Journal of the History of Ideas* 43:1 (Jan.-Mar. 1982): 91–103.

Grossberg, Benjamin Scott. "'The Tender Passion was Very Rife among Us': Coverdale's Queer Utopia and *The Blithedale Romance.*" *Studies in American Fiction* 28:1 (Spring 2000): 3–25.

Guarneri, Carl J. "The Americanization of Utopia: Fourierism and the Dilemma of Utopian Dissent in the United States." *Utopian Studies* 5:1 (1994), 72–88.

———. "Reconstructing the Antebellum Communitarian Movement: Oneida and Fourierism." *Journal of the Early Republic* 16 (Fall 1996): 463–485.

———. *The Utopian Alternative: Fourierism in Nineteenth-Century America.* Ithaca: Cornell UP, 1991.

Habegger, Alfred. *The Father: A Life of Henry James, Sr.* New York: Farrar, Straus, and Giroux, 1994.

The Harbinger. Boston and New York: 1845–1849.

Hawthorne, Julian. *Nathaniel Hawthorne and His Wife: A Biography.* 2 vols. 2nd ed. Boston: James R. Osgood and Company, 1885.

Hawthorne, Nathaniel. *The American Notebooks.* The Centenary Edition of the Works of Nathaniel Hawthorne, vol. 8. Ed. Claude M. Simpson. Ohio: Ohio State UP, 1972.

——. *The Blithedale Romance and Fanshawe.* 1852 and 1828. The Centenary Edition of the Works of Nathaniel Hawthorne, vol. 3. Ed. William Charvat, Roy Harvey Pearce, and Claude Simpson. Ohio: Ohio State UP, 1964.

——. *The House of the Seven Gables.* 1851. The Centenary Edition of the Works of Nathaniel Hawthorne, vol. 2. Ed. William Charvat, Roy Harvey Pearce, and Claude Simpson. Ohio: Ohio State UP, 1965.

——. *The Letters, 1843–1853.* The Centenary Edition of the Works of Nathaniel Hawthorne, vol. 16. Ed. Thomas Woodson, L. Neal Smith, and Norman Holmes Pearson. Ohio: Ohio State UP, 1985.

——. *Miscellaneous Prose and Verse.* The Centenary Edition of the Works of Nathaniel Hawthorne, vol. 23. Ed. Thomas Woodson, Claude Simpson, and L. Neal Smith. Ohio: Ohio State UP, 1994.

——. *Mosses from an Old Manse.* 1846. The Centenary Edition of the Works of Nathaniel Hawthorne, vol. 10. Ed. William Charvat, Roy Harvey Pearce, and Claude Simpson. Ohio: Ohio State UP, 1974.

——. *The Scarlet Letter.* 1850. The Centenary Edition of the Works of Nathaniel Hawthorne, vol. 1. Ed. William Charvat, Roy Harvey Pearce, and Claude Simpson. Ohio: Ohio State UP, 1962.

——. *The Snow Image and Uncollected Tales.* 1851. The Centenary Edition of the Works of Nathaniel Hawthorne, vol. 11. Ed. Fredson Bowers, L. Neal Smith, John Manning, and J. Donald Crowley. Ohio: Ohio State UP, 1974.

——. *Twice-Told Tales.* 1837, 1842. The Centenary Edition of the Works of Nathaniel Hawthorne, vol. 9. Ed. William Charvat, Roy Harvey Pearce, and Claude Simpson. Ohio: Ohio State UP, 1974.

Helgerson, Richard. *Adulterous Alliances: Home, State, and History in Early Modern European Drama and Painting.* Chicago: U of Chicago P, 2000.

Herbert, T. Walter. *Dearest Beloved: The Hawthornes and the Making of the Middle-Class Family.* Berkeley: U of California P, 1993.

Howe, Daniel Walker. *The Political Culture of the American Whigs.* Chicago: U of Chicago P, 1979.

Hunt, Andrew E. "The Wisconsin Phalanx: A Forgotten Success Story." *Canadian Review of American Studies* 28:2 (1998), 119–43.

Idol, John L., Jr., and Jones, Buford, eds. *Nathaniel Hawthorne: The Contemporary Reviews.* Cambridge: Cambridge UP, 1994.

James, Henry. *Hawthorne.* 1879. Ithaca: Cornell UP, 1997.

Jameson, Fredric. *The Political Unconscious: Narrative as a Socially Symbolic Act.* Ithaca: Cornell UP, 1981.

Kanter, Rosabeth Moss. *Commitment and Community: Communes and Utopias in Sociological Perspective.* Cambridge: Harvard UP, 1972.

Kesselring, Marion. *Hawthorne's Reading: 1828–1850.* New York: New York Public Library, 1949.

Kingsley, Charles. *Alton Locke, tailor and poet.* 1850. London: Macmillan and Company, 1890.

Knadler, Stephen. "Hawthorne's Genealogy of Madness: *The House of Seven Gables* [sic] and Disciplinary Individualism." *American Quarterly* 47:2 (June 1995): 280–308.

Kropotkin, Peter. *The Conquest of Bread.* Trans. Paul Avrich. London: Penguin Press, 1972.

Labanyi, Jo. "Adultery in the Exchange Economy." *Scarlet Letters: Fictions of Adultery from Antiquity to the 1990s.* Ed. Nicholas White and Naomi Segal. New York: St. Martin's Press, 1997. 98–108.

Lawrence, D. H. *Studies in Classic American Literature.* 1923. London: Penguin Books, 1971.

Lefcowitz, Alan and Barbara. "Some Rents in the Veil: New Light on Priscilla and Zenobia in *The Blithedale Romance.*" *Nineteenth-Century Fiction* 21 (1966), 263–275.

Levine, Robert S. "Of Sympathy and Reform in The Blithedale Romance." *The Cambridge Companion to Nathaniel Hawthorne.* Ed. Richard H. Millington. Cambridge: Cambridge UP, 2004. 207–229.

Loman, Andrew. "'That Narrow Strip of Sunlight, which we call Now': Hawthorne's 'The Prophetic Pictures' and the Writing of History." Nathaniel Hawthorne Society Conference. Boston. June, 2000.

Luedtke, Luther. *Nathaniel Hawthorne and the Romance of the Orient.* Bloomington: Indiana UP, 1989.

Mackenzie, Manfred. "Colonization and Decolonization in *The Blithedale Romance.*" *University of Toronto Quarterly* 62:4 (Summer 1993): 504–21.

Mandeville, Bernard. *The Fable of the Bees and Other Writings.* Ed. E. J. Hundert. Indianapolis: Hackett Publishing Company, Inc., 1997.

Martin, Robert K. "Fourier in America." Unpublished article.

———. "Haunted by Jim Crow: Gothic Fictions by Hawthorne and Faulkner." *American Gothic: New Interventions in a National Narrative.* Ed. Robert K. Martin and Eric Savoy. Iowa City: Iowa UP, 1998.

Marx, Karl. *The Communist Manifesto.* 1848. Trans. Helen Macfarlane. *The Adventures of the Communist Manifesto.* Ed. Hal Draper. Berkeley: Center for Socialist History, 1994.

Marx, Karl and Engels, Friedrich. *The Marx-Engels Reader.* Ed. Robert C. Tucker. 2nd ed. New York: W. W. Norton and Company, 1978.

Matthiessen, F. O. *American Renaissance: Art and Expression in the Age of Emerson and Whitman.* Oxford: Oxford UP, 1941.

Mellow, James R. *Nathaniel Hawthorne in His Times.* Baltimore: Johns Hopkins UP, 1980.

Miller, J. Hillis. *Hawthorne and History: Defacing It.* Oxford: Basil Blackwell, 1991.

M'Laren, Donald C. *Boa Constrictor; or, Fourier Association Self-Exposed as to Its Principles and Aims.* Rochester: Canfield and Warren, 1844.

Milton, John. *Paradise Lost.* 1674. *The Riverside Milton.* Ed. Roy Flanagan. Boston: Houghton Mifflin, 1998.

Morton, Nathaniel. *New Englands Memoriall.* 1669. Ed. Howard J. Hall. New York: Scholars' Facsimiles and Reprints, 1937.

Mueller, Monika. *"This Infinite Fraternity of Feeling": Gender, Genre, and Homoerotic Crisis in Hawthorne's The Blithedale Romance and Melville's Pierre.* Madison: Fairleigh Dickinson UP, 1996.

Nawrocki, Gerard. *"The Blithedale Romance* and Charles Fourier." *Studia Anglica Posnaniensia: An International Review of English Studies* 29 (1994): 199–209.

Orton, Stephen Noyes. *Banning the Tribes: Emily Dickinson and the Communitarian Movement.* Diss. U of North Carolina at Chapel Hill, 1998.

Orvis, Marianne Dwight. *Letters from Brook Farm, 1844–1847.* Ed. Amy L. Reed. The American Utopian Adventure. Philadelphia: Porcupine P, 1972.

Person, Leland S. "The Dark Labyrinth of Mind: Hawthorne, Hester, and the Ironies of Racial Mothering." *Studies in American Fiction* 29:1 (Spring 2001): 33–48.

Pfister, Joel. *The Production of Personal Life: Class, Gender, and the Psychological in Hawthorne's Fiction.* Stanford: Stanford UP, 1991.

Pitzer, Donald E., ed. *America's Communal Utopias.* Chapel Hill: U of North Carolina P, 1997.

Poldevaart, Saskia. "Theories about Sex and Sexuality in Utopian Socialism." *Journal of Homosexuality* 9:2/3 (1995): 41–67.

Prospectus of The Anti-Jacobin; or, Weekly Examiner. London: 1797.

Reynolds, David S. *Beneath the American Renaissance: The Subversive Imagination in the Age of Emerson and Melville.* Cambridge: Harvard UP, 1988.

——. *Walt Whitman's America: A Cultural Biography.* New York: Vintage Books, 1996.

Reynolds, Larry J. *European Revolutions and the American Literary Renaissance.* New Haven: Yale UP, 1988.

Rubin, Gayle. "The Traffic in Women: Notes on the 'Political Economy of Sex.'" *Toward an Anthropology of Women.* Ed. Rayna Reiter. New York: Monthly Review P, 1975, 157–210.

Ryan, Mary P. *Cradle of the Middle Class: The Family in Oneida County, New York, 1790–1865.* New York: Cambridge UP, 1981.

Schaer, Ronald, Claeys, Gregory, and Sargent, Lyman Tower, eds. *Utopia: The Search for the Ideal Society in the Western World.* New York: New York Public Library, Oxford UP, 2000.

Sellers, Charles. *The Market Revolution: Jacksonian America, 1815–1846.* Oxford: Oxford UP, 1991.

Sherbo, Arthur. "Albert Brisbane and Hawthorne's Holgrave and Hollingsworth." *NEQ* 27 (1954): 531–4.

Smith, Adam. *An Inquiry into the Nature and Causes of The Wealth of Nations.* 1776. Ed. Edwin Cannan. Chicago: U of Chicago P, 1976.

Smith, Adam. "Of Licentious Systems." 1759. *Private Vices, Publick Benefits? The Contemporary Reception of Bernard Mandeville.* Ed. J. Martin Stafford. Solihull: Ismeron, 1997.

Smith, Shawn Michelle. *American Archives: Gender, Race, and Class in Visual Culture.* Princeton: Princeton UP, 1999.

Smith-Rosenberg, Carroll. *Disorderly Conduct: Visions of Gender in Victorian America.* New York: Alfred A. Knopf, 1985.

Spurlock, John C. *Free Love: Marriage and Middle-Class Radicalism in America, 1825–1860.* New York: New York UP, 1988.

Stanley, Amy Dru. *From Bondage to Contract: Wage Labor, Marriage, and the Market in the Age of Slave Emancipation.* Cambridge: Cambridge UP, 1998.

———. "Home Life and the Morality of the Market." *The Market Revolution in America: Social, Political, and Religious Expressions, 1800–1880.* Ed. Melvyn Stokes and Stephen Conway. Charlottesville: UP of Virginia, 1996. 74–96.

Stanton, Elizabeth Cady and Anthony, Susan B. *The Elizabeth Cady Stanton and Susan B. Anthony Reader: Correspondence, Writings, Speeches,* rev. ed. Ed. Ellen Carol Dubois. Boston: Northeastern UP, 1992.

Stoehr, Taylor, ed. *Free Love in America: A Documentary History.* New York: AMS Press, 1979.

———. *Hawthorne's Mad Scientists: Pseudoscience and Social Science in Nineteenth-Century Life and Letters.* Hamden: Archon Books, 1978.

Swift, Lindsay. *Brook Farm: Its Members, Scholars, and Visitors.* Secaucus: Citadel P, 1973.

Taylor, Barbara. *Eve and the New Jerusalem: Socialism and Feminism in the Nineteenth Century.* 1983. Harvard Paperback ed. Cambridge: Harvard UP, 1993.

Tomasek, Kathryn Manson. *"The Pivot of the Mechanism": Women, Gender, and Discourse in Fourierism and the Antebellum United States.* Diss. U of Wisconsin-Madison, 1995.

Tompkins, Jane. *Sensational Designs: The Cultural Work of American Fiction, 1790–1860.* Oxford: Oxford UP, 1985.

Trachtenberg, Alan. "Seeing and Believing: Hawthorne's Reflections on the Daguerreotype in *The House of the Seven Gables.*" *American Literary History* 9:3 (Fall 1997): 460–81.

Valenti, Patricia Dunlavy. *Sophia Peabody Hawthorne: A Life, 1809–1847.* Columbia, MO: U of Missouri P, 2004.

Von Abele, Rudolph. *The Death of the Artist: A Study of Hawthorne's Disintegration.* The Hague: Nijhoff, 1955.

Waggoner, Hyatt. *Hawthorne: A Critical Study.* Cambridge: Harvard UP, 1963.

White, Allon. *The Uses of Obscurity: The Fiction of Early Modernism.* London: Routledge and Kegan Paul, 1981.

Williams, William Carlos. *In the American Grain*. New York: Albert and Charles Boni, 1925.

Wineapple, Brenda. *Hawthorne: A Life*. New York: Albert A. Knopf, 2003.

Zucchi, John E. *The Little Slaves of the Harp: Italian Child Street Musicians in Nineteenth-Century Paris, London, and New York*. Kingston: McGill-Queen's UP, 1992.

Index